Feedback in Second Language Writing

THE CAMBRIDGE APPLIED LINGUISTICS SERIES

Series editors: Michael H. Long and Jack C. Richards

This series presents the findings of work in applied linguistics that are of direct relevance to language teaching and learning and of particular interest to applied linguists, researchers, language teachers, and teacher trainers.

Feedback in Second Language Writing
Contexts and Issues

Edited by

Ken Hyland
University of London

Fiona Hyland
University of London

CAMBRIDGE
UNIVERSITY PRESS

CAMBRIDGE UNIVERSITY PRESS
Cambridge, New York, Melbourne, Madrid, Cape Town, Singapore, São Paulo

Cambridge University Press
32 Avenue of the Americas, New York, NY 10013-2473, USA

www.cambridge.org
Information on this title: www.cambridge.org/9780521856638

First published 2006

Printed in the United States of America

A catalog record for this publication is available from the British Library.

Library of Congress Cataloging in Publication Data

Feedback in second language writing : contexts and issues / edited by Ken Hyland,
Fiona Hyland.
  p.   cm. – (Cambridge applied linguistics series)
Includes bibliographical references and index.
ISBN-13: 978-0-521-85663-8
ISBN-10: 0-521-85663-9
ISBN-13: 978-0-521-67258-0 (pbk.)
ISBN-10: 0-521-67258-9 (pbk.)
1. Language and languages – Study and teaching (Higher)   2. Rhetoric – Study and
teaching (Higher)   3. Second language acquisition.   I. Hyland, Ken.
II. Hyland, Fiona.   III. Series.
P53.27.F44   2006
418.0071′1 – dc22   2006042605

ISBN-13   978 0 521 85663 8 hardback
ISBN-10   0 521 85663 9 hardback

ISBN-13   978 0 521 67258 0 paperback
ISBN-10   0 521 67258 9 paperback

This book is for our parents, Barbara, Gwen,
Les, and Mac.
For so many things.

Contents

III NEGOTIATING FEEDBACK: INTERPERSONAL AND INTERACTIONAL DIMENSIONS   183

Contributors

Joan Carson, *Georgia State University, United States*

Caroline Coffin, *The Open University, England*

Dana Ferris, *California State University, Sacramento, United States*

María C. M. de Guerrero, *Inter American University, Puerto Rico*

Lynn Goldstein, *The Monterey Institute of International Studies, United States*

Liz Hamp-Lyons, *University of Hong Kong and University of Melbourne, Australia*

Fiona Hyland, *University of London, England*

Ken Hyland, *University of London, England*

Ann Hewings, *The Open University, England*

Ann M. Johns, *San Diego State University, United States*

Ilona Leki, *University of Tennessee, United States*

John Milton, *Hong Kong University of Science and Technology*

Gayle Nelson, *Georgia State University, United States*

Christine Tardy, *DePaul University, United States*

Olga S. Villamil, *Inter American University, Puerto Rico*

Paige D. Ware, *Southern Methodist University, United States*

Mark Warschauer, *University of California, Irvine, United States*

Robert Weissberg, *New Mexico State University, United States*

Series editors' preface

Approaches to second language writing pedagogy have traditionally attributed a primary role to feedback, whether generated by the learner, a peer, a computer, or a teacher and whether occurring through error correction, self-editing, peer feedback, or conferencing. However, as the field of second language writing instruction has changed its focus from skills to process and then to genre, and most recently to sociocultural considerations, issues related to the nature, form, and value of feedback have had to be reexamined. The papers in this book provide the basis for such a reexamination by presenting a variety of research-based perspectives on the status and practice of feedback in second language writing.

Research into the role of feedback in L2 writing reveals that there are no simple answers to questions such as which activities merit feedback, how and when to give feedback, and what the benefits of giving feedback are. These questions are examined from different perspectives in this book, particularly in relation to writing in academic settings. The nature of feedback and revision, the effects of feedback on student writing, strategies for the delivery of feedback, the role of teachers' and learners' beliefs and expectations, as well as the influence of social, cultural, and contextual factors, are shown to be relevant to our understanding. The contributors draw on an extensive body of research to clarify the issues involved in understanding the nature of feedback and to draw implications for the teaching of L2 writing. This book provides a valuable source of information for researchers, teachers, and others interested in the role of feedback in the development of composition skills and confidence for second language students.

Michael H. Long
Jack C. Richards

Preface

Providing feedback to students, whether in the form of written commentary, error correction, teacher-student conferencing, or peer discussion, has come to be recognized as one of the ESL writing teacher's most important tasks, offering the kind of individualized attention that is otherwise rarely possible under normal classroom conditions. Teachers are now very conscious of the potential feedback has for helping to create a supportive teaching environment, for conveying and modeling ideas about good writing, for developing the ways students talk about writing, and for mediating the relationship between students' wider cultural and social worlds and their growing familiarity with new literacy practices.

However, despite the major part feedback plays in modern writing classrooms and in the lives of all teachers and learners, book-length treatments of the topic are rare, and much of the research published in journals fails to find its way to teachers. This volume sets out to address these gaps by providing readers with a clear synthesis of theory and practice, highlighting what is conceptually and pedagogically significant and offering a clear picture of the key issues in feedback today. We attempt to bring together theoretical understandings and practical applications of feedback for teachers, researchers, and others working in the fields of second language teaching and literacy studies.

We do this by focusing such key issues through three broad lenses. The first situates feedback in the context of the wider institutional, social, political, and cultural factors which have been found to influence how feedback is received and given. The second looks more closely at the "how" and "what" of feedback – the ways it is shaped through its modes of delivery and its form. The third is concerned with the negotiation of feedback in the relationships between providers and receivers, addressing issues that arise in the social interactions around feedback itself. These three lenses are not meant to imply divisions among context, delivery, and interaction, as it is evident that every act of feedback will involve a complex interaction among all three. They do, however, allow the authors to focus on one or another salient feature of the process and what each means for participants.

Another important feature of the book is that it takes a broad view of feedback on writing. In the following chapters, distinguished figures in the field of second language writing go beyond discussions of grammar and error correction to look at responses by peers, teachers, computers, and the self; to explore modes such as oral, written, computer-modeled, and electronically mediated feedback; to examine the kinds of commentary given on form, organization, academic conventions, and meaning; to study the preferences students have for different kinds of interaction and commentary; and to analyze the kinds of comments that are given and the issues that teachers consider when framing them. While the book provides no clear-cut, unequivocal answers to many questions raised by the practical use of feedback in second language writing classrooms, it nevertheless poses the most interesting of those questions and shows that there is a vast array of *potential* answers that we might explore.

Finally, we have tried to make the volume as useful to teachers and researchers as possible. Rather than dwell on the abstract benefits of various feedback practices, the authors take care to link research with practice, highlighting what the research tells us about feedback and exploring its relevance for the classroom. The volume goes a long way toward answering questions that researchers and teachers have been asking for some time. These questions include: "What shall I give feedback on?," "How shall I express it?," "What mode should I use?," "How will this affect my relationship to this student?," and "Will this make a difference to students' writing?" Thus, each chapter gives teachers and researchers a clear, complete perspective on current issues that can provide a basis for classroom practice or research into this fascinating and fundamental area.

Ken Hyland and Fiona Hyland

1 Contexts and issues in feedback on L2 writing: An introduction

Ken Hyland
Fiona Hyland

Feedback is widely seen in education as crucial for both encouraging and consolidating learning (Anderson, 1982; Brophy, 1981; Vygotsky, 1978), and this significance has also been recognized by those working in the field of second language writing. Its importance is acknowledged in process-based classrooms, where it forms a key element of the students' growing control over composing skills, and by genre-oriented teachers employing scaffolded learning techniques. In fact, over the past 20 years, changes in writing pedagogy and research have transformed feedback practices, with teacher comments often supplemented with peer feedback, writing workshops, conferences, and computer-delivered feedback. Summative feedback, designed to evaluate writing as a product, has generally been replaced by formative feedback that points forward to the student's future writing and the development of his or her writing processes. More widely, there is a growing awareness of the social and political implications of teacher and peer response.

Although feedback is a central aspect of ESL writing programs across the world, the research literature has not been unequivocally positive about its role in instruction, and teachers often have a sense that they are not making use of its full potential. This book addresses this incongruity, and in this introductory chapter we offer an overview of some key issues and preview the book's organization.

Some historical context

The importance of feedback emerged with the development of learner-centered approaches to writing instruction in North American L1 composition classes during the 1970s. The "process approach" gave greater attention to teacher-student encounters around texts and encouraged teachers to support writers through multiple drafts by providing feedback and suggesting revisions during the process of writing itself, rather than at the end of it. The form feedback took was extended beyond the teacher's marginal notes to include oral interaction involving the teacher or the students themselves. The focus moved from a concern with mechanical accuracy and control of language to a greater emphasis on the development and discovery of meaning through the experience of writing and rewriting. Feedback came to be viewed as having a powerful potential, with the possibility for "a revision of cognition itself that stems from response" (Freedman, 1985, p. xi).

Feedback practices and issues were also increasingly influenced by interactionist theories, which emphasized the significance of the individual reader and the dialogic nature of writing. Rather than asking students to write for an idealized general audience, the interpretation and response of a specific reader was seen as important in giving meaning to a text and assisting writers to shape their texts for real people. Without a reader, there is only "potential for meaning" but no meaning itself (Probst, 1989, p. 69). This perspective places a high value on reader response and encourages the use of peer feedback and multiple feedback sources to provide a real rather than a visualized audience.

More recently, feedback has been seen as a key element of students' growing control over writing skills in genre-oriented approaches, where sociocultural theories of scaffolded instruction and learning as a social practice are important. Here feedback is important in providing students with the rhetorical choices central to new academic or professional literacy skills and as a way of assisting students in negotiating access to new knowledge and practices. This view of feedback also means confronting issues of teacher control and social and political dominance. Bartholomae (1986, p. 12) has discussed "the difficult and often violent accommodations that occur when students locate themselves in a discourse that is not 'naturally' or immediately theirs." In such contexts feedback may be seen as either denying students their own voice and imposing teachers' own requirements on them, or as empowering them to produce texts that appropriately address the expectations needed to succeed in a particular discourse community.

But while response to student writing has been a subject of considerable interest to teachers and researchers for more than 30 years, research into response in L2 writing, as opposed to error correction, did not really begin until the early 1990s, and many questions remain only partially answered. Several key questions continue to be hotly debated. What kinds of feedback are most appropriate in different contexts? What are the most effective teacher practices? How do students perceive and respond to feedback? How do cultural factors influence response? And does feedback improve student writing in the long term? L2 writers obviously work within a complex context, where language proficiency, diverse cultural expectations, new teacher-learner experiences, and different writing processes can interact in significant ways with the cognitive demands of interpreting feedback and negotiating revisions. As a result, research has tended to explore some key issues of difference between L1 and L2 writing contexts, such as peer response, teacher-student conferencing, and the effects of teachers' written feedback.

An overview of key issues

Teacher feedback to L2 writers

Surveys of students' feedback preferences indicate that ESL students greatly value teacher written feedback and consistently rate it more highly than alternative forms, such as peer feedback and oral feedback in writing conferences (Leki, 1991; Saito, 1994; Zhang, 1995). Even though students themselves are positive about written feedback and appear to value comments and corrections on all aspects of their texts, its contribution to students' writing development is still unclear. Ferris (1997), for instance, found that although three quarters of substantive teachers' comments on drafts were used by students, only half of their revisions in response to these could be considered as improvements and a third actually made matters worse. A similarly mixed success rate emerged from Conrad and Goldstein's (1999) study of the revisions of three case study subjects.

In the L2 context, the effectiveness of feedback that focuses on error correction is seen as particularly important, and the question of whether such feedback is beneficial to students' development, in both the short and long term, has become a major issue of contention. Early L2 writing researchers, influenced by process theories, argued that feedback on error was both discouraging and unhelpful. Zamel (1985, p. 96), for instance, advised teachers to rein in their "reflex-like reactions to surface level concerns and give priority to meaning." Others suggested that error correction had few positive effects on student writing (Kepner, 1991; Polio, Fleck, and Leder, 1998; Robb et al., 1986; Semke, 1984; Sheppard, 1992). In a well-known summary of this literature, Truscott (1996) saw very little benefit in this kind of feedback and argued strongly that it is the responsibility of teachers to change student attitudes regarding the benefits of error correction by adopting a "correction-free approach" in their classrooms (Truscott, 1999).

But while process approaches emphasize the need for writing uninhibited by language correction, grammar errors can be an obvious problem for L2 writers, and it is not surprising that teachers often feel the need to respond to them. ESL students themselves, particularly those from cultures where teachers are highly directive, generally welcome and expect teachers to notice and comment on their errors and may feel resentful if their teachers do not do so. This is a particularly pressing issue where students are learning to write for business or academic audiences for whom accuracy is important (Hyland, 2003). A number of survey studies, for instance, suggest that university subject teachers have little tolerance of typical ESL errors and that these can influence their overall grading of papers (e.g., Janopoulos, 1992).

It has also been suggested that ESL students have less of their self worth invested in their L2 writing than L1 writers have in their native language, and that language corrections therefore are not as discouraging to them as they would be to native speakers (Leki, 1991; Schachter, 1991). The idea that "error" has different connotations for L2 learners is one that needs further investigation, but it is clear that the practice of response is not so clear-cut as was first thought. The picture is further complicated by the fact that teachers respond to students in their comments and not just to texts. Hyland (1998), for example, found that teachers consider not only the errors they find in a piece of writing but also the student responsible for them, basing their comments and what they choose to address on their relationship with the student and what they know of his or her background, needs, and preferences.

In other words, we cannot ignore either our students or their immediate needs to produce texts that are regarded as competent and successful by their intended audiences and to become self-sufficient in constructing acceptably accurate prose. Admonishments to teachers to focus exclusively on meaning therefore seem misplaced, the result of a view of writing that sees ideas and language as distinct. In fact, the separation of form and content is largely an artificial one, of dubious theoretical value, and impossible to maintain when responding to writing.

We should not be surprised, therefore, that other researchers disagree with Truscott's views on error correction, arguing instead that form-focused feedback can be effective, especially when accompanied by classroom instruction (Master, 1995; White, Spada, Lightbown, & Ranta, 1991). Studies measuring student improvement longitudinally suggest that students who receive error feedback over a period of time can improve their language accuracy (Fatham & Whalley, 1990; Ferris, 2002; Ferris & Helt, 2000; Ferris & Roberts, 2001). In one study, for example, Chandler (2003) tracked students' writing over one semester and found that both underlining and direct correction reduced grammatical and lexical errors in subsequent writing. Although it is unlikely that feedback alone is responsible for long-term language improvement, it is almost certainly a highly significant factor.

Another key area of investigation has been the stance teachers take when giving feedback. Leki (1990) suggests that L2 teachers may be fulfilling several different and possibly conflicting roles as they respond to student writing. When giving feedback, then, we have to choose the appropriate language and style to accomplish a range of informational, pedagogic, and interpersonal goals. Studies of L2 students' reactions to teacher feedback show that learners remember and value encouraging remarks but expect to receive constructive criticism rather than simple platitudes (Ferris, 1995; Hyland, F., 1998). However, many teachers are very conscious of the potentially damaging effect of critical comments, and this awareness can translate into a reluctance to address issues directly. Hyland and Hyland (2001) suggest that teachers often seek to mitigate the full force of their criticisms and suggestions, taking the sting out of them with hedges, question forms, and personal attribution. However, this kind of indirection also carries the very real danger that students may miss the point of the comment and so misinterpret the feedback.

Writing conferences

Research indicates that, to be effective, feedback should be conveyed in a number of modes and should allow for response and interaction (e.g., Brinko, 1993). Among the most extensively employed of these modes is the writing conference, an approach lauded by L1 researchers as a dialogue in which meaning and interpretation are constantly being negotiated by participants and as a method that provides both teaching and learning benefits. Writing conferences with teachers have been visualized as "conversational dialogues" (Freedman & Sperling, 1985), with the emphasis on two-way communication. At the heart of the writing conference is the Vygotskian concept of *scaffolding*, the ways that the feedback delivered through the dialogue between teacher and student can be used by the student writer to develop both a text and his or her writing abilities (Williams, 2002). The interactive nature of the conference also gives teachers a chance to respond to the diverse cultural, educational, and writing needs of their students, clarifying meaning and resolving ambiguities, while saving them the time spent in detailed marking of papers. Writing conferences can give students a clearer idea of their strengths and weaknesses, develop their autonomy, allow them to raise questions on their written feedback, and help them construct a revision plan (Hyland, F., 2000).

Both teachers and students tend to be positive about the opportunities for detailed discussion that conferences offer, and research suggests that students typically receive more focused and usable comments than through written feedback (Zamel, 1985). But conferences vary considerably in the extent to which they improve student writing, and the literature stresses the need for careful planning to ensure that students participate actively. Where they are successful, however, oral conferences can not only lead to revisions in subsequent drafts but also have lasting effects on improving writing in later assignments (e.g., Patthey-Chavez & Ferris, 1997).

Some teachers have expressed reservations about oral conferences, however, because L2 students are not always in a good position to make the most of these opportunities to get individual attention and discuss their writing face-to-face with their teachers. Conferences differ considerably from the typical classroom situation, and some students may lack the experience, interactive abilities, or aural comprehension skills to benefit. There is also the issue of power relations in the conference and the ways that this may affect student participation and negotiation of meaning (Powers, 1993). Some learners have cultural or social inhibitions about engaging informally with authority figures, let alone questioning them (Goldstein & Conrad, 1990), and this can result in students passively and unreflectively incorporating the teacher's suggestions into their work. For teachers there are the disadvantages that conferences consume considerable amounts of time and require specialized interaction skills that have not been fully defined. There is, therefore, a need for further investigation of the effectiveness of the feedback offered in conferences and the nature of the oral interaction between teachers and students.

Peer feedback and L2 writers

Another important issue in L2 feedback is the role of peer response. From a socio-cognitive perspective, peer review can be seen as a formative developmental process that gives writers the opportunities to discuss their texts and discover others' interpretations of them.

Although peer response was introduced into L2 settings from L1 contexts on the assumption that what was good for one would be good for the other, subsequent research has not confirmed this optimism. Chaudron (1984), for instance, found the influence of teacher and peer feedback on writing improvement to be about the same, while Zhang (1985) found that teacher feedback was more effective for improving grammatical errors than peer or self-feedback, and Connor and Asenavage (1994) discovered that peer feedback made only a marginal difference to student writing. Other studies, however, have been more positive. Paulus (1999), for instance, established that peer feedback influenced student revision significantly and led to improved texts, and Mendonca and Johnson (1994) found that students used their peers' comments in more than half their revisions. Affective factors are also important in the success of peer feedback, and studies have suggested that whereas students might value peer feedback, they prefer teacher feedback to all other types (Saito, 1994; Sengupta, 1998; Zhang, 1995).

These studies have taught us to avoid idealizing L2 peer group interactions as sites of constructive interaction, since the reality can be quite different. An important factor in the success of peer response seems to be student training, with instruction encouraging a greater level of engagement with the task and more helpful and concrete advice (e.g., Keh, 1990; Stanley, 1992). In fact, training appears to benefit both the writer and the reader in peer dyads, with students who receive training to give peer feedback also making higher quality revisions to their own writing (Berg, 1999).

Some problems with peer response are specific to the L2 situation. It is suggested that student editors, for example, are more likely to address surface errors than problems of meaning (Keh, 1990) and that inexperienced L2 students may find it hard to judge the validity of their peers' comments (Leki, 1990). Students might also have difficulties identifying problem areas in other students' writing and offer them inaccurate or misleading advice (Horowitz, 1986), while writers may react negatively and defensively to critical comments from their peers (Amores, 1997). But studies looking specifically at the kinds of advice given by L2 editors have found relatively small amounts of miscorrection (Jacobs, 1989). Caulk (1994), for example, concluded that L2 peer commentary appeared to offer valuable and complementary suggestions when compared with teachers' comments, with only 6 percent of peer suggestions offering bad advice. The comments made covered different concerns from the teacher comments and gave less general and more specific advice.

Peer response studies have focused on the nature of peer interactions in writing workshops (Guerrero & Villamil, 1994; Lim & Jacobs, 2001; Ohta, 1995). In their study of peer interactions by Spanish speakers in an EFL writing workshop, for instance, Villamil and Guerrero (1996) found a complex and productive scaffolded peer help process, conducted largely in the students' L1. The authors argue that a crucial aspect of peer interactions is "affectivity," which includes "camaraderie, empathy and concern for not hurting each other's feelings" (1996, p. 65). Hyland's (2000) examination of writing workshop interactions found that the aspects of peer feedback mentioned most positively by the students in interviews were related to informal peer support mechanisms. Rather than focusing on a finished product, these interactions functioned mainly at the affective level, with students informally providing each other with support and advice during the writing process.

An important but contentious issue in examinations of peer-group interactions is a focus on the problems that can arise from the variety of cultural and educational backgrounds that L2 peer groups may contain. According to Allaei and Connor (1990, p. 24), "conflict, or at the very least, high levels of discomfort may occur in multi-cultural collaborative peer response groups." Students from different cultures may have different expectations about fundamental aspects of the group situation, such as the roles of the members, the mechanics of the group, and interpersonal interaction strategies (Carson & Nelson, 1994, 1996; Nelson & Carson, 1995, 1998; Nelson & Murphy, 1992). These differences can make it difficult for multicultural groups to reach a consensus about what to focus on and how to convey information and may affect the extent to which students incorporate their peers' suggestions. If the members of the group cooperate, the writers are more likely to make changes, but if the interaction is poor or the writers become defensive, they are less likely to do so (Nelson & Murphy, 1993).

As we can see, the research so far has not been conclusive on the central issue of whether peer response is an effective means of improving L2 writing or revision strategies. However, many writing teachers of L2 students feel instinctively that it has benefits, since it provides an audience for writers and seems to develop students' evaluative skills. Although it remains an important source of feedback in many writing courses, there is clearly a need for further investigation.

Computer-mediated feedback

As technology develops and computer facilities become more widely available, the role of the computer in delivering and mediating feedback has become a focus for research. In addition, changes in university sources of funding and student demographic distributions have meant a marked increase in the provision of distance courses and online research supervision. In more local contexts of instruction, writing workshops have also been extended through the use of computer networks that allow students to exchange writing with each other and with the teacher and receive comments without the need for face-to-face interaction.

Some researchers claim that these technological developments can empower students and make writing classes more collaborative. According to Warschauer et al. (1996), computer-mediated communication (CMC) allows students to take a more active and autonomous role when seeking feedback, since they can raise questions when they want to and take the initiative in discussions. Student conferencing is also said to make discussion more "student centered," foster a sense of community, encourage a sense of group knowledge, and increase student participation, since there are more opportunities for student-student interaction with the teacher as facilitator (Warschauer, 2002). CMC may also have particular advantages for empowering disadvantaged and less able students (Belcher, 1990; Hartman et al., 1991) and may be particularly motivating for L2 students (Warschauer, 2002; Greenfield, 2003). Some researchers also claim that it can lead to better writing products and more focused and better-quality peer feedback (Braine, 1997; Sullivan & Pratt, 1996).

However, there are also some concerns about CMC as a substitute for more traditional forms of feedback, since its benefits have not yet been clearly established by research. Belcher (1999) has cautioned that although many students respond well to CMC, it can disadvantage the technologically challenged and those lacking access to good computer facilities at home. The lack of face-to-face communication and the time pressure may also have a negative effect on the quality of peer inter-action in the CMC mode. Liu and Sadler (2003) looked at comments made by peer reviewers in technology-enhanced and traditional face-to-face contexts and found that students using CMC, especially those using real-time communication in online chat rooms, made a greater number of comments, but that these were more superficial, perhaps due to the pres-sure to respond immediately. Face-to-face interaction resulted in a more positive response with more focused feedback and more questions and interaction among peers. The future role of electronic peer review may be as part of a two-step peer review process, combined with traditional face-to-face activities rather than as a replacement for them.

Another area with a growing impact on approaches to feedback is the development of software that is either programmable or capable of scan-ning student text. Going beyond the often misleading and prescriptive information provided by early grammar checkers, several programs now offer students feedback in a wide variety of areas, including grammar. Programs such as the Criterion Online Writing Service (Burston et al., 2004), for instance, automatically evaluate essay responses, and e-rater (Burston, 2003) provides a holistic score for an essay with real-time feed-back about grammar, usage, style, organization, and development. Such programs offer the potential for integrated and systematic feedback on language problems, although their value has not yet been fully demon-strated. The goal of producing automated feedback on L2 writing is still the holy grail of software developers, and the problem of parsing natural language in completely reliable ways remains an area of ongoing activity and research (Hearst, 2000).

Another kind of automated feedback program is the type offered in the Respond module of the widely used Daedalus Integrated Writing Environment (Daedalus, 2005). The program steers students through an evaluative process using a series of modifiable prompts. Learners revise their drafts, with questions appearing in the upper half of a window; students respond in the lower half while consulting their text in another window. Once again, research is sparse regarding the effectiveness of the program, but the fact that students as well as teachers are able to con-struct questions that focus on fine-tuning writing or highlighting common problems can be a productive way of using the medium.

Computers are also influencing feedback on writing through the use of electronic corpora, which are becoming increasingly important as teach-ing becomes less a practice of imparting knowledge and more one of providing opportunities for learning. Concordancers offer interesting possibilities for innovative uses of feedback, allowing students to access numerous examples of particular features in large collections of texts so they can focus on typical patterns in writing. If students submit their writing electronically, teachers can hyperlink errors directly to a concordance file where students can examine the contexts and collocations of the words they have misused (Milton, 1999). This kind of reflective, active response to a teacher's feedback can be extremely useful for raising students' awareness of genre-specific conventions, developing independent learning skills, and improving writing products (Hyland, K., 2003; Milton, 2004) and is an area for further investigation.

Contexts and issues of feedback

It is clear that many areas of feedback remain unresolved. The main reason for this is that feedback on students' writing, whether by teachers or peers, is a form of social action designed to accomplish educational and social goals. Like all acts of communication, it occurs in particular cultural, institutional, and interpersonal contexts, between people enacting and negotiating particular social identities and relationships, and is mediated by various types of delivery. The fact that participants respond differently to these factors means that the effectiveness of feedback is difficult to pin down, and it is these factors that are explored in this book.

We need, then, to go beyond the individual act of feedback itself to consider the factors that influence feedback options and student responses. Although the choices are affected by what responders see on the page or screen, they are also socially shaped and constrained by the possibilities made available by their previous experiences, by their preferences for certain cultural and institutional practices, by the type of feedback mode they employ, and by their assumptions and beliefs about writing, learning, and individual writers.

The difficulties of specifying relevant aspects of context are considerable and have been discussed at length in the literature (e.g., Goodwin & Duranti, 1992; Levinson, 1983). Although such aspects of teaching writing and learning to write are not fully understood, it is clear that we can only appreciate them by considering both the immediate interaction in which they take place and the larger world that has an impact on participants' behaviors. Context is therefore a frame that surrounds feedback and provides resources for its appropriate interpretation. This volume seeks to further our understanding of what we do when we respond to second language students' writing, how we do it, what perceptions come into play, and the effects feedback has on teachers, learners, and writing. To do this involves examining how feedback is situated, shaped, and negotiated, and for us this means looking at three key dimensions of

feedback: the wider sociocultural context, the ways tha
delivered, and the interactions among participants. Alth
categories are obviously not watertight, we believe the
way of conceptualizing feedback practices and exploring
second language writing.

Situating feedback: Sociocultural dimensions

All acts of communication are embedded in wider sociocultural beliefs
and practices that selectively activate knowledge and prompt specific
processes. Cultural factors, particularly experiences and backgrounds,
help shape participants' understandings of teaching and learning and are
likely to have a considerable impact on the feedback offered and how it is
taken up in subsequent writing. Whether teachers decide to focus on form
or content, look to praise or criticize student writing, establish an equal
or hierarchical affiliation, or adopt an involved or remote stance, they
are at least partly influenced by the dominant ideologies of their institutions and the beliefs acquired as a result of their cultural backgrounds
and educational experiences. These ideologies help establish cohesion
and coordinate understanding through mutual expectations, but cultural
variations in these assumptions can intrude into classrooms through the
expectations that teachers and students have about instruction and the
meanings they attach to the feedback they are given.

Culture, however, is something of a controversial concept. Generally
understood as a historically transmitted and systematic network of meanings that allows us to understand, develop, and communicate our knowledge and beliefs about the world (Lantolf, 1999), it is often regarded
as "reductionist" and static by postmodern theorists (Atkinson, 1999;
Clifford, 1992). It has been argued that an over-reliance on culture as
an explanatory tool may lead researchers to downplay the importance of
other complex and constantly changing sociocultural factors. Students
have individual identities beyond the language and culture they were
born into and may resist or ignore cultural patterns. We are all members of many communities and social groups whose cultures are fluid,
diverse, and non-determining, so individual beliefs and practices cannot
simply be labeled as typical of a culture. But we should avoid labeling
teachers or students according to crude cultural stereotypes, we cannot ignore perspectives that might help us understand the ways students
and teachers may prefer to interact, teach, and learn. We do not have
to lump L2 students together as an undifferentiated group, restrict the
idea to broad ethnic or geographical dispositions, nor regard cultural
norms as decisive to see explanatory and pedagogic value in the concept.
Language and learning are inextricably bound up with culture (Kramsch,
1993), mainly because our routine experiences foreground certain

aken-for-granted conceptions of writing and the ways it is learned in a second language. These conceptions can, in turn, influence our representations about feedback, trigger assumptions about participant relationships in teaching-learning situations, and affect our ideas about how response should be structured and negotiated. Although teachers and students are not prisoners of their origins or of the communities in which they habitually participate, human cognition and learning is rooted in cultural environments and influenced by the discursive practices of their social groups.

Even though the notion of culture is problematic and contested, it has played an important explanatory role in feedback research, most notably in studies of peer response, as an explanation for mismatches in teacher-learner expectations, and in the issues surrounding ownership of writing. Chapters in the first section of the book draw on these ideas and focus on related research.

- Olga Villamil and Maria de Guerrero emphasize the critical role of interaction in developing students' writing skills in peer response groups. Providing sample episodes from a long-term research project on peer interaction, the authors illustrate how sociocultural theory helps us to understand peer feedback and propose ways in which it can be most effectively used in the L2 writing classroom.
- Gayle Nelson and Joan Carson also examine culture and peer feedback in L2 writing classrooms. Revisiting peer response studies (including their own), the authors address the controversy this issue raises and argue for the relevance of cultural considerations in peer group interactions, showing how they might interfere with the effectiveness of such groups.
- Christine Tardy takes a different angle on culture, exploring different facets of "appropriation." Tardy expands on the traditional view of appropriation – that writing can be "stolen" from a writer by the teacher's comments (Knoblauch & Brannon, 1984) and explores the tensions between promoting dominant discourses and encouraging individuals to preserve their own ways of writing. Describing dialogic models of appropriation, she argues that teachers and students should focus on the complex ways in which ownership, identity, community, and expertise interact in feedback and revision.

Shaping feedback: Delivery and focus dimensions

The second section of the book looks at shaping feedback in the immediate context of response, concentrating in particular on the mode in which feedback is delivered and on the focus of that delivery. It explores the *how* and *what* of feedback. The issue of focus is obviously a crucial dimension, and the various ways in which teachers and peers provide feedback can also have a considerable impact on its meaning and value to students.

The chapters in this section therefore examine the key ways in which feedback can be presented, the issues it might target, and how effective it is. Of importance here is the kind of feedback provided, whether oral, written, computer-mediated, or a variety, and how language is used, both as the object of focus (as when it is attended to in terms of error correction) and as a resource in the feedback itself (such as when it is modeled as appropriate form and good writing). The section begins with the long-running debate concerning the effectiveness of teacher-written feedback on student drafts and expands to consider various other feedback delivery systems, including electronic, corpus-assisted portfolios and self-feedback techniques.

- Dana Ferris examines the value of responding to student language errors. Analyzing more than 200 preliminary and revised drafts by 92 L2 undergraduates, along with questionnaire and interview data, she explores teacher feedback strategies and their effectiveness in improving students' immediate and long-term writing accuracy.
- Paige Ware and Mark Warschauer focus on electronic response by summarizing and analyzing three main strands of research on computer-based feedback in second language writing: software-generated feedback, computer-mediated feedback, and key aspects of differentiation within electronic modes.
- John Milton describes a suite of computer-based tools integrated to support students in the writing process through effective feedback. He shows how technology can give novice L2 writers and their teachers access to important lexical and grammatical aspects of English, reduce the tedium of error correction, make feedback more timely, consistent and adequate, and assist language teachers in prioritizing and identifying error.
- Liz Hamp-Lyons examines feedback in portfolio writing contexts, illustrating how portfolios make feedback a central aspect of teaching and learning by encouraging students to reflect on their writing and the criteria employed for judging it before revising and resubmitting their assignments.
- Ann Johns explores "self-feedback" through a research assignment called the I-Search paper. The I-Search process helps students to assess their knowledge before and after their research; record their search activities; identify their planning, reading, note-taking, and other strategies; reflect on their processes; and consider future improvements.

Negotiating feedback: Interpersonal and interactional dimensions

As all teachers are aware, giving feedback is more than selecting a delivery mode and deciding which aspects of writing to attend to. The interpersonal and interactional dimension refers to the relationships that participants construct, confront, and deal with as they engage in the situated processes of giving feedback. The kinds of institution, the ethos of the classroom, students' purposes in learning to write, their proficiencies, and the genres they are studying are often important though neglected variables in feedback studies (Ferris, 2003). Even though controlled experiments may simply ignore this dimension, response always takes place within a classroom context of instruction and interaction, in which students and teachers have particular goals and preferences and in which they develop personal relationships. Participants' identities and roles, the place that feedback has in instruction, the channel that is employed, and the goals students are trying to achieve in learning to write in a foreign language are all important aspects of feedback environments.

The papers in this section focus on the negotiation of feedback: the ways in which the processes and purposes of the event unfold and how the participants experience this.

- Lynn Goldstein argues for the importance of understanding the individual teacher and student in three feedback contexts. She highlights the ways in which teachers construct feedback in terms of their perceptions of each student, how individual students interact with this feedback, and the factors that can influence students' using feedback effectively.
- Ken Hyland and Fiona Hyland examine the interpersonal dimensions of teacher-written feedback through a detailed text analysis of two teachers' written feedback as praise, criticism, and suggestions. They explore the pedagogic and interpersonal motivations for these comments and the ways in which students responded to them.
- Caroline Coffin and Ann Hewings look at the interactional roles of teacher and students in a computer-mediated conferencing environment, arguing that the interactive nature of the medium encourages an awareness of argument strategies and helps develop students' writing and reasoning skills.
- Bob Weissberg turns to the value of oral teacher feedback in one-on-one encounters with students in writing-center tutorial sessions and teacher-student conferences, examining how instructor and student cooperate in building conversational scaffolds to develop advanced writing skills.

- Ilona Leki explores the perceptions of 20 graduate students on the feedback practices they experienced in both disciplinary and writing courses during their first semester of study in the United States.

Conclusion

Feedback is a key component of teaching second language writing, with process, social constructivist, and academic literacy approaches all employing it as a central part of their instructional repertoires. This means that response does not represent a single theory or method but a collection of ways by which teachers can assist students toward a better understanding of their texts, their readers, their writing processes, and their learning and so develop their awareness of writing and language use more generally. Actual classroom practices are influenced and intimately related to the three dimensions sketched in this introduction. In the following chapters, the ways that feedback is situated, shaped, and negotiated are explored in some detail to reevaluate the role and significance of response in second-language writing instruction and to locate feedback clearly within current research, classroom practice, and theoretical perspectives about teaching and learning.

References

Allaei, S., & Connor, U. (1990). Exploring the dynamics of cross-cultural collaboration. *The Writing Instructor, 10*, 19–28.

Amores, M. J. (1997). A new perspective on peer editing. *Foreign Language Annals, 30*(4), 513–523.

Anderson, J. R. (1982). Acquisition of cognitive skill. *Psychological Review, 89*, 369–406.

Atkinson, D. (1999). TESOL and culture. *TESOL Quarterly, 33*, 625–654.

Bartholomae, D. (1986). Inventing the university. *Journal of Basic Writing, 5*(1), 4–23.

Belcher, D. (1990). Peer vs. teacher response in the advanced composition class. *Issues in Writing, 2*, 128–150.

Belcher, D. (1999). Authentic interaction in a virtual classroom: Leveling the playing field in a graduate seminar. *Computers and Composition, 16*, 253–267.

Berg, E. C. (1999). The effects of trained peer response on ESL students' revision types and writing quality. *Journal of Second Language Writing, 8*, 215–241.

Braine, G. (1997). Beyond word processing: Networked computers in ESL writing classes. *Computers and Composition, 14*, 45–58.

Brinko, K. T. (1993). The practice of giving feedback to improve teaching. *Journal of Higher Education, 64*(5), 574–593.

Brophy, J. (1981). Teacher praise: A functional analysis. *Review of Educational Research, 51*, 5–32.

Burstein, J. (2003). The *e-rater*® scoring engine: Automated essay scoring with natural language processing. In M. D. Shermis & J. Burstein (Eds.), *Automated essay scoring: A cross-disciplinary perspective*. Hillsdale, NJ: Lawrence Erlbaum.

Burstein, J., Chodorow, M., & Leacock, C. (2004). Automated essay evaluation: The Criterion online writing service. *AI Magazine, 25(3)*, 27–36.

Carson, J., & Nelson, G. (1994). Writing groups: Cross-cultural issues. *Journal of Second Language Writing, 3*, 17–30.

Carson, J., & Nelson, G. (1996). Chinese students' perceptions of ESL peer response group interaction. *Journal of Second Language Writing, 5*, 1–19.

Caulk, N. (1994). Comparing teacher and student responses to written work. *TESOL Quarterly, 28(1)*, 181–187.

Chandler, J. (2003). The efficacy of various kinds of error correction for improvement of the accuracy and fluency of L2 student writing. *Journal of Second Language Writing, 12*, 267–296.

Chaudron, C. (1984). The effects of feedback on students' composition revisions. *RELC Journal, 15(2)*, 1–15.

Clifford, J. (1992). Traveling cultures. In C. Grossberg, C. Nelson, and P. Triechler (Eds.), *Cultural Studies* (pp. 96–116). New York: Routledge.

Connor, U., & Asenavage, K. (1994). Peer response groups in ESL writing classes: How much impact on revision? *Journal of Second Language Writing, 3(3)*, 257–276.

Conrad, S. M., & Goldstein, L. M. (1999). Student revision after teacher written comments: Text, contexts and individuals. *Journal of Second Language Writing, 8*, 147–180.

Daedalus Integrated Writing Environment (2005). Computer software. Austin, TX: The Daedalus Group.

Fathman, A., & Whalley, E. (1990). Teacher response to student writing: Focus on form versus content. In B. Kroll (Ed.), *Second language writing: Research insights for the classroom* (pp. 178–190).

Ferris, D. R. (1995). Student reactions to teacher response in multiple-draft composition classrooms. *TESOL Quarterly, 29(1)*, 33–53.

Ferris, D. R. (1997). The influence of teacher commentary on student revision. *TESOL Quarterly, 31*, 315–339.

Ferris, D. R. (2002). *Treatment of error in second language student writing*. Ann Arbor, MI: University of Michigan Press.

Ferris, D. R. (2003). *Response to student writing*. Mahwah, NJ: Lawrence Erlbaum.

Ferris, D. R., & Helt, M. (2000). *Was Truscott right? New evidence on the effects of error correction in L2 writing classes*. Paper presented at American Association of Applied Linguistics Conference, Vancouver, BC.

Ferris, D. R., and Roberts, B. (2001). Error feedback in L2 writing classes: How explicit does it need to be? *Journal of Second Language Writing, 10*, 161–184.

Freedman, S. W. (Ed.). (1985). *The acquisition of written language. Response and revision*. Norwood, NJ: Ablex.

Freedman, S., & Sperling, M. (1985). Teacher student interaction in the writing conference: Response and teaching. In S. Freedman (Ed.), *The acquisition of written language: Response and revision* (pp. 106–130). Norwood, NJ: Ablex.

Goldstein, L. M., and Conrad, S. M. (1990). Student input and negotiation of meaning in ESL writing conferences. *TESOL Quarterly, 24(3),* 443–460.

Goodwin, C., & Duranti, A. (1992). Rethinking context: An introduction. In A. Duranti & C. Goodwin (Eds.), *Rethinking context: Language as an interactional phenomenon* (pp. 1–37). Cambridge, UK: Cambridge University Press.

Greenfield, R. (2003). Collaborative e-mail exchange for teaching secondary ESL: A case study in Hong Kong. *Language Learning and Technology, 7(1),* 46–70.

Guerrero, M. C. M. de, & Villamil, O. S. (1994). Social-cognitive dimensions of interaction in L2 peer revision. *The Modern Language Journal, 78(4),* 484–496.

Guerrero, M. C. M. de, & Villamil, O. S. (2000). Activating the ZPD: Mutual scaffolding in L2 peer revision. *The Modern Language Journal, 84,* 51–68.

Hartman, K., Neuwith, C., Kiesler, S., Sproull, L., Cochran, C., Palmquist, M., & Zubrow, D. (1991). Patterns of social interaction and learning to write: Some effects of network technologies. *Written Communication, 8,* 79–113.

Hearst, M. (2000). The debate on automated essay grading. *Intelligence Systems, 15(5),* 22–37.

Horowitz, D. (1986). Process, not product: Less than meets the eye. *TESOL Quarterly, 20(1),* 141–144.

Hyland, F. (1998). The impact of teacher written feedback on individual writers. *Journal of Second Language Writing, 7(3),* 255–286.

Hyland, F. (2000). ESL writers and feedback: Giving more autonomy to students. *Language Teaching Research, 4,* 33–54.

Hyland, F., & Hyland, K. (2001). Sugaring the pill: Praise and criticism in written feedback. *Journal of Second Language Writing, 10(3),* 185–212.

Hyland, K. (2003). *Second language writing.* New York: Cambridge University Press.

Jacobs, G. (1989). Miscorrection in peer feedback in writing class. *RELC Journal, 20(1),* 68–75.

Janopoulos, M. (1992). University faculty tolerance of NS and NNS writing errors. *Journal of Second Language Writing, 1,* 109–122.

Keh, C. (1990). Feedback in the writing process: A model and methods for implementation. *ELT Journal, 44(4),* 294–305.

Kepner, C. (1991). An experiment in the relationship of types of written feedback to the development of writing skills. *The Modern Language Journal, 75,* 305–313.

Kramsch, C. (1993). *Context and culture in language teaching.* Oxford: Oxford University Press.

Kroll, B. (Ed.). (1990). *Second language writing: Research insights for the classroom.* Cambridge, UK: Cambridge University Press.

Lantolf, J. P. (1999). Second culture acquisition: Cognitive considerations. In E. Hinkel (Ed.), *Culture in second language teaching and learning* (pp. 28–46). Cambridge, UK: Cambridge University Press.

Leki, I. (1990). Coaching from the margins: Issues in written response. In B. Kroll (Ed.), *Second language writing: Research insights for the classroom* (pp. 57–68).

Leki, I. (1991). The preferences of ESL students for error correction in college level writing classes. *Foreign Language Annals, 24(3)*, 203–218.

Lim, W. L., & Jacobs, G. M. (2001). *An analysis of students' dyadic interaction on a dictogloss task.* ERIC Document Reproduction Service, ED 456 649.

Levinson, S. (1983). *Pragmatics.* Cambridge, UK: Cambridge University Press.

Liu, J., & Sadler, R. (2003). The effect and affect of peer review in electronic versus traditional modes on L2 writing. *Journal of English for Academic Purposes, 2*, 193–227.

Master, P. (1995). Consciousness raising and article pedagogy. In D. Belcher and G. Braine (Eds.), *Academic writing in a second language: Essays on research and pedagogy* (pp. 183–205). Norwood, NJ: Ablex.

Mendonca, C. O., & Johnson, K. E. (1994). Peer review negotiations: Revision activities in ESL writing instruction. *TESOL Quarterly, 28(4)*, 745–768.

Milton, J. (1999). Lexical thickets and electronic gateways: Making text accessible by novice writers. In C. N. Candlin & K. Hyland (Eds.), *Writing: Texts, processes and practices* (pp. 221–243). London: Longman.

Milton, J. (2004). From parrots to puppet masters: Fostering creative and authentic language use with online tools. In B. Holmberg, M. Shelly, & C. White (Eds.), *Distance education and language: Evolution and change* (pp. 242–257). Clevedon, UK: Multilingual Matters.

Nelson, G., & Carson, J. (1995). Social dimensions of second-language writing instruction: Peer response groups as cultural context. In D. Rubin (Ed.), *Composing social identity in written communication* (pp. 89–109). Hillsdale, NJ: Lawrence Erlbaum.

Nelson, G., & Carson, J. (1998). ESL students' perceptions of effectiveness in peer response groups. *Journal of Second Language Writing, 7*, 113–131.

Nelson, G., & Murphy, J. M. (1992). An L2 writing group: Task and social dimensions. *Journal of Second Language Writing, 1(3)*, 171–193.

Nelson, G., & Murphy, J. M. (1993). Peer response groups: Do L2 writers use peer comments in revising their drafts? *TESOL Quarterly, 27(1)*, 135–141.

Patthey-Chavez, G. G., and Ferris, D. (1997). Writing conferences and the weaving of multi-voiced texts in college composition. *Research in the Teaching of English, 31*, 51–90.

Paulus, T. (1999). The effect of peer and teacher feedback on student writing. *Journal of Second Language Writing, 8*, 265–289.

Polio, C., Fleck, C., & Leder, N. (1998). "If I only had more time": ESL learners' changes in linguistic accuracy on essay revisions. *Journal of Second Language Writing, 7*, 43–68.

Powers, J. (1993). Rethinking writing center conferencing strategies for the ESL writer. *Writing Center Journal, 13*, 39–47.

Probst, R. E. (1989). Transactional theory and response to student writing. In C. Anson (Ed.), *Writing and response* (pp. 68–79). Urbana, IL: NCTE.

Robb, T., Ross, S., & Shortreed, I. (1986). Salience of feedback on error and its effect on EFL writing quality. *TESOL Quarterly, 20(1)*, 83–91.

Saito, H. (1994). Teachers' practices and students' preferences for feedback on second language writing: A case study of adult ESL learners. *TESL Canada Journal, 11(2)*, 46–70.

Schachter, J. (1991). Corrective feedback in historical perspective. *Second Language Research, 7(2)*, 89–102.

Semke, H. D. (1984). The effects of the red pen. *Foreign Language Annals, 17,* 195–202.

Sengupta, S. (1998). Peer evaluation: "I am not the teacher." *ELT Journal, 52(1),* 19–28.

Sheppard, K. (1992). Two feedback types: Do they make a difference? *RELC Journal, 23,* 103–110.

Stanley, J. (1992). Coaching student writers to be effective peer evaluators. *Journal of Second Language Writing, 1(3),* 217–233.

Sullivan, N., & Pratt, E. (1996). A comparative study of two ESL writing environments: A computer assisted classroom and a traditional oral classroom. *System, 24,* 491–501.

Truscott, J. (1996). The case against grammar correction in L2 writing classes. *Language Learning, 46,* 327–369.

Truscott, J. (1999). The case for "the case against grammar correction in L2 writing classes." A response to Ferris. *Journal of Second Language Writing, 8,* 111–122.

Villamil, O. S., & de Guerrero, M. C. M. (1996). Peer revision in the L2 classroom: Social-cognitive activities, mediating strategies, and aspects of social behaviour. *Journal of Second Language Writing, 5(1),* 51–75.

Vygotsky, L. S. (1978). *Mind in society: The development of higher psychological processes.* Cambridge. MA: Harvard University Press.

Warschauer, M. (2002). Networking into academic discourse. *Journal of English for Academic Purposes, 1,* 45–58.

Warschauer, M., Turbee, L., & Roberts, B. (1996). Computer learning networks and student empowerment. *System, 24(1),* 1–14.

White, L., Spada, S., Lightbown, P. M., & Ranta, L. (1991). Input enhancement and L2 question formation. *Applied Linguistics, 12(4),* 416–432.

Williams, J. (2002). Undergraduate second language writers in the writing center. *Journal of Basic Writing, 21, 2,* 73–91.

Zamel, V. (1985). Responding to student writing. *TESOL Quarterly, 19(1),* 79–101.

Zhang, S. (1985). *The differential effects of sources of corrective feedback on ESL writing proficiency.* Occasional paper series no 9. Honolulu: University of Hawaii at Manoa, Department of English as a Second Language.

Zhang, S. (1995). Re-examining the affective advantages of peer feedback in the ESL writing class. *Journal of Second Language Writing, 4(3),* 209–222.

PART I:
SITUATING FEEDBACK: SOCIOCULTURAL DIMENSIONS

2 Sociocultural theory: A framework for understanding the social-cognitive dimensions of peer feedback

Olga S. Villamil
María C. M. de Guerrero

Part of the great popularity that peer feedback enjoys today in L2 writing classrooms comes no doubt from its potential in providing learners with rich and extended assistance during the writing process. Peer response is thus often welcomed by teachers because it involves students sharing the responsibility of feedback. Part of the great appeal of peer feedback is also derived, in our view, from its strong foothold in theoretical principles relating social interaction and mediation to individual development. These principles are best expressed in the sociocultural theory (SCT) of the developmental psychologist Lev Vygotsky.

In this paper, we summarize our long-term research on peer feedback in the L2 writing classroom with a focus on how SCT contributes to illuminating and explaining the social-cognitive[1] dimensions of L2 writing development. Within this framework, we discuss some salient aspects of our research on peer feedback, such as patterns of joint interaction and self-regulation; forms of mediation during interaction, development and internalization; and cultural issues in peer feedback.

The sociocultural theory framework

Traditionally associated with the work of Vygotsky (1978, 1986; see also Wertsch, 1979a), SCT is a system of ideas on the origin and development of the mind. Mind and consciousness are, from an SCT perspective, predominantly social in nature. They are fundamentally the result of the internalization of socially and temporally bound modes of thinking, feeling, and behaving. Within this theory, learning is also a social phenomenon embedded in specific cultural, historical, and institutional contexts. Whereas other theories of learning recognize the importance of social factors in learning and particularly in L2 acquisition, SCT, unlike other approaches to mind, such as the information-processing approach, views the social element as constitutive of cognition – and thus of learning – not just as one more variable affecting processes that reside mainly in the learner's head.

Central to SCT is the notion that higher forms of thinking and the ability to perform certain complex skills originate in and are shaped by social interaction. However, SCT stands in sharp contrast to interactionist theories of learning, in which interaction is seen merely as an exchange of information between partners or as a means of modifiying "input" for the learner. In these theories, the learner takes from social interaction what is of benefit and processes that information alone. From an SCT perspective, in contrast, social interaction (with both humans and artifacts participating dialogically) is internalized, the external-dialogic becomes the internal-dialogic, and a socially constructed dialogic mind emerges.

Some key concepts of sociocultural theory

Several SCT concepts are useful in analyzing peer feedback, in particular the concepts of mediation, internalization, developmental change, and cultural embeddedness. First, SCT postulates that the adult human mind is *mediated*. It is the result of the transformation of lower forms of thinking (elementary perception, involuntary attention, natural memory) into higher forms of thinking (voluntary attention, logical reasoning, planning, problem solving) through cultural mediation. SCT does not deny the existence of biological requirements and constraints on intellectual development, but it does argue that, to operate at a high level of intellectual activity, the mind must necessarily be socioculturally mediated. Vygotsky was particularly interested in the use of signs as a psychological mediating tool. In actuality, however, three forms of mediation can be distinguished in SCT: mediation by others, mediation by the self, and mediation by artifacts (Lantolf, 2000). These forms of mediation are heavily dependent on language (or symbols), and all are sociocultural in origin and nature.

To operate at the level of higher intellectual functions, individuals must go through a process of *internalization* of mediational means. As Vygotsky (1978) remarked, internalization entails a long series of developmental processes resulting in the radical alteration of the nature of psychological activity on the basis of sign mediation (p. 57). He believed that social interaction, such as takes place in schooling, is essential in the internalization of external actions. In Vygotsky's view, an optimal scenario for development, and hence internalization, is the *zone of proximal development* (ZPD). In the ZPD, those areas that are sensitive to development, that is, "those functions that have not yet matured but are in the process of maturation" (1978, p. 86), have the potential to grow and develop through mediation by others. Vygotsky did not limit mediation in the ZPD to that of teachers or adults but, significantly, made *peer* mediation an essential means for internalization and development.

We propose that an essential feature of learning is that it creates the zone of proximal development; that is, learning awakens a variety of internal developmental processes that are able to operate only when the child is interacting with people in his environment and in cooperation with his peers. Once these processes are internalized, they become part of the child's developmental achievement. (1978, p. 90)

One way of conceptualizing movement within the ZPD, which is useful in our analysis of peer feedback, has been Wertsch's (1979a, 1979b) categorization of stages of regulation, or control over intellectual actions. Wertsch has proposed that, in the transition from interpsychological to intrapsychological activity, the learner moves from other-regulation to complete self-regulation. When other-regulated, the learner can perform with assistance from others. The learner achieves self-regulation when, in the course of ZPD interactions, he or she can take control of external actions and is capable of independent problem solving. In the absence of other-regulation or when not responding to other-regulation, the learner may be at a stage of object-regulation (Wertsch, 1979b, p. 90), a stage in which the learner is easily regulated by objects in the environment.

Because assistance in the ZPD is extended as long as other-regulation persists but is removed once the learner can function independently, it has been metaphorically conceived as a form of *scaffolding*. Traditionally, the concept of scaffolding has referred to the supportive behaviors by which an expert can help a novice learner achieve higher levels of regulation (see, for example, Lidz, 1991; Stone, 1993; Wood et al., 1976).

Starting with Donato (1994), several studies in the L2 literature have explored the effects of "mutual" rather than unidirectional peer scaffolding (Antón & DiCamilla, 1998; DiCamilla & Antón, 1997; Lim & Jacobs, 2001; Ohta, 1995). In Guerrero and Villamil (2000), for example, our purpose was to identify the mechanisms of bidirectional scaffolded help in peer revision. To observe these mechanisms, we employed a microgenetic analysis, an approach that allowed us to perceive closely how scaffolding assistance shifted hands and peer revision behaviors developed throughout the interaction. For Vygotsky (1978), both *microgenesis*, the observation of moment-to-moment changes in behavior (p. 61), and *ontogenesis*, development over the course of a lifetime, are indispensable in understanding the genesis of higher psychological functions.

A final concept of SCT that is of great value in the study of peer feedback is that human activity is always embedded in particular cultural, historical, and institutional settings. Thus, no aspect of learning can be fully and appropriately understood without taking into account the sociocultural context in which it takes place. As John-Steiner, Panofsky, and Smith (1994) explain, development is always shaped by the tools, strategies, values, and practices routinely enacted by specific communities. In their view, to acknowledge this means also to recognize that "activity settings vary greatly both within and between cultures" (p. 11). The notion that human activity and development are always culturally, temporally, and spatially bound is fundamental within activity theory, a theoretical framework that grew out of Vygotsky's original proposals and was expanded by A. N. Leontiev (1981). Activity theory proposes that attempts to understand human actions must take into account not only the socio-historical-cultural settings but also the particular motivations and goals that drive people to do what they do. An important contribution, then, of activity theory is in assigning agency to learners, that is, the capacity to establish personal goals, set up conditions, and choose the means that best suit their motives or needs in learning (Lantolf & Pavlenko, 2001). In short, an activity theory framework highlights the situated, intentional, and goal-directed nature of human learning.

In this paper, we highlight four distinct areas of our research in which an SCT framework proved most illuminating: (a) patterns of interaction and regulation during peer revision, (b) mediated assistance during interaction, (c) development and internalization of revision behaviors, and (d) the role of cultural situatedness in peer revision

Aims, participants, and data collection

In 1993 we embarked on a research project designed to gather data that would throw light on the social-cognitive dimensions of peer revision. Broadly, our aim was to find out how individual development in L2 writing could be impacted by the social experience of writing and revising among peers. From the beginning, we were clear that SCT, because of its critical emphasis on the interrelatedness of the social and the cognitive aspects of learning, would constitute the most appropriate theoretical framework for our goals. Fifty-four intermediate ESL college learners enrolled in a writing class taught by one of the researchers at a large private university in San Juan, Puerto Rico, participated in the study. Data were collected in two revision sessions scheduled one month apart.

Before each revision session, five classes were presented to train students in two rhetorical modes – narration and persuasion – and in how to revise their own as well as their peers' drafts.

After composing sessions for each mode were conducted, first drafts were collected and randomly paired. Two external raters determined independently which paper needed more revision. Students were then paired for each review session and instructed to record their interactions as they revised the draft. Each pair consisted of a "writer" (the author of the composition which needed more revision) and a "reader" (the other member of the pair, whose task was to assist the writer), although these roles were not explicitly mentioned to the students. There was no mention as to the language of interaction to be used in the session.

The participants started their interaction with the writer reading the paper aloud to the reader. After the session, drafts were returned to the participants, who worked on their final versions at home, then submitted them to the instructor a week later. The 40 audio-recorded interactions, together with the written texts that were obtained (first drafts, joint revised texts, final versions), would prove to be an exceedingly rich source of insights and information on peer revision.

Patterns of interaction and regulation during peer revision

In our first study (Guerrero & Villamil, 1994), we explored the cognitive stages of regulation that emerged when participants engaged in peer review. We focused on the different patterns of interaction and the social relationships that resulted from the participants' stages of regulation. We observed that learners displayed particular behaviors that would characterize them as self-regulated, other-regulated, and object-regulated during interaction. Self-regulated participants were capable of solving problems independently, identifying trouble sources, initiating revision, and providing scaffolding, as well as displaying an attitude of self-confidence in terms of content, language use, tasks, and procedures. Other-regulated learners did not seem to have a complete grasp of task goals and were unable to undertake revision on their own initiative; however, they could achieve a certain degree of control over the task as they let themselves be guided by their partners. Object-regulated learners were controlled by their drafts and could not see ways to improve them, nor could they respond to prompts of revision made by peers or engage in constructive dialogue. They were satisfied with their rudimentary first drafts and failed to understand the overall purpose of the revision session.

The categories of self-, other-, and object-regulation already described were used to code the participants' behavior during their interaction in the peer sessions. Prior to this coding, each interaction was transcribed and segmented into episodes. Each episode was then coded in terms of cognitive stages of regulation for individual participants, as well as in terms of the social relationships that resulted from their interaction.[2]

Participants' comments during the process are illustrative of various stages of regulation and throw light on the nature of regulatory behavior. Comments from self-regulated participants suggest leadership, self-assurance, and willingness to share knowledge.

"Let's read from the beginning so we can get the ideas."
"With this sentence you can start another paragraph because you see ... this is something else you are going to talk about."
"Just check and tell me if what you understood is what I meant."

In contrast, remarks from other-regulated members may indicate a certain degree of hesitancy, a need to be taken by the hand, and despair when not knowing what to do.

"And how can I explain that?"
"But this is in the past, do you think it should be in the present tense?"
"We can change this word, feel, well, I don't know, I really don't know."
"Oh God, I have an idea ... that this goes here, but ... oh my God, what is this ... ?"

Representative comments from object-regulated participants seem to demonstrate lack of interest in the task at hand and a need to justify limitations by avoiding the task or by turning to jokes or off-task behavior.

"I don't know, details, you mean? To tell you the truth, all of this writing in English and Spanish (starts singing) ... I always do so bad."
"I don't care about details. I am not a good observer, besides, I don't like to say much."

Cognitive regulation fluctuated during the course of interaction. Students found themselves immersed in a situation where they not only had to exercise control over the task but also regulate and be regulated by another. Fluctuation of regulation was dependent on several task factors: L2 knowledge, awareness of goals, mastery of rhetorical mode, the role adopted (reader or writer), and the presence of a collaborator who could engage in as much regulatory behavior. In our data we found 39.34 percent other-regulation, 2.31 percent object-regulation, and 58.35 percent self-regulation. The relatively high percentage of self-regulation could be attributed to the training students received prior to the revision sessions and to the students' frequent use of their L1 as a mediating tool to facilitate communication and achievement of goals. We also found that other-regulation predominated among writers, although self-regulation predominated among readers.

Different patterns of social relationships resulted from the participants' stages of cognitive regulation, as demonstrated by the audio recordings. Symmetrical interactions occurred when both participants were at the same stage of regulation and shared control of the task to the same degree. Asymmetrical interactions took place when partners

Table 2.1. *Symmetrical and asymmetrical peer interactions*

Symmetrical interactions	
Both participants are self-regulated, other-regulated, or object-regulated.	
SER–SER	Both participants are self-regulated.
OTR–OTR	Both participants are other-regulated.
OBR–OBR	Both participants are object-regulated.
Asymmetrical interactions	
Each participant in a student pair is at a different level of regulation.	
SER–OTR	Self-regulated vs. other regulated
OTR–OBR	Other-regulated vs. object-regulated
OBR–SER	Object-regulated vs. self-regulated

were at a different level of regulation and one of them had larger control over the task (see Table 2.1). An analysis of asymmetrical relationships revealed a majority (55%) of self-regulated (SER)–other-regulated (OTR) interactions. This relationship re-creates a social situation that recapitulates Vygotsky's ZPD, in which learning is fostered by the more skilled peer's assisting a partner in solving particular textual problems.

Within the self- and other-regulated category, 83 percent of the interactions were of a collaborative nature. Collaborative interactions were those in which both individuals recognized and respected the other's perspective and both felt free to present their views for the creation of meaningful text. In most cases, the self-regulated participant tried to see the text through the eyes of the author in order to help the partner achieve the task goals. This peer thus became a strategic assistant who promoted transition toward self-regulation through scaffolded assistance. Collaboration could be observed when partners commented, for example, "What do you mean when you say . . . ?" (reader); "I don't know if this is correct, what do you think?" (writer); and "You see, we can work better this way . . . when I work alone, sometimes I don't know what to do, but two heads think better than one" (writer). These comments reveal that partners understood that through negotiation and compromise goals could be achieved. Compromise was also evident in the frequent use of "we" and in the interchangeability of roles – either partner could read, compose, jot down comments, or initiate or lead revision.

A crucial aspect in collaborative interactions was affectivity. Readers and writers showed camaraderie, empathy, and concern for each other's feelings. Congratulatory comments such as, "Wow, you know how to revise well," "Your composition does not have as many errors as you think," or "This is quite good" served to stimulate both participants to collaborate. We believe that because of its collaborative nature and scaffolded assistance, this type of asymmetrical self- and other-regulated interactions appears to be the most conducive to learning within a ZPD perspective.

In contrast, non-collaborative interventions (only 17 percent of the self- and other-regulated interactions) were characterized by authoritative attitudes or resistance to collaboration. In some cases, the self-regulated member controlled the task and imposed personal views. These authoritative attitudes led to personality clashes or to cases of readers appropriating the writers' texts or writers struggling for and finally relinquishing their authorial control. Resistance to collaboration could also be seen when one of the partners showed indifference or unwillingness to participate in the revision task.

Mediated assistance during interaction

One way in which SCT bore insights in our analysis was in identifying the nature of mediation during peer interaction. Three main forms of mediation were used by the students as they worked jointly on revising a text: artifact-mediation, self-mediation, and other-mediation. Artifact-mediation (see Villamil & Guerrero, 1996) includes the use not only of language (L1 and L2), the most fundamental of all culturally constructed artifacts, but also of other symbolic tools. These include asterisks, numbers, parentheses, arrows, and brackets to mark texts for revision and external resources, such as dictionaries and prompt sheets provided for the occasion. It is important to note the role that the L1 (Spanish) played in the interactions. In 95 percent of the interactions, the L1 was the chief tool of mediation, being instrumental for a variety of purposes: making meaning of text, helping retrieve words in the L2, exploring and expanding ideas, guiding the action through the task, and keeping conversation going.

In addition to mediation by artifacts, mediation sometimes came from the self and was directed to the self. Despite being in a situation where joint work was required, the learners were occasionally observed to engage in solo behavior, either working silently, presumably through inner speech, or regulating their thinking through vocalized private speech. Self-directed, private speech in the form of repetitions, questions, self-reminders, and affective comments appeared to fulfill two purposes: to guide behavior and to release some of the affective load generated by the task (Villamil & Guerrero, 1996).

Most other-mediation proceeded from learners who were assigned as partners in the revision sessions, although occasionally assistance was also procured from the teacher.[3] To pursue the nature of other-mediation in depth, we conducted a microgenetic study of one pair's interaction as the partners were revising a narrative text written by one of them (Guerrero & Villamil, 2000).

The participants were two male college learners selected from 54 participants enrolled in an intermediate English writing course. (See the Aims, Participants, and Data Collection section in this paper.) The notion of scaffolding, operationally defined as "those supportive behaviors by which one partner in a semiotically mediated interactive situation can help another achieve higher levels of competence and regulation," was instrumental in the analysis of other-mediation. To help us identify these supportive scaffolding behaviors in the interaction, we drew from previously established categories and features of assistance in the ZPD (mainly those in Donato, 1994; Lidz, 1991; Villamil & Guerrero, 1996; and Wood et al., 1976).

Several scaffolding mechanisms were employed by the students in helping each other revise the composition. Early in the interaction, it was the reader who engaged in two crucial mediating behaviors: *recruiting interest in the task* and *marking critical aspects or discrepancies* (Donato, 1994; Wood et al., 1976). The reader took the lead by calling the writer's attention to two critical features in the text – lack of paragraph indentation and illegible handwriting: "You have to leave a space.... Before starting you have to indent.... That's an *i*, isn't it? It looks like a *d*." The reader's behavior reveals *intentionality* (Lidz, 1991), a feature of mediated assistance whose main goal is to influence other-performance and that is characterized by conscious efforts to engage a partner's attention, keep the interaction going, and maintain goal orientation.

Another important scaffolding behavior displayed by the reader was *task regulation* (Lidz, 1991), that is, manipulating the task in such a way as to facilitate problem solving by stating a principle of solution or introducing a partner into strategic thinking. In the following episode, the reader regulates the task by calling attention to a trouble source (a faulty use of the future tense [*I'll*]) and resorting to *instructing* (Villamil & Guerrero, 1996) and *modeling solutions* (Wood et al., 1976).[4]

1. R(eader): Here it says "**I didn't thought that I'll come back.**" It says that I will come back [*regresaré*], that you would come back [*regresarías*], you mean, right?

2. W(riter): Exactly.

3. R: That is, you mean, that when you went to Utuado to practice **rappeling**, you did not think you would come back with a good appreciation of Puerto Rico, so it is *would*.... "**We'd come back**," would come back [*regresaría*].

4. W: It's that ... grammar kills me, in Spanish and English.

5. R: Remember that *would* corresponds to the ending *ría* in (Spanish) verbs.

6. W: Ah.... That's something new I learned.

7. R: I'll come back [*regresaré*] you are going to do it in the future.

8. W: Hmm...
9. R: I'll come back, you'll come back, he'll come back [*yo regresaré, tú regresarás, él regresará*] with a better appreciation of Puerto Rico. It's *I would come back*, [*regresaría*], because you went back in that moment.

In the above segment, the reader is modeling a solution to the trouble source (how to conjugate verbs in the conditional) and guiding the writer to the correct revision. In the process, he is displaying his own heuristics for dealing with the task and thus equipping his partner with a rule that he might transfer to other situations. In response, the writer acknowledges his limitations (line 4) and gives evidence that learning of an important grammar rule might have occurred (line 6).

Two scaffolding behaviors – *contingent responsivity* and *psychological differentiation* (Lidz, 1991) – were particularly important in keeping high levels of affective involvement during the interaction. In the following episode, the reader displays *contingent responsivity*, that is, the ability to "read the [partner]'s cues and signals related to learning, affective, and motivational needs, and then to respond in a timely and appropriate way" (Lidz, 1991, p. 109). The reader seems to sense the writer's uneasiness at being corrected too much.

10. R: "We were at over..."
11. W: We were over one hundred twenty feet high...
12. R: At...this *at* is unnecessary because...
13. W: We were...
14. R: We were over one hundred twenty, this *at*, I mean...I don't...
15. W: We were over...
16. R: I mean, you..., I want you to give me your opinion...
17. W: No...
18. R: I am only revising, only revising, do you understand?
19. W: because...
20. R: As I understand it...as I understand it.... One thing is how I talk and another is how I should talk (laughter).
21. W: You make the corrections that need to be done. Don't worry....

In this episode, the reader seems to read his partner's discomfort and responds by releasing some of his tight control of the task and inviting the writer to voice his opinion. The reader also attempts to ameliorate his corrective attitude by reminding the writer that he is "only revising" (line 18). In doing so, the reader gives signs of *psychological differentiation*, that is, of making a clear distinction between his role as reader, or facilitator, and his partner's role as the author who is ultimately responsible for the text.

The reader's skillful management of the affective dimension of the interaction and the writer's willingness to consider his partner's suggestions contributed to the achievement of intersubjectivity.[5]

Intersubjectivity is an essential ingredient of work within the ZPD, because it signals a state of mutual cognition propitious for the attainment of self-regulation. Another salient scaffolding behavior that contributed to the maintenance of intersubjectivity throughout the interaction was the reader's use of *joint regard* (Lidz, 1991), that is, his continuous focusing of attention on the writer's text as if trying to see it through the writer's eyes. This behavior was clearly observed in lines such as "What is it that you want, you did it, you tell me what you were doing," "I want you to give me your opinion. You say that you passed along some houses...," and "What do you mean here?" Joint regard was also signaled by the frequent use of the pronoun *we* by both reader and writer. Revising was no longer just the reader's responsibility, or just the writer's, but a unique shared experience undertaken by both: "*We* could also put...," "What are *we* going to write?," and "*We* can say...."

Although in the first half of the revision session the reader played a crucial role as mediator, both reader and writer became active partners in the revision task with guided support moving reciprocally between them. Thus, the interaction showed that in L2 peer revision scaffolding may be mutual rather than unidirectional. In the following segment we find the participants struggling with a faulty embedded sentence ("and I was impressed at how *can* a house *could* be so far from the road"), which neither one seems to know quite how to fix. What is interesting here is that task regulation is shared between reader and writer; both give and receive feedback, thus showing the effects of mutual scaffolding.

22. R: "**And I was impressed**"... I think this *at* is not necessary.
23. W: "**And I was impressed how can a house**"... No, because then, it's like there is something missing. (--------)
24. R: ... I think that if you look... look... it says, "**and I was impressed how can a house could be so far from the road.**"
25. W: OK, but if we take out that connection (the preposition *at*), we would have to put it in quotation marks so that it looks as if I were saying it.
26. R: "**I was impressed at how can a house could be**," how can a house...
27. W: It would be then *at how a house could be*...
28. R: ... **how can a house be**...
29. W: ... again?
30. R: ... or *how can a house*...
31. W: No.
32. R: There's a very subtle detail here.
33. W: Should I ask (the teacher) or is this as we think...?
34. R: We are supposed to be the ones that revise it.
35. W: Well, then, anyway, it's all right.
36. R: **I was impressed how, how can a house be....** This doesn't sound right.
37. W: And, what about *how a house could* without *can*?
38. R: Exactly. I think it sounds better... **how a house could be**... so this *can* doesn't go there. This one, yes....

In the preceding excerpt, a symmetrical relationship between the peers is established, with both showing signs of self- and other-regulation at different times. The reader, for instance, is unsure of how to solve the verb problem in the sentence (lines 26–31) and admits a "subtle" difficulty with the text (line 32). However, he is quick to reject the writer's suggestion of calling for the teacher's help (lines 33–34). The writer, on his part, lets himself be guided in the revision by his peer but is ultimately responsible for offering the correct solution (deletion of the redundant *can*, line 37), which the reader readily accepts.

By the end of the peer session, suggestions for improvement flowed from each student so that the result was truly a joint production. In the following episode, it is evident that the partners have not only achieved a state of mutual cognition and are working as one but have also attained a significant degree of meta-conscious awareness about the benefits of collaboration, most clearly seen in their jointly constructed comments that "Two heads think better than one" and "When one works alone [reader's words] . . . one gets stuck [writer's words]" (lines 49 and 50).

39. R: "There are some places that . . .
40. W: . . . have to stay untouched by human hands.
41. R: I don't know. This seems to need **it**.
42. W: It already has **this**.
43. R: Oh, yeah, yeah, right. "**This leads me to believe there are some places that** . . ."
44. W: . . . "**have to stay untouched.**"
45. R: This must be **must**.
46. W: We could also put . . .
47. R: It's an obligation.
48. W: *Must remain*, we could also put here *remain* . . .
49. R: Exactly, **that must remain . . . untouched**. This way we can work better because, you see, two heads think better than one. When one works alone, one thinks and thinks and doesn't know what to do.
50. W: Exactly. One gets stuck.

Development and internalization of revision behaviors

The microgenetic approach to the data described in the preceding section allowed us to observe movement within the students' ZPDs. Particularly striking was the development of self-regulation in the writer. As can be seen in Figure 2.1, in the course of the 16 episodes that constituted the revision session for the pair described, a mostly other-regulated (OTR) writer (Oswald) at the beginning of the interaction became increasingly self-regulated (SER) as the interaction proceeded. During the first half of the interaction, 75 percent (six out of eight) of the writer's behaviors were OTR (as defined by the data analysis in Guerrero & Villamil, 1994),

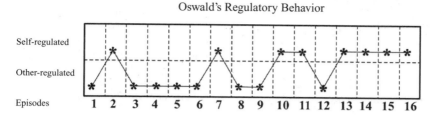

Figure 2.1. Writer's development of regulatory behavior during revision session.

whereas during the second half the situation was reversed: The writer was SER in 75 percent of the episodes.

As the interaction unfolded, we saw a rather passive and acquiescent writer gradually adopt behaviors associated with self-regulation, such as increasing disinhibition to make or reject suggestions for change and a more active role in initiating revision and repairing trouble sources on his own. In short, throughout the interaction, we witnessed the emergence of the writer's self-regulation and his growth as a more independent writer and reviser. The task not only benefited the writer; it also gave the reader the opportunity to grow in aspects of L2 writing and revising as well as in strategic assistance and collaboration. The task allowed both reader and writer to consolidate and reorganize knowledge of the L2 in structural and rhetorical aspects and to make this knowledge explicit for each other's benefit. As already pointed out, the effects of scaffolding in this interaction were mutual. As the students reciprocally extended support and the task regulation became more symmetrical, important lessons were shared and new knowledge was learned. In short, through microgenesis, we were able to study advancement within the ZPD and the developmental outcomes of moment-to-moment behavioral changes in peer revision.[6]

In an attempt to further observe how peer feedback could contribute to the development of revision behaviors in our student population, we designed a third study (Villamil & Guerrero, 1998), in which we looked at the impact of peer collaboration on final drafts. Impact was measured by the extent to which writers incorporated their peers' suggestions and worked on their final drafts on their own. Results showed that peer assistance had a substantial effect on revising, as the majority of trouble sources revised during interaction (74%) were incorporated into final versions.

An example of an incorporated revision (adopted in peer session and incorporated without changes in the final version) follows. The incorporated revision type is grammar/form of sentence.

Draft version: *Legalize them, it would be to invite everybody to use them....*
In-session revision (audiotaped):

Reader: Here, in this place, you should say "to legalize them"
          and you should eliminate this "it"...because
          "legalized, then comma, and this 'it'" does not make
          sense.

Writer: Circle it then. [Changes appear marked in text.]

Final version: *To legalize them would be to invite everybody to use them....*

In our study, we did not attempt to measure long-term ontogenesis, that is, whether development of revision behaviors was sustained far beyond the peer revision sessions. Thus, we interpret the writers' incorporation of changes into final drafts as only tentative evidence of actual growth. However, some signs of independent writing performance were provided by our writers' further revisions, adopted in session and further developed at home, or self revisions, performed at home but not discussed in session.

The presence of "further revisions" (6%) and "self revisions" (39%) in final drafts indicates that writers, before turning in their final versions, worked considerably on their own on the basis of previous peer work. What the writers did after peer interaction may be taken as symptomatic of self-regulatory behavior. In other words, the writers' reformulation of the changes made in sessions and all other revisions made on their own might be indicative of the effect that other-regulation (peer assistance) had on self-regulation (independent performance), as already suggested.

The role of cultural situatedness in peer revision

All learning situations are unique and highly variable. Interaction during peer revision is no exception to the rule, as it can be multifaceted and unpredictable. As Grabe (2001) and Grabe and Kaplan (1996) stated, the diversity of student populations, their L2 proficiency, their distinct cultural dispositions and instructional socialization, as well as their own beliefs about writing, may lead to different results. All of these characteristics may give occasion to collaborative and non-collaborative situations in the classroom, which could be analyzed within the SCT framework.

The issue of collaboration seems to be highly correlated to the social context of the instructional situation. In our studies on dyadic revision, collaborative interventions predominated among our participants. In general, the students tried to establish a working atmosphere that would lead them to complete the task. We believe that our students' spirit of camaraderie and compromise was mainly generated because joint work and collaboration are culturally perceived as pleasurable and beneficial in Puerto Rico (Nine-Curt, 1993). Furthermore, interactions were conducted in the languages our students share (Spanish and English), so breakdowns in communication that additional languages may have introduced were minimized.

However, this cultural scenario with a homogeneous population may not be repeated in all teaching contexts. Cultural disposition toward peer work might differ in other places. In fact, non-collaborative interactions, which may make peer feedback ineffective, have been documented in the literature. In 1992, Carson expressed the difficulties that peers of various language backgrounds could experience because of different cultural orientations and instructional systems. She stated that when Japanese and Chinese students come to the United States, they may be confused about the purpose and effectiveness of methods employed in the classroom. Other studies, by Carson and Nelson (1994, 1996), Nelson and Carson (1998), and Nelson and Murphy (1992), have shown how the behavior of culturally heterogeneous individuals within a group may affect revision. Japanese and Chinese students "may say what the writer wants to hear or may not speak at all rather than say what might be helpful to the writer but might hurt the writer's feelings or damage the cohesiveness of the group" (Carson & Nelson, 1994, p. 23). In terms of cultural differences, Nelson and Carson (1998) contended that students from these countries would depend on group consensus to guide decisions about changes. If they perceived different opinions about a particular trouble source, changes to the text would not be performed.

As a human activity, peer revision has to be embedded in a particular cultural, historical, and institutional setting. In other words, it cannot be fully understood or explained without observing the sociocultural contexts in which it takes place. SCT helps to illuminate those culture-specific interactions and to explain not only what seems to prove effective but also what does not. In fact, as Lantolf and Pavlenko (2001) point out, an SCT and activity-theory perspective offers a "complex view of second language learners as agents, whose actions are situated in particular contexts and are influenced by their dynamic ethnic, national, gender, class and social identities" (p. 155).

Pedagogical implications

Given the pivotal role of social mediation in the development of cognitive functions, peer feedback emerges as an indispensable component of the L2 writing classroom. Our research has informed us of several pedagogical considerations that must be taken into account in the implementation of peer response.

- To ensure progress within the learners' ZPDs, teachers should provide students with opportunities to interact with a variety of peers so that other-mediation can be effectively extended. What one peer may not be able to provide in terms of assistance, another student could. In addition, teachers should keep in mind that individual regulation is highly variable and dependent on a number of factors (L2 knowledge, rhetorical mode, role adopted during the interaction, nature of the trouble source, and others), so that no learner is at all times completely self-regulated, other-regulated, or object-regulated. Peer revision allows learners to fluctuate contingently in terms of regulation and to extend and receive strategic assistance accordingly.
- Teachers need to become aware of those strategic behaviors that may contribute to successful scaffolding or other-mediation during peer revision. While some of these behaviors, such as maintaining a partner's interest in the task, marking critical differences, and keeping psychological differentiation, may come naturally to some individuals as they position themselves in roles of other-mediation, it is our belief that educators as well as learners may benefit from heightened awareness and open discussion of these behaviors in the classroom. Students and tutors, in particular, need to have these behaviors modeled and encouraged in peer training sessions so that they can then reproduce them with their partners.
- It is imperative that teachers take the students' sociocultural contexts and learning backgrounds into account to determine the extent to which peer feedback may be most successfully brought into the classroom, assess students' training needs, and make the necessary adjustments to actual classroom implementation. In particular, to minimize clashes or behaviors that would impede collaborative dialogue, educators must be aware of the differences students might bring with them to the instructional context. Issues such as distinct cultural socialization patterns and belief systems, conceptualizations of writing, understanding of audience awareness, and cultural practices in textual organization, to name just a few, need to be addressed openly in the classroom.

Conclusion

In our long-term study of peer revision, we were able to observe the social-cognitive dimensions of L2 writing development through patterns of social interaction and regulation, mediated assistance, and development and internalization of revising behaviors in a particular sociocultural context. SCT helped us understand the importance of social mediation in learning. Specifically, it showed how individual development in the second language could be transformed by the social experience of talking about writing, as well as writing and revising, with a partner.

This social experience provided our students with a unique opportunity to assist each other in the development of writing skills and discourse strategies. The peer revision task allowed both reader and writer to consolidate and reorganize knowledge of the L2 and make this knowledge explicit for each other's benefit. It was through the exchange of ideas that peers were able to do the following: (a) acquire strategic competence in revising a text, (b) discuss textual problems, (c) internalize the demands of two rhetorical modes, (d) develop self-regulatory behaviors, (e) acquire a sense of audience, and (f) become sensitive to the social dimension of writing. The observed peer activities constitute the social bases for the development of cognitive processes that are necessary for revision. As we have said elsewhere, the importance of these activities as performed jointly during interaction resides in their role as precursors of the conscious, volitional processes that characterize individual writing activity.

Notes

1. In using the term "social-cognitive," we do not imply that the social and the cognitive dimensions of learning exist as two separate and independent realms. Rather, we want to emphasize our view of the mind as a social construction in which the cognitive and the social are dialectically inseparable (Guerrero & Villamil, 2002).
2. Extensive statistical and qualitative analyses of the data were performed in relation to stages of cognitive regulation and patterns of social relationships. The reader is invited to locate this information in Guerrero & Villamil (1994).
3. After giving instructions at the beginning of the revision session, the teacher was available for intervention when called upon.
4. Because the students' interactions were mostly in Spanish, an English version of the transcripts is presented here. In addition, the following notations have been used to facilitate understanding:

italics	Italics are employed to cite a letter, word, or phrase as a linguistic example, including Spanish words.
[brackets]	Brackets enclose Spanish words spoken by students.
(parentheses)	Explanation by authors
. . .	Sequence of dots indicates a pause.
boldface	Words spoken in English (text not in boldface was spoken in Spanish)
"quotation marks"	Quotation marks indicate participants are reading from the text.
(_ _ _ _ _ _ _ _ _)	An enclosed line indicates that an ensuing segment of the interaction has been deleted for brevity's sake.

5. Intersubjectivity is a concept used by Rommetveit (1985) to signify that subjects participating in a common task have a shared understanding of the situation and are in tune with one another.
6. Not all movement within the ZPD in the writing classroom implies advancement toward prescribed language and rhetorical forms. It is possible for L2 learners to regress to lower forms, rather than advance in their development, when interacting with a peer who is less knowledgeable in certain aspects and when there is no certainty regarding the language feature revised.

References

Antón, M., & DiCamilla, F. (1998). Socio-cognitive functions of L1 collaborative interactions in the L2 classroom. *Canadian Modern Language Review, 54,* 314–342.

Carson, J. G. (1992). Becoming biliterate: First language influences. *Journal of Second Language Writing, 1,* 37–60.

Carson, J. G., & Nelson, G. L. (1994). Writing groups: Cross-cultural issues. *Journal of Second Language Writing, 3,* 17–30.

Carson, J. G., & Nelson, G. L. (1996). Chinese students' perceptions of ESL peer response group interaction. *Journal of Second Language Writing, 5,* 1–19.

DiCamilla, F. J., & Antón, M. (1997). Repetition in the collaborative discourse of L2 learners: A Vygotskian perspective. *Canadian Modern Language Review, 53,* 609–633.

Donato, R. (1994). Collective scaffolding in second language learning. In J. P. Lantolf & G. Appel (Eds.), *Vygotskian approaches to second language research* (pp. 33–56). Norwood, NJ: Ablex.

Grabe, W. (2001). Notes toward a theory of second language writing. In T. Silva & P. K. Matsuda (Eds.), *On second language writing* (pp. 39–57). Mahwah, NJ: Lawrence Erlbaum.

Grabe, W., & Kaplan, R. B. (1996). *Theory and practice of writing.* London: Longman.

Guerrero, M. C. M. de, & Villamil, O. S. (1994). Social-cognitive dimensions of interaction in L2 peer revision. *The Modern Language Journal, 78,* 484–496.

Guerrero, M. C. M. de, & Villamil, O. S. (2000). Activating the ZPD: Mutual scaffolding in L2 peer revision. *The Modern Language Journal, 84,* 51–68.

Guerrero, M. C. M. de, & Villamil, O. S. (2002). Metaphorical conceptualizations of ESL teaching and learning. *Language Teaching Research, 6,* 95–120.

John-Steiner, V., Panofsky, C. P., & Smith, L. W. (1994). Introduction. In V. John-Steiner, C. P. Panofsky, & L. W. Smith (Eds.), *Sociocultural approaches to language and literacy: An interactionist perspective* (pp. 1–33). New York: Cambridge University Press.

Lantolf, J. P. (2000). Second language learning as a mediated process. *Language Teaching, 33,* 79–96.

Lantolf, J. P., & Pavlenko, A. (2001). Second language activity theory: Understanding second language learners as people. In M. P. Breen (Ed.), *Learner contributions to language learning: New directions in research* (pp. 141–158). New York: Pearson Education.

Leontiev, A. N. (1981). The problem of activity in psychology. In J. V. Wertsch (Ed.), *The concept of activity in Soviet psychology* (pp. 37–71). Armonk, NY: Sharpe.

Lidz, C. S. (1991). *Practitioner's guide to dynamic assessment.* New York: Guilford Press.

Lim, W. L., & Jacobs, G. M. (2001). *An analysis of students' dyadic interaction on a dictogloss task.* ERIC Document Reproduction Service, ED 456 649.

Nelson, G. L., & Carson, J. G. (1998). ESL students' perceptions of effectiveness in peer response groups. *Journal of Second Language Writing, 7,* 113–131.

Nelson, G. L., & Murphy, J. M. (1992). An L2 writing group: Task and social dimensions. *Journal of Second Language Writing, 1,* 171–193.

Nine-Curt, C. J. (1993). Intercultural interaction in the Hispanic-Anglo classroom from a nonverbal perspective. In J. Fayer (Ed.), *Puerto Rican communication studies* (pp. 99–109). San Juan, Puerto Rico: Fundación Arqueológica, Antropológica e Histórica.

Ohta, A. (1995). Applying sociocultural theory to an analysis of learner discourse: Learner-learner collaborative interaction in the zone of proximal development. *Issues in Applied Linguistics, 6*(2), 93–121.

Stone, C. A. (1993). What is missing in the metaphor of scaffolding? In E. A. Forman, N. Minick, & C. A. Stone (Eds.), *Contexts for learning: Sociocultural dynamics in children's development* (pp. 169–183). New York: Oxford University Press.

Rommetveit, R. (1985). Language acquisition as increasing linguistic structuring of experience and symbolic behavior control. In J. Wertsch (Ed.), *Culture, communication, and cognition: Vygotskian perspectives* (pp. 183–204). Cambridge: Cambridge University Press.

Villamil, O. S., & de Guerrero, M. C. M. (1996). Peer revision in the L2 classroom: Social-cognitive activities, mediating strategies, and aspects of social behavior. *Journal of Second Language Writing, 5,* 51–75.

Villamil, O. S., & de Guerrero, M. C. M. (1998). Assessing the impact of peer revision on L2 writing. *Applied Linguistics, 19,* 491–514.

Vygotsky, L. S. (1978). *Mind in society: The development of higher psychological processes.* Cambridge, MA: Harvard University Press.

Vygotsky, L. S. (1986). *Thought and language* (A. Kozulin, Trans.). Cambridge, MA: MIT Press. (Original work published 1934.)

Wertsch, J. V. (1979a). From social interaction to higher psychological processes: A clarification and application of Vygotsky's theory. *Human Development, 22,* 1–22.

Wertsch, J. V. (1979b). The regulation of human action and the given-new organization of private speech. In G. Zivin (Ed.), *The development of self-regulation through private speech* (pp. 79–98). New York: John Wiley & Sons.

Wood, D., Bruner, J. S., & Ross, G. (1976). The role of tutoring in problem solving. *Journal of Child Psychology and Psychiatry, 17,* 89–100.

3 Cultural issues in peer response: Revisiting "culture"

Gayle Nelson
Joan Carson

Revision is widely understood to be the key to effective writing, but the quality of the revision depends crucially on the quality of the feedback that the writer receives, whether from self, peers, tutors in a writing center, or a writing instructor. In writing classrooms, a frequent source of feedback is peer response groups, a pedagogical technique that originated in L1 writing and was subsequently adopted in L2 classrooms. Given the differences between L1 and L2 writing, researchers and L2 teachers were eager to know if peer response was as effective in L2 settings as it was in L1 contexts. Although many of the research studies on peer response indicate mixed results, researchers have concluded, after two decades of examining the issue, that peer response can be beneficial for L2 writers under certain conditions (Ferris, 2003; Hyland, 2003; Liu & Hansen, 2002).

In this chapter we will consider factors that contribute to effective peer response, with a focus on the role that culture may play in peer group interaction. Based on the review of literature and our own research, we suggest the possibility that students with a common language and cultural expectations tend to have more successful peer response interactions than students in heterogeneous cultural groupings. Because our previous work on this topic (Carson & Nelson, 1994, 1996; Nelson & Carson, 1995, 1998) has elicited some negative reaction, we will address both this criticism and the difficulty in talking about culture at all. This chapter concludes with pedagogical and research suggestions.

Contextual factors in effective peer response

L2 researchers have teased apart some of the contextual factors that contribute to more or less effective peer response group interaction and feedback. Not all peer response groups are equally successful, and the quality of the feedback that writers receive is influenced by a number of factors. One factor highlighted in research studies is the importance of training students in peer response and of structuring peer response sessions (Hedgcock & Lefkowitz, 1992; Paulus, 1999; Villamil & Guerrero,

1998; Zhu, 1995). Training has been found to result in more revisions related to meaning (as opposed to surface) revisions (Berg, 1999), the inclusion of more peer suggestions in revisions (Nelson & Murphy, 1993; Stanley, 1992), and higher quality revisions (Berg, 1999). These studies counterbalance a tendency to assume that groupwork of any type will necessarily achieve the desired outcome. As this body of research clearly indicates, structuring the context of peer review is an important factor in student success.

Training students in peer response techniques and structuring peer response group interaction becomes even more important given that other studies have consistently found that students prefer teacher feedback to peer and self feedback. In several studies (Amores, 1997; Chaudron, 1984; Sengupta, 1998; Zhang, 1995), students cited their own and peers' lack of expertise as the reason for their preference for teacher feedback. Students who approach peer review unconvinced of its value at best, or antagonistic to the process at worst, are unlikely to benefit from peer response group activities. However, researchers have pointed out that self, peer, tutor, and teacher feedback are not mutually exclusive categories and that multiple types of feedback including peer feedback are useful for students. If not asked to choose between teachers and peers, students have reported peer review to be a useful activity in a number of studies of successful peer groups (e.g., Jacobs et al., 1998; Mendonça & Johnson, 1994; Rothschild & Klingenberg, 1990).

However well the students are trained and however well the peer review session is structured, though, a significant factor in the effectiveness of peer response is the contextual element of the *interaction* of the group itself and the quality of that interaction. A number of research studies have noted the sometimes problematic social nature of peer response groups. Both Amores (1997) and Jacobs (1987) found tension among students who expressed discomfort with other students' acting like teachers and with disagreement among their peers. The negative social dynamics of one writing group examined by Nelson and Murphy (1992) were found to have hindered its effectiveness and influenced students' attitudes about the peer response process. Studies by Lockhart and Ng (1993) and by Mangelsdorf and Schlumberger (1992) found that students who took a collaborative stance in response to peer review activities fared better, achieving better understanding of the writing process and higher grades, than did those students with other stances (e.g., interpretive or prescriptive).

Group dynamics are complex, and it is unlikely that any one factor is ever the cause of successful or unsuccessful peer group interaction and outcomes. Studies, however, have implicated several possibilities. Chavez (2000) in her study of peer response group outcomes found that gender had a significant effect. Females in female-dominated classrooms were more likely than females in male-dominated ones to change their oral responses to the teacher's questions based on peer feedback, and males were more likely to change responses in male-dominated classrooms than in female-dominated ones.

The language used in peer interaction was also found to be a factor in several studies. In her study of peer response groups composed of native speakers (NS) and nonnative speakers (NNS), Zhu (2001) found that nonnative speakers took fewer turns and produced fewer language functions than native speakers during oral discussions, although they were comparable in their written responses. In a classroom of Chinese L1 students, Huang (1995) found that students participating in peer response groups in their L1 were more confident in their peers' ability to provide effective feedback, believed more firmly in the value of peer response, and were more convinced that peer feedback helped them revise than were students participating in peer response groups in their L2 (English). Levine, Oded, Connor, and Asons (2002) compared the results of a linguistically homogenous EFL peer response group in Israel with a linguistically heterogeneous ESL group in the United States Although the Israeli group made briefer written responses, the researchers' evaluation of their response sheets suggested a higher degree of cooperation in revising behavior than did the scores of the ESL group. The researchers also found that the ESL group tended to be more critical, and the ESL teacher noted an atmosphere of conflict in the group. The Israelis, on the other hand, were more supportive of each other, perhaps because they could discuss their drafts in a common language and everyone understood the verbal exchanges. In an analysis of Puerto Rican students' interactions in pairs at a university in Puerto Rico, Villamil and Guerrero (1996) found that students stayed on task and talked about each other's drafts during pair interactions. Most frequently, they talked about problems in the drafts, and they often did so in a collaborative manner (i.e., they respected each other as readers and writers).

Culture as context

The results of these last three studies – the Israeli / EFL study, the Puerto Rican study, and to an extent the Chinese L1 study – suggest the intriguing possibility of a bond among group participants that may have contributed to the group's success by creating a collaborative environment. The bond may have been a common language or it may have been shared cultural expectations that somehow facilitated the social interaction, or both. It is reasonable to assume that a shared pattern of socialization or culture among students participating in peer response groups contributes to the context of peer review and that culture may be a factor in peer group effectiveness.

In our studies of peer response group interaction (Carson & Nelson, 1996; Nelson & Carson, 1998), we found a surprising amount of similarity in the perceptions of the three female Chinese students participating in three different response groups. The other students in the groups were from Argentina, Mexico, Laos, Iran, Bangladesh, Thailand, and Haiti. Using key informant interviews as our primary data collection procedure, we viewed videotapes of peer response groups with the Chinese student informants who participated in the groups. The interviewer used a remote control to stop the videotape after each exchange initiated by the informant, after each exchange directed at the informant, and at other times when the interviewer had questions about what the informant was thinking or feeling in response to peers' interactions. These interviews were audiotaped, transcribed, and analyzed. Each student expressed the desire for a positive group climate and worked toward the goal of maintaining the harmony of the group. This goal affected their interactions with their peers, including not criticizing others' drafts. For example, one student would not criticize another student's draft during peer response group interactions because she did not want to cause an argument.

The reason why I keep my questions [to myself] sometimes is . . . because some of them are quite tricky . . . so I write it down. I don't want to embarrass the writer or arouse an argument. (Carson & Nelson, 1996, p. 8)

Students were also reluctant to disagree with a peer's comment. A second student did not agree with a peer's comment, but she would not say anything in the group. To the interviewer she said, "It's really hard for me to say that I don't agree with someone; . . . it's like I'm really mad at him or her or really angry" (p. 10). Another student explained to the interviewer that she would not make a change unless more than one student agreed on what needed to be done. The interviewer asked, "You wouldn't do it?"

No . . . because nobody agreed . . . if somebody in the group agree with somebody's opinion then I would think about it. (Nelson & Carson, 1998, p. 126)

We interpreted this need for consensus as part of the Chinese students' perceived need for harmonious group relations. These Chinese students, then, appeared reluctant to speak because of not wanting to embarrass the writer and wanting to create and maintain harmonious group relations. In turn, they seemed reluctant to use their peers' comments unless there was group consensus.

Other researchers have found similar patterns of behavior with Chinese students in peer response groups. In her peer response study, Hyland (2000) attributes the lack of negative feedback among Chinese to cultural issues. One of her participants, Zhang, a Chinese student, commented on the lack of feedback he received on his oral presentation.

I just given a presentation and just now I asked Chan for some comments for my presentation. Well, he said "oh it's all right." Nothing important, nothing useful. Maybe he didn't like to comment. Especially for Chinese, for Chinese people you know they seldom comment on some other people's work.

Hyland (2003) includes the following sentiments from a Hong Kong learner.

The conference is not so useful because our group members just give good comments. We just say the essay is OK. Perhaps suggest a small change sometimes, especially grammar mistake. We don't usually make a criticism to our classmate. (p. 42)

Tang & Tithecott (1999) noted that in their journal entries Asian students often commented on their worries about criticizing others' work. One student wrote:

[It is] very difficult to tell the person who write the essay negative things frankly because I don't want to hurt his or her feelings. (p. 31)

We hypothesize that the cultural backgrounds of these Chinese students may have influenced their behaviors in the groups. In peer response groups, students share drafts with each other to get guidance and feedback on their writing as their drafts are developing. It is assumed that the guidance will result in improved essays. But what happens if, during group interactions, few suggestions are given? What happens if students are more interested in being polite and maintaining positive group relations than in making suggestions about each other's drafts?

Individuals, groups, and culture in educational systems

In our earlier work we explained the Chinese students' behavior in terms of the social-psychological dimensions of collectivism and individualism (Triandis, 1995), broad generalizations that require numerous caveats, many of which will be made in following sections of this chapter. Briefly stated, collectivism is characterized as individuals' subordinating their personal goals to the goals and for the good of the group (Triandis, 1995). It has been defined as a "social pattern of closely linked individuals who see themselves as parts of one or more collectives ... and emphasize their connectedness to members of these collectives" (p. 2). Collectivists belong to few groups, but the groups one belongs to define one's identity (e.g., I am a member of a certain family; I am a member of a certain group).

Important values for collectivists are maintaining cohesion and harmony within the group. In contrast, individualism is a social pattern characterized by individuals' subordinating the goals of the collective to personal goals. People are primarily motivated by their own preferences and needs, believe they have the right to self-fulfillment and freedom of choice, and are expected to take care of themselves and their immediate families. Important values for individualists are self-assertion and achievement (Triandis, 1995).

Given the reputed emphasis on groups in Chinese culture, it seems reasonable to assume that Chinese students would function well in peer response groups. However, as usually implemented in the United States, peer response groups function in a way that may be antithetical to the values of many Chinese, because they more often function for the benefit of the individual writer than for benefit of the group (i.e., each student gets feedback on a draft for individual benefit). Giving other students negative feedback on their drafts during a peer response interaction might be difficult for a Chinese student who is accustomed to attending to the feelings of others and obtaining correction from the teacher.

More important education systems, classrooms, teaching methodologies, student-teacher interactions, and so forth are all components of culture. In fact, students are socialized into cultures through various institutions, and education is one of the primary socializing institutions. A body of research on culture and education (or pedagogy) has developed that focuses on the culture of learning, a term that both suggests a more manageable amount of information and overlaps with the superordinate culture in which the culture of learning exists. This relationship may be apparent to some, but Cheng (2000), for example, argues that in an Asian "teacher-centred teaching and learning environment, the learners are doomed to reticence" because they "have had a *long learning experience* in such an environment...." (italics added, p. 442), not because of their culture. This long learning experience is the culture of learning. A culture of learning has been defined in this way:

... socially transmitted expectations, beliefs, and values about what good learning is. The concept draws attention to the usually taken-for-granted cultural ideas about the roles and relations of teachers and learners, and about appropriate teaching and learning styles and methods, about the use of textbooks and materials, and about what constitutes good work in classrooms. (Jin & Cortazzi, 1998a, p. 749)

In an extensive study carried out in China between 1993 and 1995, Jin and Cortazzi (1998b) observed classrooms in schools and universities, conducted interviews, administered questionnaires, and analyzed students' essays, all with a focus on the perceptions of native English-speaking teachers (from Australia, Britain, New Zealand, and North America) about Chinese students' behaviors and ways of learning and Chinese students' perceptions of the native English-speaking teachers' behaviors and ways of teaching. Their results indicate that "Western" teachers perceived students as unwilling to work in groups but willing to work as a whole class or to do individual work. Students perceived "Western" teachers' use of group discussion as fruitless, as wasting time, and as dangerous because they risked learning errors from others. This negative view of groupwork may have been shared by the three Chinese students in our studies and, in part, accounted for their reluctance to participate.

Jin and Cortazzi (1998a) also propose the maintenance of *face* as a component of one of the Chinese cultures of learning. Many of the students in their study explained their reluctance to ask questions in class in terms of not wanting to lose face by asking questions that might appear stupid or by asking a smart question that might be seen as showing off. The Chinese concept of face, however, has other sides. Liu (2001) characterizes the Chinese sense of face less as concern for self and more as concern for others, noting that Chinese face emphasizes "the harmony of individual conduct with views and judgments of the community" (p. 205). Triandis (1995) has referred to this concern for the community or saving the face of the group as "other-face concern" (p. 118) and notes that it is associated with compromise and avoiding conflict. The three Chinese students in our study frequently referred to concerns of face as reasons for their lack of participation in the peer response groups. They preferred not to vocalize their thoughts because they did not want to embarrass, hurt, or disagree with the writer or others in the group.

Homogeneity

Although the Chinese learners in these heterogeneous groups were not enthusiastic about criticizing other students in peer response groups, researchers have found that homogeneous groups often work well in contexts other than peer response. Jones (1995), who worked with Cambodian students in self-access language centers, and Ho and Crookall (1995), who studied group interaction with Chinese students in a large-scale simulation, both found that their students worked successfully in groups. Furthermore, the studies cited earlier (Huang, 1995; Levine et al., 2002; Villamil & Guerrero, 1996) suggest that linguistic and cultural homogeneity may be an important factor in successful peer response group interaction. The reasons that these homogeneous groups work well are not clear, but one possibility suggested by Nelson (1997) relates to the importance of maintaining everyone's face in peer response groups. Because such "face work" may lead to indirect responses, she asserts, speakers of the same language and cultural backgrounds will better understand the nuances and subtleties of each other's messages, allowing for both group harmony and improved writing.

The problem of culture

We have hypothesized that the three Chinese students in our study exhibited similar interaction styles that may have been a result of their shared culture. It is unlikely that the socialization processes that have affected and helped form the identities of students would not affect the social interactions of peer response groups. Peer response groups are not culturally neutral, and if we agree that the context of peer feedback includes what each person brings to the group, we need to be able to talk about the role that culture plays in peer group interaction.

Investigating cultural influences and their potential effects can help us to understand the ways in which peer response can be used successfully. However, unlike gender and language, the cultural backgrounds that students bring to group interactions are somewhat opaque. They are opaque to us as teachers because we are not usually members of the sociocultural group or myriad sociocultural groups that our students represent, and because cultural influences are variable within specific sociocultural groups themselves. Much of the difficulty of examining cultural influences, however, lies with the construct of "culture" itself.

Across academic disciplines, the concept of culture has been critiqued by postmodern, post-structuralist, and postcolonial theorists as essentialist – consisting of fixed characteristics that do not allow for variation within the culture or group. In fact, the anthropologist Abu-Lughod (1991), in *Writing Against Culture*, argues that the concept of culture has outlived its usefulness. Asserting that anthropology as a discipline has been "built on the historically constructed divide between the West and the non-West" (p. 139), she observes that it continues to be the West that studies the non-West, the West that has constituted the non-West, and the West that has held the position of dominance.

This argument has been made by others, notably Edward Said (1978), who criticizes the West's (i.e., the Occident's) construction of the Orient. "The essence of Orientalism," asserts Said, "is the ineradicable distinction between Western superiority and Oriental inferiority" (p. 42). Said continues, arguing that this construction of the Orient "is contained and represented by dominating frameworks" (p. 40). According to Abu-Lughod, Said, and others (e.g., Kubota, 1999, 2001; Pennycook, 2001), this construction of the Orient has resulted in its reification. A culture (e.g., the Orient) becomes thinglike, static, homogeneous, coherent, and timeless. Atkinson (1999) refers to this view of culture as the "received" view, a notion that sees cultures in their most typical forms "as geographically (and quite often nationally) distinct entities, as relatively unchanging and homogeneous, and as all-encompassing systems of rules or norms that substantially determine personal behavior" (p. 626). This received view of culture has been an easy target for critics who point out that cultures are in motion (Rosaldo, 1989), permeable and permeating (Clifford, 1992), unbounded and unstable (Appadurai, 1996), fragmented and subjective (Foucault, 1982), heterogeneous (Atkinson, 1999), and incoherent and changing (Abu-Lughod, 1991).

Because of these critiques of culture, anthropologists, philosophers, and practitioners of applied linguistics are questioning the use of the term or construct "culture" at all. Some scholars have suggested what appears to be alternate terminology. For example, Atkinson (1999) and Clifford (1992) have suggested that many educational researchers have substituted the term *identity* for culture. The concept of culture can be recognized easily in Hall's (2002) discussion of identity.

> Even the geographical region in which we are born provides us with a
> particular group membership and upon our birth we assume specific identities
> as Italian, Chinese, Canadian, or South African, etc. Within national
> boundaries, we are defined by membership in regional groups, and we take on
> identities as, for example, northerners or southerners. (p. 32)

Norton's (2000) notion of identity, on the other hand, is one of relationships in an inequitably structured world in which individuals are marginalized for gender, race, class, and ethnicity, and power is continually being renegotiated. She states, "I use the term identity to reference how a person understands his or her relationship to the world, how that relationship is constructed across time and space, and how the person understands the possibilities for the future." Continuing, she argues for a conception of identity "that is understood with reference to larger, and frequently inequitable, social structures which are reproduced in day-to-day interaction" (p. 5).

Appadurai (1996) is troubled by the term *culture* as a noun but comfortable with the adjectival form of the word, *cultural*. He contends that the noun form implies that culture is a kind of object or thing, whereas the adjective *cultural* "moves into the realm of differences, contrasts, and comparisons that is more helpful" and "builds on the context-sensitive, contrast-centered heart of Saussurean linguistics" (p. x). Appadurai (1991) also suggested global *ethnoscapes*, a term that implies important central features – the changing social, territorial, and cultural reproduction of cultural identity as groups migrate, regroup, and reconstruct histories. Specifically, an ethnoscape is "the landscape of persons who make up the shifting world in which we live: tourists, immigrants, refugees, exiles, ..." (p. 191).

Discourse is the word of choice for many, including Abu-Lughod (1991), in that it enables scholars to analyze social life without presuming the degree of coherence that the concept of culture has come to represent. *Discourse*, as Abu-Lughod uses the term, refers to "notions of discursive formations, apparatuses, and technologies . . . and draws attention to the social uses by individuals of verbal resources" (pp. 147–148). Gee (1996) presents a broader view of the term *discourse*.

. . . ways of behaving, interacting, valuing, thinking, believing, speaking, and often reading and writing that are accepted as instantiations of particular roles (or "types of people") by specific *groups by people*, whether families of a certain sort, lawyers of a certain sort, . . . and so on. . . . Discourses are ways of being "people like us." They are "ways of being in the world"; they are "forms of life." They are, thus, always and everywhere *social* and products of social histories. (p. *viii*)

Are scholars using terms such as *identity*, *cultural*, or *discourse* as a means to sidestep the post-structural quagmire of culture? At times, it appears so. For example, Hall's (2002) view of identity with its focus on geographical boundaries resembles Scollon and Scollon's (1995) definition of culture that includes what large groups of people have in common, from histories to worldviews to languages to geographical locations. On the surface, Gee's (1996) construction of discourse as "ways of being in the world" and "products of social histories" is similar to Martin and Nakayama's (2001) definition of culture as "learned patterns of perception, values, and behaviors, shared by a group of people, that is also dynamic" (p. 26). Both refer to a socialization process that provides members of a group with norms for perceiving (i.e., interpreting), valuing, behaving, and believing in the world. However, scholars such as Norton (2000), Gee (1996), and other critical theorists do not appear to be substituting one word for another or even modifying existing paradigms. They assume a different kind of social world, one that is not coherent and organic, but is instead fragmented and subjective – a social world, as Norton (2000) explains, that is inequitably structured and in which power operates at the macro level of powerful institutions and the micro level of everyday social encounters.

Our point here is not to summarize critical theory but to illustrate the types of issues being discussed in connection to culture. By attempting to find a new way to write about what is socially shared by a group of humans, many who are wary of the old ways of discussing culture are looking for new ways of thinking about culture and new terms for referring to culture; others have ceased addressing culture altogether. For many, the search for a new way to talk about culture illustrates the need to recognize the existence of a loosely woven fabric of cultural identity within members of social groups. As Shore (1996) notes:

Without a robust concept of culture, . . . a significant aspect of human life remains undertheorized and underexamined. The poststructuralist critique of traditional conceptions of culture is potentially of great importance . . . , but only if it is used to refine the notion of culture rather than to discard it. (p. 9)

A central issue, then, is how to talk about what members of a particular group share while acknowledging that the group is in motion, permeable and permeating, unbounded and unstable, fragmented, heterogeneous, incoherent, and changing. Or as Mannheim and Tedlock (1995) asked, How do we recognize that "cultural forms have their own principles of organization without resorting to a crude essentialism"? (p. 10).

Culture in peer response groups

The real problem of culture, though, is not that we do not agree on what it is, although this question is far from settled. Rather, the problem of culture is that stereotypes associated with specific cultures are used to maintain unjust social structures, because the power structure defines cultures in ways that maintain its power (the more privileged cultures) and disadvantage others (the less privileged cultures). Kubota (1999) argues that the representation of culture is always political, since the question of what defines a culture depends crucially on the power relations between those who are doing the defining and those who are defined. For Spack (1997) cultural labels "preserve a system that situates people in dominant and subordinate positions" (p. 766) by conflating culture with difference and leads their defenders "inevitably to identify U.S. culture as the norm from which students are deviating" (p. 767). She argues that *because* the culture-stereotype connection can lead to social inequities, we should abandon the use of culture as a lens through which to examine student behavior. Spack maintains that identifying students as belonging to a specific cultural group has negative effects.

[a]t worst, ... may imply that we sanction an ethnocentric stance. At the very least, it can lead us to stigmatize, to generalize, and to make inaccurate predictions about what students are likely to do as a result of their language or cultural background. (p. 765)

Spack's "at worst" and "at the very least" scenarios, neither of which have acceptable outcomes, set up a dichotomy that leaves little room for other perspectives. Kubota (2001) also argues against a "cultural differences" position for the same reasons that Spack does. She claims that our pointing out the potential negative influences of collectivism on peer response group interaction (Carson & Nelson, 1994, 1996; Nelson & Carson, 1995, 1998) assumes a cultural differences position (p. 13). At the same time, however, she cites other studies (e.g., Harklau, 2000; Leki, 1999; Zamel, 1995) in which culture is used as an explanatory variable and labels these studies as providing an "institutional problem" perspective in which the student's cultural attributes are seen as neutral, and the institution's unwillingness to accommodate those students is seen as the problem. In other words, thinking about students in terms of cultural influences is good if the conclusion is that the institution is bad. But thinking about students in terms of cultural influences is bad if the conclusion is that cultural constructs (e.g., collectivism and individualism) that could lead to negative stereotypes might explain observed student behaviors. Kubota's conclusions make sense, given that she had previously stated (Kubota, 1999) that the influences of collectivism and individualism proposed in Carson & Nelson (1994) assume that there is "a systematic, culturally determined way in which all members in a certain culture think, behave, and act" (p. 14).

If our research on possible cultural effects in peer group response interaction exploited the negative stereotypes associated with collectivism, then Kubota would be correct. Trying to account for the role of culture in peer response groups would lead to inequities *if* collectivism were defined as the inability to think for oneself, and individualism as the ability to think critically, and *if* Confucian influence on education meant that knowledge is preserved only by passive learners and that Socratic education meant that knowledge is created only by engaged learners. These stereotypes do essentialize; they delineate differences as deficit. However, they do not represent our understanding of culture as an influence on social practices rather than as a determinant of "inferior" or "unproductive" behaviors.

We recognize that dominant discourses are inequitably maintained and distributed in schools and thus reproduce fundamentally unjust social structures. As a microcosm, a peer response group could also be seen as one of those unjust social structures. Peer response is a classroom practice socially constructed by the educational power structure. To the extent that these groups are based on an individualist ideology, the collectivist-influenced behaviors of some students place them at a disadvantage. If maintaining harmony in a group is highly valued, then criticism of a peer's writing will be avoided and the goals of peer review – revision based on that criticism – will be unattainable.

Those who work in critical theory ask legitimate questions and raise legitimate concerns. But these questions and concerns should not blind us to inequities that may result from common culturally influenced behaviors. As practitioners and researchers, we have to weigh the dangers of overgeneralization against the benefits of assessing possible culture-related behaviors that need to be taken into consideration when we design classroom activities. We also need to examine our own – too often unexamined – culturally influenced behaviors that may result in inequities (e.g., favoring one student or group of students over another) in spite of all our good intentions.

The context of classrooms and pedagogical practices comprises complex variables, including what Atkinson (1999) describes as "individuals-in-context (who) do not exist separately from their social worlds"

(p. 642). Peer review can be an effective pedagogical practice in developing L2 writing abilities, but not in all of its manifestations, as the research has shown. One of the factors that must be considered is how these "individuals-in-context" interact with their peers in soliciting and providing quality feedback. Because our identities are influenced by culture, we need to understand the ways in which culture may affect student behavior in peer response groups.

"[S]uch articulated knowledge of who students are individually-culturally leads logically to the need to develop *appropriate pedagogies* – approaches to learning and teaching that dynamically respond to that knowledge. (p. 643)

Pedagogical implications

Silva and Brice (2004), writing on the current status of L2 writing, highlight a transition away from a one-size-fits-all approach to writing pedagogy to an approach that recognizes variation among writers, contexts, and text types. Specifically, if writing instructors decide to use peer response groups, they would do well to heed Ferris's (2003) advice to "form pairs or groups thoughtfully" (p. 165). In making decisions about using peer response groups, it is important to consider the cultural influences that may affect student behaviors in peer response groups, including the following:

- Communication style
- The importance of face in maintaining social harmony
- The cultures of learning that students bring to second / foreign language classrooms

Once the decision to use peer response has been made, teachers can assist in the following ways:

- Explain the purpose of peers' responding to each others' drafts so students understand your objectives.
- Train students in effective peer response strategies (written and verbal).
- If teaching a heterogeneous class, try to put students from the same cultures together because, as several studies in this chapter indicate, students who understand the nuances of each others' communication styles tend to have more successful group interactions.
- Perhaps put students in pairs instead of groups of three or four students. The issue of group dynamics can complicate the task of providing feedback to each other on drafts.
- Give students enough time to provide written feedback before they meet in pairs or as a group. With time to think and write, they can

phrase their criticisms or suggestions in a way that softens the criticism and is less hurtful to the writer.

- If using electronic feedback, use asynchronous communication (e.g., e-mail or Web postings) rather than synchronous communication (e.g., chat rooms) to give students ample reflection and response time.
- Adjust your peer response procedures based on feedback from students.

Suggestions for further research

In reviewing the literature on peer response groups and critiques of culture for this chapter, we became aware of the need for researchers to ask what it means to look at peer response with a view of culture that is in motion (Rosaldo, 1989), permeable and permeating (Clifford, 1992), unbounded and unstable (Appadurai, 1996), fragmented and subjective (Foucault, 1982), heterogeneous (Atkinson, 1999), and incoherent and changing (Abu-Lughod, 1991). In responding to this question, what kinds of studies would researchers devise? We believe that taking this approach to culture would result in qualitative studies that would include the following considerations:

- Present students' views of their socially constructed realities in peer response groups as writers and readers of writing.
- A variety of settings (e.g., EFL, immigrant, refugee, elementary and secondary school, adult).
- Factors such as culture, ethnicity, gender, socioeconomic positioning, language proficiency, and future career and life goals of writers and their peers.
- A longitudinal view to observe the actual value of peer response for L2 reading and writing from both the students' and instructors' points of view and to note different types of changes over time, taking into consideration that individual identities change over time.
- Cross-cultural, possibly involving collaboration among teachers and researchers in several locations around the world with the probability of different types of educational backgrounds, educational experiences, linguistics expertise, and so forth.

Examining and taking into account the potential influence of language and culture on peer group interaction might help researchers and practitioners alike to better understand the context in which feedback contributes to the development of second language writing competence.

Acknowledgments

We would like to thank Fiona and Ken Hyland for asking the tough questions that helped us clarify our point of view; Diane Belcher for her honest, yet encouraging, comments during various stages of the manuscript; and Dwight Atkinson for pushing us to go further. A special thanks to Yanbin Lu for her meritorious editing skills and careful attention to detail.

References

Abu-Lughod, L. (1991). Writing against culture. In R. Fox (Ed.), *Recapturing anthropology: Working in the present* (pp. 137–162). Santa Fe, NM: School of American Research Press.

Amores, M. J. (1997). A new perspective on peer-editing. *Foreign Language Annals, 30(4)*, 513–522.

Appadurai, A. (1991). Global ethnoscapes: Notes and queries for a transnational anthropology. In R. Fox (Ed.), *Recapturing anthropology: Working in the present* (pp.191–210). Santa Fe, NM: School of American Research Press.

Appadurai, A. (1996). *Modernity at large: Cultural dimensions of globalization* (*Vol. 1*). Minneapolis, MN: University of Minnesota Press.

Atkinson, D. (1999). TESOL and culture. *TESOL Quarterly, 33(4)*, 625–654.

Berg, E. C. (1999). The effects of trained peer response on ESL students' revision types and writing quality. *Journal of Second Language Writing, 8*, 215–241.

Carson, J., & Nelson, G. (1994). Writing groups: Cross-cultural issues. *Journal of Second Language Writing, 3*, 17–30.

Carson, J., & Nelson, G. (1996). Chinese students' perceptions of ESL peer response group interaction. *Journal of Second Language Writing, 5*, 1–19.

Chaudron, C. (1984). The effects of feedback on students' composition revision. *RELC Journal, 15(2)*, 1–14.

Chavez, M. (2000). Teacher and student gender and peer group gender composition in German foreign classroom discourse: An exploratory study. *Journal of Pragmatics, 32*, 1019–1058.

Chen, G. (1995). Differences in self-disclosure patterns among Americans versus Chinese: A comparative study. *Journal of Cross-Cultural Psychology, 26*, 84–91.

Cheng, X. (2000). Asian students' reticence revisited. *System, 28*, 435–446.

Clifford, J. (1992). Traveling cultures. In L. Grossberg, G. Nelson, & P. Treichler (Eds.), *Cultural studies* (pp. 96–116). New York: Routledge.

Ferris, D. (2003). *Response to student writing: Implications for second language students*. Mahwah, NJ: Lawrence Erlbaum.

Foucault, M. (1982). Afterword: The subject and power. In H. Dreyfus & P. Rabinow (Eds.), *Michel Foucault: Beyond Structuralism and Hermeneutics* (pp. 208–226). Chicago: University of Chicago Press.

Gee, J. (1996). *Social linguistics and literacies: Ideology discourses*, 2nd ed. London: Routledge.

Hall, J. K. (2002). *Teaching and researching language and culture*. London: Longman.

Harklau, L. (2000). From the "good kids" to the "worst": Representations of English language learners across educational settings. *TESOL Quarterly, 34,* 35–67.

Hedgcock, J., & Lefkowitz, N. (1992). Collaborative oral/aural revision in foreign language writing instruction. *Journal of Second Language Writing, 1(3),* 255–276.

Ho, J., & Crookall, D. (1995). Breaking with Chinese cultural traditions: Learner autonomy in English language teaching. *System, 23(2),* 235–243.

Huang, S.-Y. (1995). *The efficacy of using writing groups to help students generate ideas for writing and revising drafts in an EFL university writing class.* ERIC Document. Reproduction Service No: ED 397654.

Hyland, F. (2000). ESL writers and feedback: Giving more autonomy to students. *Language Teaching Research, 4,* 33–54.

Hyland, K. (2003). *Second language writing.* Cambridge: Cambridge University Press.

Jacobs, G. (1987). First experiences with peer feedback on compositions: Student and teacher reaction. *System, 15(3),* 325–333.

Jacobs, G. M., Curtis, A., Braine, G., & Huang, S. (1998). Feedback of student writing: Taking a middle path. *Journal of Second Language Writing, 7,* 307–317.

Jin, L., & Cortazzi, M. (1998a). Dimensions of dialogue: Large classes in China. *International Journal of Educational Research, 29,* 739–761.

Jin, L., & Cortazzi, M. (1998b). The culture the learner brings: A bridge or a barrier. In M. Byram & M. Fleming (Eds.), *Language learning in intercultural perspective: Approaches through drama and ethnography* (pp. 98–118). Cambridge: Cambridge University Press.

Jones, J. F. (1995). Self-access and culture: Retreating from autonomy. *ELT Journal, 49, 3,* 228–234.

Kubota, R. (1999). Japanese culture constructed by discourse: Implications for applied linguistics research and ELT. *TESOL Quarterly, 33,* 9–35.

Kubota, R. (2001). Discursive construction of the images of U.S. classrooms. *TESOL Quarterly, 35,* 9–38.

Leki, I. (1999). "Pretty much I screwed up": Ill-served needs of a permanent resident. In L. Harklau, K. M. Losey, & M. Siegal (Eds.), *Generation 1.5 meets college composition: Issues in the teaching of writing to U.S.-educated learners of ESL* (pp. 17–43). Mahwah, NJ: Lawrence Erlbaum.

Levine, A., Oded, B., Connor, U., & Asons, I. (2002). Variation in EFL-ESL peer response. *TESL-EJ, 6(3),* Retrieved August 18, 2004, from www-writing.berkeley.edu/TESL-EJ/ej23/a1.html.

Liu, J. (2001). *Asian students' classroom communication patterns in U.S. universities: An emic perspective.* Westport, CT: Ablex Publishing.

Liu, J., & Hansen, J. (2002). *Peer response in second language writing classrooms.* Ann Arbor, MI: The University of Michigan Press.

Lockhart, C., & Ng, P. (1993). How useful is peer response? *Perspectives, 5(1),* 17–29.

Mangelsdor, K., & Schlumberger, A. (1992). ESL student response stances in a peer-review task. *Journal of Second Language Writing, 1(3),* 235–254.

Mannheim, B., & Tedlock, D. (1995). Introduction. In D. Tedlock & B. Mannheim (Eds.), *The dialogic emergence of culture* (pp. 1–32). Urbana & Chicago: University of Illinois Press.

Martin, J. N., & Nakayama, T. K. (2001). *Experiencing intercultural communication: An introduction.* Mountain View, CA: Mayfield.

Mendonça, C. O., & Johnson, K. E. (1994). Peer review negotiations: Revision activities in ESL writing instruction. *TESOL Quarterly, 28(4),* 745–769.

Nelson, G. L. (1997). How cultural differences affect written and oral communication: The case of peer response groups. In D. L. Sigsbee, B. W. Speck, & Bruce Maylath (Eds.), *Approaches to teaching non-native English speakers across the curriculum* (pp. 77–84). San Francisco: Jossey-Bass.

Nelson, G., & Carson, J. (1995). Social dimensions of second-language writing instruction: Peer response groups as cultural context. In D. Rubin (Ed.), *Composing social identity in written communication* (pp. 89–109). Hillsdale, NJ: Lawrence Erlbaum.

Nelson, G., & Carson, J. (1998). ESL students' perceptions of effectiveness in peer response groups. *Journal of Second Language Writing, 7,* 113–131.

Nelson, G., & Murphy, J. (1992). An L2 writing group: Task and social dimension. *Journal of Second Language Writing, 1,* 171–192.

Nelson, G., & Murphy, J. (1993). Peer response groups: Do L2 writers use peer comments in revising their drafts? *TESOL Quarterly, 27,* 135–142.

Norton, B. (2000). *Identity and language learning: Gender, ethnicity and educational change.* Essex, UK: Pearson Education Ltd.

Paulus, T. M. (1999). The effect of peer and teacher feedback on student writing. *Journal of Second Language Writing, 8(3),* 265–289.

Pennycook, A. (2001). *Critical applied linguistics: A critical introduction.* Mahwah, NJ: Lawrence Erlbaum.

Rosaldo, R. (1989). *Culture & truth: The remaking of social analysis.* Boston: Beacon Press.

Rothschild, D., & Klingenberg, F. (1990). Self and peer evaluation of writing in the interactive ESL classroom: An exploratory study. *TESL Canada Journal, 8(1),* 52–65.

Said, E. (1978). *Orientalism: Western conceptions of the Orient.* London, UK: Penguin Books.

Scollon, R., & Scollon, S. W. (1995). *Intercultural communication.* Oxford, UK: Blackwell.

Sengupta, S. (1998). Peer evaluation: "I am not the teacher." *ELT Journal, 52(1),* 19–28.

Shore, B. (1996). *Culture in mind: Cognition, culture, and the problem of meaning.* New York: Oxford University Press.

Silva, T., & Brice, C. (2004). Research in teaching writing. In M. McGroarty (Ed.), *Annual Review of Applied Linguistics: Advances in Language Pedagogy,* Vol. 24, pp. 70–106. New York: Cambridge University Press.

Spack, R. (1997). The rhetorical construction of multilingual students. *TESOL Quarterly, 31,* 765–774.

Stanley, J. (1992). Coaching student writers to be effective peer evaluators. *Journal of Second Language Writing, 1(3),* 217–233.

Tang, G. M., & Tithecott, J. (1999). Peer response in ESL writing. *TESL Canada Journal, 18(2),* 20–38.

Triandis, H. C. (1995). *Individualism and collectivism.* Boulder, CO: Westview Press.

Villamil, O., and de Guerrero, M. C. M. (1998). Assessing the impact of peer revision on L2 writing. *Applied Linguistics 19(4),* 491–514.

Villamil, O., & de Guerrero, M. C. M. (1996). Peer revision in the L2 classroom: Social-cognitive activities, mediating strategies, and aspects of social behavior. *Journal of Second Language Writing, 5(1)*, 51–75.

Zamel, V. (1995). Strangers in academia: The experiences of faculty and ESL students across the curriculum. *College Composition and Communication, 46*, 506–521.

Zhang, S. (1995). Reexamining the affective advantage of peer feedback in the ESL writing class. *Journal of Second Language Writing, 4(3)*, 209–222.

Zhu, W. (1995). Effects of training for peer response on students' comments and interaction. *Written Communication, 12*, 492–528.

Zhu, W. (2001). Interaction and feedback in mixed peer response groups. *Journal of Second Language Writing, 10*, 251–276.

4 Appropriation, ownership, and agency: Negotiating teacher feedback in academic settings

Christine Tardy

I recently attended a new faculty seminar at my university, at which everyone was asked to describe a person or event that had led us into the field of teaching. Our seminar leader began by sharing his experience in attempting to publish his first paper. He described receiving his draft from his dissertation advisor and being horrified initially to find it covered in red ink with "not a line untouched." But after reading through the comments, he was struck with a feeling of amazement that his advisor had cared enough about his work to so fully invest his interest and time in responding to the draft. As we worked our way around the seminar room, one of my new colleagues shared another story that seemed to counter the paper-saturated-in-red-ink story that had begun the discussion. He described an English teacher who wrote next to nothing on his papers. Despite his initial disappointment at not receiving the feedback he had wanted and expected, he found that the teacher's minimal response had freed him to write and given him a sense of independence that eventually led him to believe in his own writing. These two stories interested me because they illustrated such dramatically different approaches to teaching and responding to writing, yet had equally strong, positive impacts on the writers.

Just over a decade ago, Reid (1994) examined what she called the "myths of appropriation" – the seeming dichotomy of under-responding and over-responding to texts, specifically addressing the prevailing fear of taking away ownership of, or appropriating, students' writing. In the time since Reid's article, the term *appropriation* has not disappeared from discussions of feedback. As second language writing research has shown an increased interest in both sociopolitical concerns and issues of identity and voice, appropriation has become an important concern for teachers. This chapter reviews the issue of appropriation and feedback in EAP (English for academic purposes) settings, offering a new lens through which to view the interactions of learner and teacher voices in student writing. I begin by outlining traditional definitions of appropriation as unidirectional and more recent theories of appropriation as dialogical, then I draw upon my own case study research to illustrate how teachers and learners may appropriate one another's texts. I conclude with a

60

discussion of how EAP researchers and teachers can address this complex issue in concrete ways.

Monologic definitions of appropriation

To appropriate another's words is to take those words and inject one's own meaning into them, to take ownership of those words for one's own purposes. Through appropriation, prior texts and discourses assume new meanings, identities, and ideologies, often serving the intentions of the appropriator. In writing research, the term *appropriation* has been used in various ways, but it always invests power in the hands of the appropriator.

Because it involves the intermingling of voices, appropriation is imbued with power. Whose voice takes over? Whose meaning is heard? Who has the power to repopulate or resist another's words? In the case of teacher feedback on students' texts, power is unequally distributed – it is generally the teacher who decides what the learner will write about, the length of time allowed for composing, the criteria by which the text will be evaluated, and the grade to be given. It is this power differential that has prompted concern in both L1 composition studies (e.g., Brannon & Knoblauch, 1982; Onore, 1989; Sommers, 1982) and L2 writing (e.g., Conrad & Goldstein, 1999; Goldstein, 2004; Reid, 1994), leading teachers to question their own approaches to student feedback.

When teachers respond to learners' texts, they do so with various goals in mind: to illustrate how readers may respond to the text, to show alternative expressions, or to suggest how the text may conform more closely to the expert's view of successful writing. Because of the hierarchical nature of the teacher-student relationship, students may feel pressured to follow teacher directives, even when students do not understand or agree with the feedback (e.g., Hyland, 1998) so that "the student's attention dramatically shifts from 'This is what I want to say,' to 'This is what you the teacher are asking me to do'" (Sommers, 1982, p. 150).

In her article, Reid (1994) described a vicious cycle in which her fear of taking ownership of her students' work led her to write less on their papers, resulting in a fear that she had become a fraudulent teacher who was failing to help students improve their writing. But after closely examining early theories of appropriation, Reid concluded that these theories were often flawed because they exaggerated claims and overlooked the role of social context. Emphasizing the importance of discourse community in teaching academic writing, Reid saw the teacher as a "cultural informant" and liaison between the student-writer and the target discourse community. She therefore contended that "we must introduce students to ways in which they can learn to gain ownership of their writing while at the same time considering their readers" (p. 217). In other words, Reid at least partially neutralized the fear of appropriation by arguing that feedback provides important scaffolding for learning to write for an academic community, by giving students a sense of how the community might respond to their texts.

Since the mid-1990s, however, traditional EAP approaches to teaching have been questioned for their tendency to reproduce the power structures of academic institutions (Benesch, 2001; Pennycook, 1997). By the turn of the millennium, Pennycook (2000) argued that "It is impossible to believe any longer in the myth that teaching English can be reduced to helping people gain access to social and economic power. Rather, we are part of complex social, economic, and political relations that flow back and forth through our classroom walls" (p. 95). In this view, monologic or unidirectional definitions of appropriation – that is, those that focus on the teacher's appropriation of the learner's text – are insufficient, accounting for the teacher's agency but not the learner's. Dialogic models of appropriation, on the other hand, offer rich vocabularies and heuristics for understanding the sociopolitical relations and the cross-directional flows of ownership and agency that permeate writing.

Appropriation and voice: Sociocultural models of appropriation

Second language writing scholarship has given increased recognition to the social, cultural, and political dimensions of writing – considerations of how a writer's unique experiences influence his or her writing. Bakhtin's theory of language as dialogic embodies this social mingling of texts, seeing "the unique speech experience of each individual [as] shaped and developed in continuous and constant interaction with others' individual utterances" (Bakhtin, 1986, p. 89). In Bakhtin's view, texts exist both in literal dialogue – responding to a prior utterance and preceding a subsequent utterance – and also as interwoven voices and discourses.

Our speech, that is, all our utterances (including creative works), is filled with others' words, varying degrees of otherness or varying degrees of "our-own-ness," varying degrees of awareness and detachment. These words of others carry with them their own expression, their own evaluative tone, which we assimilate, rework, and re-accentuate. (p. 89)

As writers ventriloquize, re-envoice, or re-accentuate the words of others, they create and assert their own voice and identity. The voices that writers reclaim are those that they encounter in their classrooms, textbooks, pleasure reading, social spaces, workplaces, and professional meetings.

They are the voices of peers, friends, icons, adversaries, mentors, and teachers.

Feedback on writing then becomes a part of writers' intertextual and "intermental" (Ivanič, 1998) encounters, having the power to shape – and be shaped by – writers in unique ways. Situating appropriation within other streams of voices acknowledges the agency that writers have in their own writing, an element largely absent from the monologic theories already described. The three sociocultural models of appropriation described in the following sections consider not merely the ways in which teachers may take over student-writers' texts but also the ways in which student-writers may appropriate the multiple texts that they encounter in their lives. These models emphasize the agency of the writer as well as the teacher.

Typology of appropriation: Kamberelis & Scott (1992)

Drawing extensively on Bakhtin's (1981, 1986) work, Kamberelis and Scott (1992) define a typology of six ways in which voices may be appropriated (by writers) to take on different meanings and intentions. Their typology outlines a relatively broad definition of appropriation, ranging from practices that adopt others' words in a more or less uncritical manner to more transformative practices like parody.

Applying this typology to analyze the multivoiced texts of two children writing in their first language, Kamberelis and Scott show how the first three strategies in their typology (*direct quotation, adoption*, and *stylization*) function to establish social alignments or solidarity with other individual or group discourses, whereas the latter three strategies (*parody, hidden polemic*, and *idealization*) offer means for asserting power *over* other discourses. Further, parody and hidden polemic, the authors claim, can be used to resist ideologies or actions advocated by others. Because Kamberelis and Scott use this model to understand how children appropriate more powerful discourses, it is unclear how it might apply to the appropriation of less powerful voices (e.g., teachers appropriating student writing). Nevertheless, the model offers a very broad definition of appropriation, considering it as consisting of multiple ways of weaving together the voices that surround writers, for both alignment and resistance.

Appropriation as strategy of textual negotiation: Canagarajah (2002)

Appropriation figures prominently in Canagarajah's (2002) work as a component of critical writing – writing that asks learners to, for example, question the conventions of dominant discourses and those favored by the learners, interrogate received knowledge, and use language in creative ways to represent their own interests and values. Canagarajah classifies appropriation as one of several "strategies of textual negotiation" that multilingual writers use to mediate their own vernacular-based voices in the face of dominant (mainstream) discourses. Each of these strategies may adopt monologic or dialogic voices, index critical or uncritical ideologies, and result in varying degrees of textual coherence.

Within this taxonomy, appropriation is characterized by a dialogical voice, a critical ideology, and a coherent text. According to Canagarajah, appropriation "takes over the dominant / alien discourse and shapes it for achieving one's own purposes" (p. 115), offering multilingual writers a means of persuasively adding their own voices to academic conversations. While it is used here to describe the textual negotiation of learners, this view of appropriation may also be applied to understand the textual negotiation of collaborators or even teachers.

One potential weakness of Canagarajah's model is that it appears to idealize appropriation as a preferred strategy. Quite often, writers will be unwilling (or unable) to take the risks involved in this practice, depending on the demands, constraints, or stakes involved in the writing task. Canagarajah does acknowledge that writers turn to different strategies in different contexts, and he brings in Peirce's (1995) notion of *investment* to account for these differences. Extending the economic metaphors of symbolic capital (Bourdieu, 1977), Peirce uses investment to illustrate that "when language learners speak, they are not only exchanging information with target language speakers but they are constantly organizing and reorganizing a sense of who they are and how they relate to the social world" (p. 18). Writers and teachers may have an investment in accommodating, opposing, or appropriating discourses, depending on their roles and motives within a particular social context.

Modes of appropriation and participation: Prior (1998)

Prior's (1998) theoretical view of writing is firmly grounded in the sociohistoric theories of Bakhtin (1981, 1986), Voloshinov (1973), and Wertsch (1991), which emphasize "that none of us have 'our own words' to put our thoughts into and that even our most innovative knowledge is heavily mediated by cultural tools not of our making" (Prior, 1998, p. 100). Through his study of disciplinary writing with both L1 and L2 writers, Prior leans heavily on the concept of appropriation and points to a need for a more complex understanding of that concept.

Using intertextual tracing of writers' texts and discourse-based interviews with writers and mentors, Prior details the "modes of appropriation" adopted by different writers. Such modes may include, at one extreme, borrowing others' words verbatim without truly aligning oneself with those words (similar to *stylization* in Kamberelis and Scott's 1992 model) and, at the other extreme, borrowing and transforming others' words while aligning oneself with the larger disciplinary community. While the former mode illustrates a rather limited participation in disciplinary activity (what Prior calls *procedural displays*), the latter exemplifies deeper participation (labeled *deep participation*) with a sense of belonging to the community. Feedback figures into Prior's model as one of the many voices that writers engage in. This model seems to me to be the most dialogic of the three, as Prior explicitly illustrates how appropriation can flow from teachers to learners and back to teachers, as they collaborate and influence one another. Yet while the theoretical model appears to be quite powerful in describing the postgraduate settings with which Prior works, it is a bit more difficult to imagine its application in contexts where relationships may be characterized by more marked power differentials.

Appropriation, ownership, and language rights

Relying on the metaphor of voice, the three models all emphasize the intermingling of many voices within any one text and the resulting complexity of text ownership. With the traditional Western notions of originality and single authorship thrown into question by many writers (e.g., Howard, 1999; Pennycook, 1996; Scollon, 1995), the models instead acknowledge the multiple ways in which texts come into being in disciplinary settings and their shaping by multiple authors who exert and assert various meanings into those texts.

Recognition of the legitimacy of vernacular-based voices, including dialects and varieties of English (e.g., Canagarajah, 2002; Lu, 1994; Norton, 1997; Smitherman & Villanueva, 2003), further complicates teachers' goals and purposes in responding to student writing. Autobiographical pieces by second-language and second-dialect writers often relay feelings of alienation from dominant discourses (e.g., Belcher & Connor, 2001; Braine, 1999), but also describe the various strategies that these writers have used to accommodate, resist, or transform those discourses. Villanueva's book *Bootstraps* (1993) describes how he, as a Puerto Rican American, found his place in academic life and the study of rhetoric. As part rhetorical theory and part memoir, the writing is a compelling example of how vernacular-based voices might appropriate academic genres and discourses both critically and persuasively. As Villanueva's text blends the academic, ethnic, and racial worlds in which he lives, it illustrates possibilities for textual negotiation. Although students will not always find it desirable or even possible to bend genres to this extent, such examples provide them with a more malleable view of writing, in which alternative textual possibilities exist. Multivoiced texts like Villanueva's also foreground for researchers the many directions in which appropriation flows as writers work within dominant discourse possibilities while transforming those possibilities in new ways.

Appropriation and feedback: Illustrations

The bulk of research into teacher feedback and student response has tended to investigate types of feedback given and subsequent revisions that students do or do not make (see Ferris et al., 1997; Goldstein, 2004; and Hyland, 1998, for overviews of these findings). Issues of appropriation are generally given a nod but are not studied in depth. Research of postgraduate L2 writers, however, addresses appropriation more explicitly and illustrates the ways in which teachers and learners appropriate one another's words in a complex dialogue. Here, I detail illustrative findings from case study work, drawing on my own research with a doctoral student named "Chatri" and on previous research with similar populations.

Feedback as appropriation

Scholarship in L2 writing feedback has generally used the term *appropriation* to refer to the ways in which teachers appropriate student writing by changing the writer's intended meaning (and, therefore, the ownership) of a text. Several studies in postgraduate settings provide illustrations of when, how, and even why teachers may take ownership of students' texts; yet in these settings the "teachers" are more likely to be the writers' mentors than traditional classroom instructors.

Belcher (1994) examined three mentoring relationships between doctoral students and their advisors, arguing that the nature of these relationships can be a determining factor in the academic and professional success of the students. Belcher describes the two less successful relationships as more hierarchical and the one successful relationship as more dialogical. In the case of "Li," for example, the advisor wrote copious feedback on Li's drafts to model critical thinking and push Li to take a critical stance toward his sources. Li's response was one of opposition, dismissal, and eventual departure from academic life. At the other extreme is "Keongmee," whose advisor saw herself as a collaborator and coauthor rather than as a model to be copied. While Belcher acknowledges that mentoring relationships need not necessarily be egalitarian to be successful, her work illustrates how a hierarchical relationship can take ownership away from the student.

Indeed, L2 writers face many threats to ownership of their texts as they work through the process of publication, including those from journal editors, reviewers, and language "correctors" (Burrough-Boenisch, 2003; Flowerdew, 2000). But relationships with these gatekeepers are usually less ambiguous than that with the writer's mentor – in the case of young scholars, this is often an advisor or dissertation chair. The challenges involved in these collaborative, yet inherently hierarchical, relationships are detailed in Blakeslee's (1997) study of a collaborative writing relationship between a physics professor ("Swendsen") and his postgraduate student ("Bouzida"), a fluent L2 writer. As they worked on a series of revisions for a journal article, Swendsen took control in oral meetings, and Bouzida attempted to enact Swendsen's feedback in subsequent drafts. Frustrated by Bouzida's revisions, Swendsen eventually revised parts of the manuscript on his own, changing the article significantly and taking over ownership of the text. Like Belcher (1994), Blakeslee argues that mentors must relinquish some of their authority to provide students adequate experience with writing tasks. She notes that mentors often play the role of editor and gatekeeper, and in this role, they may (even unintentionally) constrain the learner's possibilities for negotiating texts, limiting the writer's options to less critical types of appropriation, such as stylization, adoption, or accommodation.

In my work with four writers at an American graduate school (Tardy, 2004), I saw how writers must also contend with multiple layers of ownership over their texts as they work with senior students, advisors, committees, and reviewers. This study, which followed the writers through an EAP writing course, graduate content courses, and graduate research, aimed to trace the influences on the writers' development of disciplinary writing skills; perhaps unsurprisingly, mentoring and feedback were particularly influential.[1] The writer who worked most closely with his mentors was "Chatri," a native speaker of Thai and an engineering doctoral student, who shared his writing and met with me for regular interviews over a two-year period. During this time, Chatri submitted two papers to international conferences, each step in preparation layered in interactions with both his immediate supervisor ("Roberto"), a recent doctoral graduate, and his dissertation advisor, an internationally recognized professor who directed the research lab where Chatri and Roberto worked.

The process by which Chatri usually worked on writing tasks was to compose a complete draft of the paper independently and then to revise with Roberto. Chatri described the collaborative process in this way:

Oh, I give [Roberto the] electronic file, and then I sit beside him and then he – when he writes, I will say and then, I let him write because [*laughing*] I know that his writing is better than me. I just discuss with him if his writing, I mean *his* idea, I will not argue with him about his writing, but if the *concept* is different from my idea, I will say, "No, no, not this, but this." But the style of writing, I let him go. (November 7, 2003)

Importantly, Chatri distinguished the writing from the research, which to him really defined authorship and ownership of the text. Although many of the words were revised by others, the ideas and text structure were his own. "I know – even [though] I didn't write that sentence, but I know at the time that my supervisor revised that sentence and asked me. It still preserves the idea that I want to communicate to the reader" (January 23, 2004).

At the same time, Chatri admitted to feeling uneasy with some of the changes that Roberto had suggested while revising the first conference paper. Much of the wording was revised, but the key difference that concerned Chatri was the new claim that "the accuracy in pose estimation of our new appearance-based methods *is better than* using the geometric-based approach" (emphasis mine). This revision differed, in Chatri's view, rather significantly from his original claim that "the pose estimation accuracy of our proposed methods is *at least equivalent to* the one of a current feature-based approach" (emphasis mine).

Figure 4.1 illustrates Chatri's original version of the abstract (left) and the later version revised with his supervisor (right). Words added and modified by the supervisor are underlined.

The changes to Chatri's text, in this case, illustrate Kamberelis and Scott's (1992) "hidden polemic," in which Roberto has recontextualized Chatri's original words, bringing in meanings that Chatri had not intended. Importantly, Chatri's concerns over the revision centered primarily on his own identity as a researcher and author. He explained that he preferred to avoid overstating his claims (as he felt Roberto had done) and also saw the revised knowledge claim as somewhat misleading. Unfortunately, he felt uncomfortable discussing this issue with his supervisor, both because of tight time constraints and because he viewed Roberto as a more experienced writer.

Further complicating the situation was the fact that Chatri's dissertation advisor would also be listed as a coauthor of the paper.[2] Chatri explained that he was less concerned about harming his own reputation (by overstating his claims) than he was about tarnishing the reputation of his advisor.

For *me*, I think, I'm not – I'm unknown people, right? If my work is similar to some work, okay, it's okay. But my advisor, he really well known, he is the editor in a very well-known journal. I don't want to make it too – make it... I don't know. (January 23, 2004)

In the end, neither his advisor nor the conference reviewers commented on the knowledge claim with which Chatri was so uncomfortable, and the

Abstract written by Chatri

This paper present two different object pose tracking methods which are based on an appearance model technique, called Active Appearance Model (AAM). The key idea of the first method is to utilize the AAM technique to track the feature points in a stereo image, then the 3D reconstruction and the 3D absolute orientation algorithm are applied to estimate the pose. For the second method, the AAM matching algorithm is extended to incorporate the 3D-object pose parameters as a part of minimization parameters. So while it is seeking the optimal image and the observed object image, the pose is being directly estimated. From the experiments, the results show that the pose estimation accuracy of our proposed methods is at least equivalent to the one of a current feature-based approach which has been shown as an accurate method. However, since these methods do no require the feature extraction, our both methods can be considered as the alternative approach in such a situation that the extracted features are not obvious where the feature-based approach may fail.

Abstract revised with supervisor

This paper present two different algorithms for object tracking and pose estimation. Both methods are based on an appearance model technique called Active Appearance Model (AAM). The key idea of the first method is to utilize two instances of the AAM to track landmark points in a stereo pair of images and perform 3D reconstruction of the landmarks followed by 3D-pose estimation. The second method, the AAM matching algorithm is an extension of the original AAM that incorporates the full 6 DOF pose parameters as part of the minimization parameters. This extension allows for the estimation of the 3D pose of any object, without any restriction on its geometry. We compare both algorithms with a previously developed algorithm using a geometric-based approach [14]. The results show that the accuracy in pose estimation of our new appearance-based methods is better than using the geometric-based approach. Moreover, since appearance-based methods do not require *customized* feature extractions, the new methods present a more flexible alternative, especially in situations where extracting features is not simple due to cluttered background, complex and irregular features, etc.

Figure 4.1. Contrasts in independent and collaborative writing

sentence remained in the paper's final version published in the conference proceedings.

Chatri's and Bouzida's stories highlight the multiple exigencies present in much academic writing and the ways in which a writer's mode of participation may change over time, for example, from "deep participation" at earlier stages of writing to "procedural displays," when time becomes a very immediate constraint. When the writers' participation was primarily that of procedural display, they were more likely to relinquish some ownership of their texts to others with more perceived authority. In each of these cases, issues of agency, ownership, and appropriation were complicated even more by the joint construction of the text. In such collaborative or guided writing activities, mentors are also likely to have their own (multiple) motives for the choices they make in providing feedback, including modeling professional practice, providing opportunities for legitimate peripheral participation or situated learning, supporting the development of writing skills, enacting disciplinary enculturation, and protecting one's own reputation. Although mentors may have an investment in avoiding opposition to learners' texts in some contexts, they may want to appropriate those texts in others, and these investments may at times conflict with the learner's motives and sense of identity. When learners do not share the mentor's goals or a sense of alignment with the disciplinary community, they may resist the feedback, creating a discoursal self (Ivanič, 1998) that is half their own and half others'.

Appropriation of feedback

The previous examples describe teachers' (or mentors') appropriation of learners' texts, but sociocultural theories of appropriation also provide a means to describe the learner's ownership of a text as he or she draws on multiple voices and discourses, including teacher response. Russell (1997), for example, makes an explicit connection between appropriation and learning. Writers, he argues, appropriate (pick up and learn to use) the discursive tools available within a given activity system to carry out specific tasks.

A particularly useful concept in understanding how teacher feedback may be appropriated by the student is that of *internal persuasiveness* – discourse that is "half-ours and half someone else's" (Bakhtin, 1981, p. 345) but that is semantically flexible and "able to reveal ever newer ways to mean" (p. 346). Internally persuasive discourse is contrasted with *authoritative* discourse, which is the more alien and static language of authority. Both internally persuasive and authoritative discourses interact for writers, and it is where these discourses converge that disciplinary enculturation appears to occur (Prior, 1998).

Considering what is internally persuasive to writers allows us to understand better a writer's sense of ownership over the discourses that influence his or her text. As Russell (1997) explains, individuals may personalize these discourses over time:

A newcomer may appropriate (learn) some tool, some way with words, then carry it back to a familiar activity system and put it to use there – perhaps to a very different use. There, others may appropriate it, transforming that activity system and its genres in the process. . . . Similarly, a newcomer may bring ways of acting with words from one activity system (e.g., a family or workplace) to another (e.g., a classroom or discipline), in which they might be appropriated by the collective to transform its genres. (p. 522)

Prior (1998) illustrates the ownership of others' words through his study of Moira, a sociology graduate student writing in her L1, and West, her advisor. As he traces West's responses to Moira's texts and later revisions, we see how West's words come to populate Moira's writing. But Prior's account is not simply one of word tracing. Through discourse-based interviews with both Moira and West, he is able to show how some of West's words became internally persuasive to Moira, whereas others were authoritative. The latter examples often dealt with issues of tone, as Moira resisted academic words in favor of more common synonyms. However, even when Moira adopted West's words (which she did in nearly every case), she maintained agency and ownership over her writing. At times, West's revisions helped her express the views that she intended; at other times, West's feedback became internally persuasive to Moira as her participation in the knowledge-building work of her discipline deepened.

Although Moira was writing in her L1, Chatri's experiences echoed this finding. His practices of appropriation included direct quotation, adoption, and stylization – all strategies of alignment. He described adopting many of Roberto's comments on and beliefs about writing.

[My supervisor's] writing style affect me a lot right now. Because it seems that I'm writing – 100% of my writing style is by copy. Copy, I mean that, okay, when I read this, this kind of sentence is I have some feeling that they use this kind of sentence to represent some idea. And then I remember that when I want to represent that idea, use that kind of sentence [*laughing*]. It's a kind of pattern. I have a database and try to process [it]. (June 11, 2004)

Chatri's use of strategies that promote solidarity with the dominant discourse might be explained by the extent to which Roberto's feedback was usually internally persuasive to Chatri. The feedback, therefore, served as an important learning tool for Chatri, as he gradually took increased ownership over his texts. He perceived Roberto to have rewritten about "70%" of his first conference paper but not as much, "over 50%," of his second paper. In both cases, however, he felt the work to be his own.

In his second conference paper, Chatri again faced the difficulty of negotiating a knowledge claim in the abstract written by Roberto. Similar to the claim in the previous paper, this sentence read:

Also unlike previous reports by other researchers [3, 5, 6, 9, 13], we use ground-truth to demonstrate the accuracy of our tracking algorithm.

This time, the abstract had been written solely by Roberto, as the deadline was imminent. Although he disagreed with the statement, Chatri had again allowed the sentence in the final draft because of time constraints. A few months later, however, Chatri received additional feedback through written reviews from referees. To Chatri's disappointment, the paper was rejected, but one reviewer confirmed Chatri's belief that the knowledge claim in the abstract was problematic. The reviewer wrote:

The claim that no other AAM paper has used "ground truth" to demonstrate the accuracy of tracking needs to [be] substantiated. I believe this to be a false claim (but don't have any other AAM papers at hand to provide references against this).

Chatri agreed with the reviewer; Roberto's claim that Chatri's new method outperformed previous methods was clearly *not* internally persuasive to Chatri. He not only felt the statement to be untrue but also felt uncomfortable with the particular stance created through Roberto's words, describing it as "too risky" (July 15, 2004). Chatri was caught in what Ivanič (1998) calls "a discoursal web of subjectivities, partly owned and partly disowned, designed to create a good impression on the reader without compromising the writer's integrity" (p. 244).

Although Chatri generally told Roberto when he disagreed with his revisions, he did not discuss this sentence due to time pressure. Through the review, however, Chatri seemed to gain resolve in asserting his own authority over his text. In the future, he believed he would be more forceful in discussions with Roberto, saying that "if we finally come out, we submit to a journal paper, at least I have to convince my supervisor that, 'Okay, you have to change this sentence'" (July 15, 2004). Chatri seemed to gain a clearer sense of how he might express himself in his own voice. He was beginning to learn how to balance the strategies of accommodating and resisting Roberto's construction of his identity (Ivanič, 1998).

Chatri and the other L2 writers in my study were less confident in their writing style than Moira or the writers in Ivanič's (1998) study, all L1 writers who reacted in rather strong negative ways to specific tones and stances in academic writing. In contrast, the L2 writers I studied often had difficulty determining whether mentor revisions were correcting errors, conforming to disciplinary preferences, or imposing the individual style of the teacher/mentor. When they were unsure, the writers adopted revisions without question. However, as they read more and became more immersed in disciplinary practice, they gradually became better at distinguishing idiosyncrasies and disciplinary norms in the discourses around them, giving them greater confidence in rejecting feedback that was not internally persuasive.

Chatri's story also highlights the fluid nature of both power and authority in mentoring relationships. Though he saw his supervisor as a more experienced writer, Chatri saw himself as the content expert, with more experience and reading knowledge within the specific research area. As a result, Roberto most often deferred to Chatri's ideas and intended meanings, trying only to revise the ways in which the ideas were presented in writing. Chatri's sense of agency and ownership also seemed to fluctuate as he approached different tasks. As he gained confidence over particular genres in particular settings, he was more likely to preserve his own voice and discoursal preferences; in contrast, when he approached newer genres in less familiar settings, he tended to distrust his own textual knowledge and more willingly take on the voices of his mentors. This contingent nature of expertise (see Jacoby, 1991) has important consequences for the study of feedback and appropriation, as students in EAP classrooms often hold more expertise in their subject-matter content than do writing teachers who may respond to their writing.

In sum, the stories of both Moira and Chatri illustrate how feedback from teachers or mentors may be accommodated, resisted, and later transformed by learners. Teacher feedback that does not resonate with writers' individual sense of self still becomes a part of their repertoire of voices, and they can later choose to avoid, adopt, or even transform it. Bakhtinian-based models of appropriation help illustrate the agency that the writers have in this process; they show that although utterances are multivoiced, they are always personalized through the speakers' or writers' way of making meaning out of their own social histories (Prior, 2001).

Toward a dialogical view of appropriation

The studies described here show how sociocultural theory can extend a unidirectional or monologic view of appropriation to a more dialogic construct among writers and readers. Early definitions of appropriation would give a different picture of writers like Chatri, Bouzida, or Moira, overlooking the multivoiced aspects of their texts and the ways in which writers negotiate and appropriate the voices. Dialogical theories of appropriation instead foreground the writer's agency and the contingency of expertise, integrating issues of investment, power, and social alignment. Appropriation not only acts on writers but also serves as a tool *for* writers, who may even influence those with more power, including their teachers or mentors.

Appropriation in EAP research and teaching

Appropriation is a dimension of writing that all writers contend with as they mediate the voices that constitute their texts. A more complete body of research that addresses how writers mediate these voices – particularly at the less advanced levels of EAP – would help to build a more critical understanding of L2 writing interactions and development. Ethnographic case study research (e.g., Canagarajah, 2001; Casanave, 2002) is one promising approach, particularly when it can bring in the multiple layers of influence on learner's texts, the sociopolitical dimensions of the institution, the immediate task context, and the teacher-student relationship. Approaches that integrate intertextual analysis of learners' texts with discourse-based interviews (e.g., Ivanič, 1998; Prior, 1998) also have great potential in teaching us more about how teachers and learners appropriate one another's words. Another intriguing method for classroom-based action research can be found in Atkinson's (2004) "autoethnography" of his own mentoring of graduate students in Japan. Atkinson's approach foregrounds the tensions that mentors experience as they attempt to straddle multiple roles in their teacher-student interactions, and it also adopts a more self-reflexive approach to understanding teacher response. In addition, future research must be longitudinal to show how writers negotiate and appropriate voices *over time* and in different settings as their investment in a task alters and their alignments with various power structures change.

Continuing research into appropriation and feedback will help to highlight the complexities of the issue but is unlikely to locate "the fine line between guidance and appropriation" (Blakeslee, 1997, p. 154). At the ends of this continuum lie the over-directive feedback and the hands-off feedback exemplified in the two approaches described at the opening of this chapter. However, the practices of most teachers are likely to fall somewhere between these extremes, allowing them to address issues of appropriation rather easily. Individual feedback conferences, for example, can help teachers better understand the intended meanings of students' texts before they give feedback that might mistake the writer's intentions. Engaging students in dialogue about their writing can allow them more opportunity, not only to clarify and defend their meanings, but also to build a greater sense of ownership over their texts.

Writing teachers may also consider incorporating explicit discussions of appropriation into the classroom, asking students to consider the differences between giving the teacher control over their texts and responding to teacher feedback in a way that helps readers understand the writer's intentions in a more persuasive way (Conrad & Goldstein, 1999). Clark and Ivanič (1997) advocate a pedagogy of "critical language awareness" that recognizes the relationship between writing and identity by asking students to examine the values, beliefs, and practices with which they align themselves in their texts. Students may investigate the values of target academic communities by conducting ethnographies and examining, for example, the feedback that they receive on their writing in different disciplinary environments (Ivanič, 1998). Activities like this foreground the push-and-pull exerted on writers and their texts in any given sociopolitical context, and they can help writers locate strategies for negotiating these influences.

Such activities would be of particular value in classes for postgraduate L2 writers, whose texts are quite often rewritten by advisors, as in the studies described here. Students in advanced EAP classes may be asked to analyze feedback or revisions to their own texts by teachers or mentors. Do the changes alter the grammar, the style, or the meaning of the original text? Which parts of the feedback are internally persuasive? Writers may also be encouraged to rewrite some of the revisions, perhaps drawing on published texts for examples of alternative expressions. Such an activity would also offer an excellent springboard into discussions of textual borrowing practices as they relate to the complicated issue of plagiarism. Activities such as these, which provide classroom practice in appropriating (including adopting, stylizing, or transforming) the voices of experts, can familiarize learners with strategies for negotiating texts in relatively safe environments, granting writers agency as they re-envoice the expressions and voices they encounter.

One theme that runs through discussions of appropriation is that of tension – the tensions among promoting the reproduction of dominant discourses, encouraging individuals to preserve their own voices, and helping learners succeed in their target discourse communities. These tensions are essentially the moral dilemmas that Johnston (2003) writes of, encompassing competing values about "what is good and right for the student" (p. 43). Such tension cannot be resolved, and I would argue that it is precisely that irresolvability that we should focus on in the classroom. Both teachers and students can benefit from exploring the complex ways in which agency, identity, community, and expertise interact when teachers respond to student writing and when students respond to feedback. The dialogic models of appropriation described here offer at least a preliminary means for doing so.

Notes

1. Data came from the writers' texts, oral interviews with the writers and EAP instructor, written feedback from mentors and instructors, and observations of the EAP writing classroom. Methods of analysis included qualitative coding, text analysis, and intertextual tracing.
2. Although he did not participate directly in the composing process, Chatri's advisor did read and review the paper before submission. As the director of the research lab, Chatri's advisor would be included as a coauthor, a practice that is customary in engineering and the sciences. See Prior (1998, pp. 160–179) for a more detailed discussion of the complexities of authorship in academic research.

References

Atkinson, D. (2004, May). *Mentor roles in advanced academic literacy.* Paper presented at the American Association of Applied Linguistics Conference, Portland, OR.

Bakhtin, M. M. (1981). *The dialogic imagination: Four essays by M. M. Bakhtin.* (C. Emerson & M. Holquist, Trans.; M. Holquist, Ed.). Austin, TX: University of Texas Press.

Bakhtin, M. M. (1986). *Speech genres and other late essays.* (V. W. McGee, Trans.; C. Emerson & M. Holquist, Eds.). Austin, TX: University of Texas Press.

Belcher, D. (1994). The apprenticeship approach to advanced academic literacy: Graduate students and their mentors. *English for Specific Purposes, 13,* 23–34.

Belcher, D., & Connor, U. (Eds.). (2001). *Reflections on multiliterate lives.* Clevedon, UK: Multilingual Matters.

Benesch, S. (2001). *Critical English for academic purposes: Theory, politics, and practice.* Mahwah, NJ: Lawrence Erlbaum.

Blakeslee, A. (1997). Activity, context, interaction, and authority: Learning to write scientific papers in situ. *Written Communication, 11,* 125–169.

Bourdieu, P. (1977). *Outline of a theory of practice.* (R. Nice, Trans.). Cambridge: Cambridge University Press.

Braine, G. (Ed.). (1999). *Non-native educators in English language teaching.* Mahwah, NJ: Lawrence Erlbaum.

Brannon, L., & Knoblauch, C. H. (1982). On students' rights to their own texts: A model of teacher response. *College Composition and Communication, 33,* 157–166.

Burrough-Boenisch, J. (2003). Shapers of published NNS research articles. *Journal of Second Language Writing, 12,* 223–243.

Canagarajah, A. S. (2001). Addressing issues of power and difference in ESL academic writing. In J. Flowerdew & M. Peacock (Eds.), *Research perspectives on English for academic purposes* (pp. 117–131). Cambridge: Cambridge University Press.

Canagarajah, A. S. (2002). *Critical academic writing and multilingual students.* Ann Arbor, MI: University of Michigan Press.

Casanave, C. P. (2002). *Writing games: Multicultural case studies of academic literacy practices in higher education.* Mahwah, NJ: Lawrence Erlbaum.

Clark, R., & Ivanič, R. (1996). *The politics of writing.* London: Routledge.

Conrad, S., & Goldstein, L. (1999). ESL student revision after teacher written comments: Text, contexts, and individuals. *Journal of Second Language Writing, 8,* 147–179.

Ferris, D. R., Pezone, S., Tade, C. R., & Tinti, S. (1997). Teacher commentary on student writing: Description & implications. *Journal of Second Language Writing, 6,* 155–182.

Flowerdew, J. (2000). Discourse community, legitimate peripheral participation, and the nonnative-English-speaking scholar. *TESOL Quarterly, 34,* 127–150.

Goldstein, L. M. (2004). Questions and answers about teacher written commentary and student revision: Teachers and students working together. *Journal of Second Language Writing, 13,* 63–80.

Howard, R. M. (1999). *Standing in the shadow of giants: Plagiarists, authors, collaborators*. Stamford, CT: Ablex.

Hyland, F. (1998). The impact of teacher-written feedback on individual writers. *Journal of Second Language Writing, 7*, 255–286.

Ivanič, R. (1998). *Writing and identity: The discoursal construction of identity in academic writing*. Philadelphia: John Benjamins.

Jacoby, S. (1991). The constitution of expert-novice in scientific discourse. *Issues in Applied Linguistics, 2*, 149–181.

Johnston, B. (2003). *Values in English language teaching*. Mahwah, NJ: Lawrence Erlbaum.

Kamberelis, G., & Scott, K. D. (1992). Other people's voices: The coarticulation of texts and subjectivities. *Linguistics and Education, 4*, 359–403.

Lu, M.-Z. (1994). Professing multiculturalism: The politics of style in the contact zone. *College Composition and Communication, 45*, 442–458.

Norton, B. (1997). Language, identity, and the ownership of English. *TESOL Quarterly, 29*, 9–31.

Onore, C. (1989). The student, the teacher, and the text: Negotiating meanings through response and revision. In C. Anson (Ed.), *Writing and response: Theory, practice and research* (pp. 231–260). Urbana, IL: NCTE.

Peirce, B. N. (1995). Social identity, investment, and language learning. *TESOL Quarterly, 29*, 9–31.

Pennycook, A. (1996). Borrowing others' words: Text, ownership, memory, and plagiarism. *TESOL Quarterly, 30*, 201–230.

Pennycook, A. (1997). Vulgar pragmatism, critical pragmatism, and EAP. *English for Specific Purposes, 19*, 253–269.

Pennycook, A. (2000). The social politics and the cultural politics of language classrooms. In J. K. Hall & W. G. Eggington (Eds.), *The sociopolitics of English language teaching* (pp. 89–103). Clevedon, UK: Multilingual Matters.

Prior, P. A. (1998). *Writing/disciplinarity: A sociohistoric account of literate activity in the academy*. Mahwah, NJ: Lawrence Erlbaum.

Prior, P. A. (2001). Voices in text, mind, and society: Sociohistoric accounts of discourse acquisition and use. *Journal of Second Language Writing, 10*, 55–81.

Reid, J. (1994). Responding to ESL students' texts: The myths of appropriation. *TESOL Quarterly, 28*, 273–292.

Russell, D. R. (1997). Rethinking genre in school and society: An activity theory analysis. *Written Communication, 14*, 504–554.

Scollon, R. (1995). Plagiarism and ideology: Identity in intercultural discourse. *Language in Society, 24*, 1–28.

Smitherman, G., & Villanueva, G. (Eds.). (2003). *Language diversity in the classroom: From intention to practice*. Carbondale, IL: Southern Illinois University Press.

Sommers, N. (1982). Responding to student writing. *College Composition and Communication, 33*, 148–156.

Tardy, C. M. (2004). *Exploring the interactions of writing instruction and disciplinary practice: Pathways of four multilingual writers*. Unpublished doctoral dissertation, Purdue University.

Wertsch, J. (1991). *Voices of the mind: A sociocultural approach to mediated action*. Cambridge, MA: Harvard University Press.

Villanueva, V. (1993). *Bootstraps: From an American academic of color*. Urbana, IL: NCTE.

Voloshinov, V. N. (1973). *Marxism and the philosophy of language*. (L. Matejka & I. R. Titunik, Trans.). Cambridge, MA: Harvard University Press.

PART II:
SHAPING FEEDBACK: DELIVERY
AND FOCUS DIMENSIONS

5 Does error feedback help student writers? New evidence on the short- and long-term effects of written error correction

Dana Ferris

Attitudes and approaches toward student error have been a source of debate among second language acquisition (SLA) and second language (L2) writing scholars for more than two decades. The debate has ranged from calls for correction of all student errors to prevent fossilization (e.g., Higgs & Clifford, 1982; Lalande, 1982) to a preference for selective correction that focuses on patterns of error that can be addressed productively (Bates et al., 1993; Ferris, 1995c; Hendrickson, 1978) to recommendations that all error correction be eliminated because it is unnecessary, ineffective and even counterproductive (Cook, 1991; Corder, 1981; Krashen, 1984; Selinker, 1992; Truscott, 1996).

The issue of error treatment (including error analysis, feedback, and instruction) is especially salient in the case of L2 writing classes for two reasons. First, despite disagreement on other points surrounding error correction, there is a fair amount of agreement among researchers on two counts: (1) that accuracy in writing matters to academic and professional audiences and that obvious L2 error may stigmatize writers in some contexts (Ferris & Hedgcock, 1998; Horowitz, 1986; James, 1998; Johns, 1995); and (2) that L2 student writers themselves claim to need and value error feedback from their instructors (Cohen & Cavalcanti, 1990; Ferris, 1995b; Ferris & Roberts, 2001; Hedgcock & Lefkowitz, 1994; Leki, 1991; Truscott, 1996). Second, the research base on the question of whether error feedback helps students to improve in the short run or over time is inadequate as to number of studies and inconsistent as to research design (Ferris, 1999, 2004; Polio, 1997). Given the relatively uncontested importance of accuracy and feedback to the two primary audiences (the readers and writers of L2 academic discourse) and the lack of clear-cut empirical evidence, the questions surrounding error correction in student writing deserve ongoing scrutiny.

The study described in this paper was designed to gather additional evidence on the nature and effects of error feedback in L2 writing classes[1]. In the study, conducted in 1998–99, hundreds of texts and thousands of errors produced by 92 ESL student writers at a U.S. university over the course of a 15-week semester were examined. The study was guided by the following research questions, which were generated from a review of previous studies on error correction in L2 writing classes.

- *Does error feedback from instructors help L2 writers to improve their accuracy in the short run (from one draft of a paper to the next) and in the long run (from the beginning to the end of a writing course)?*
- *Do teachers give their students accurate and complete feedback on their errors?*
- *What strategies do instructors use to give error feedback, and what is the effect of differing teacher strategies on student writing?*
- *Are different types and categories of errors affected differently by error treatment?*

A review of error correction studies

As already noted, there is disagreement, even controversy, among L2 writing researchers and teachers about whether teachers should provide any grammar correction at all to student writers and whether such feedback has any short- or long-term effects on student writing. The strongest position against grammar correction was taken by Truscott (1996; 1999), though it was foreshadowed a bit by early process advocates in ESL writing (e.g., Krashen, 1984; Zamel, 1985). Truscott (1996) makes the case against grammar correction, arguing that research findings demonstrate no positive effects for correction in L2 writing, that "practical problems" such as teacher limitations and student inattention render even the hypothetical benefits of grammar correction unlikely, and that, in the end, time spent on correction is actually harmful to student writers because it takes time and energy away from other, more important writing concerns.

In rebuttals to Truscott's argument (especially Ferris, 1999, 2004; see also Ferris, 2002, 2003), I have taken the position that the research base is not nearly as conclusive on the question of error feedback as Truscott claims and that a great deal more research is needed before anyone can claim that error feedback should be universally embraced *or* abolished. Having argued that the ultimate effectiveness of error correction in student writing is at the very least an open question (research question 1), we turn to other issues that have been raised by researchers about error correction in L2 writing classes. For instance, it has been claimed that teachers' error feedback may be incomplete, inconsistent, and inaccurate and that this is a "practical problem" (Truscott, 1996) that predicts that error correction for student writers will be ineffective (Cohen & Cavalcanti, 1990; Cohen & Robbins, 1976; Zamel, 1985). Since teacher variation is often a crucial design issue in classroom research studies, we felt it important to examine critically our instructors' feedback for comprehensiveness and accuracy (research question 2).

A number of researchers have compared different types of error feedback to see if the level of explicitness makes a difference in student adoption of teacher corrections. One important dichotomy is the distinction between *direct* and *indirect* feedback (terms taken from Hendrickson, 1978; see also Bates et al., 1993; Ferris, 1995c, 2002, 2003; Ferris & Hedgcock, 1998, 2004; Lalande, 1982). Although these terms are not always used consistently in the literature, *direct* feedback is defined for the purposes of our discussion as the provision of the correct linguistic form by the teacher to the student. Direct feedback may take various forms, including crossing out an unnecessary word, phrase, or morpheme; inserting a missing word or morpheme; or writing the correct word or form near the erroneous form (e.g., above it or in the margin). *Indirect* feedback occurs when the teacher indicates in some way that an error has been made – by means of an underline, circle, code, or other mark – but does not provide the correct form, leaving the student to solve the problem that has been called to his or her attention. Researchers have suggested that indirect error feedback is generally preferable because it forces students to engage in "guided learning and problem-solving" (Lalande, 1982) and helps them build skills as "independent self-editors" (Bates et al., 1993). However, it has also been suggested that students at lower levels of L2 proficiency may not have sufficient linguistic knowledge to self-correct errors even when they are pointed out (Brown, 1994; Ferris & Hedgcock, 1998, 2004) and that a judicious combination of direct and indirect feedback, varying according to error type, may be most helpful to students (Chaney, 1999; Ferris, 1999; Hendrickson, 1980).

Few studies have directly contrasted the effects of direct and indirect feedback, and their findings have been conflicting. For instance, Lalande (1982) reported that students who received indirect feedback reduced their errors over time, whereas those who received direct feedback did not. In contrast, Robb, Ross, and Shortreed (1986) found that four groups of students, one that received direct feedback and three that received indirect feedback in varying degrees of explicitness, showed no statistically signifcant differences in long-term gains in accuracy, though all four groups improved. Nonetheless, the claim that indirect feedback is more helpful because it engages students in reflective learning processes has intuitive appeal. Further, it is relatively easier and faster for teachers to simply underline or circle errors than to note the correct forms. Thus, the question of what type of error feedback is most beneficial to student writers deserves further scrutiny (research question 3).

An important theoretical issue raised by Truscott (1996) is that different types of linguistic forms (morphological, syntactic, and lexical) represent distinct domains of linguistic knowledge and may well go through diverse sequences or orders of acquisition. Yet, as Truscott notes, teachers often provide feedback on all categories of error in the same way. None of the studies reviewed focused specifically on the responsiveness of specific error types to particular feedback treatments, but in all of the studies in which specific categories of error were targeted for feedback and analysis, it was reported that students showed differing levels of progress depending on error type (Chaney, 1999; Ferris, 1995a; Ferris & Roberts, 2001; Frantzen, 1995; Frantzen & Rissell, 1987; Lalande, 1982; Sheppard, 1992). Because intuition, experience, and previous research all suggest that type of error may be a significant issue in examining error correction, in the present study we examined the relationships among error categories, teacher feedback strategies, and student outcomes in short-term revision and long-term improvement in accuracy (research question 4).

Thus, this study was designed not only to investigate the question raised by Truscott and others – Is error feedback worth doing at all? – but also to examine various specific issues related to how error feedback is provided by teachers and how students utilize it in the short term and benefit from it in the long run.

Study method

The following sections describe the setting, types of data collected, and data analysis methods.

Setting

Data for this study was collected in six sections of an ESL composition class taught at California State University, Sacramento, during the fall 1998 semester. The class (LS 86) was two semesters below the college (freshman) composition level. LS 86 was a three-unit, credit-optional course that met for three classroom hours per week plus one required computer lab hour. During the semester, students completed four three-draft essays on topics based on assigned readings. The task (text-based, persuasive essay writing) was basic to all four assignments, though the topics and readings varied. At the end of the semester, students had to pass an in-class exit essay examination of two hours, which was group-graded according to a standard rubric by LS 86 instructors. If a student failed the exit exam, instructors had the option to submit a portfolio of the student's best work to an appeals board; a passing score on the portfolio appeal allowed the student to pass the course.

For the individual essay assignments during the semester, teacher feedback proceeded along the lines suggested by process approach advocates

Table 5.1. *Error categories and codes used in teacher marking and in analysis*

Error type	Code	Description
Word choice	WC	Excluded spelling errors, pronouns, informal and unidiomatic usage
Verb tense	VT	
Verb form	VF	
Word form	WF	Excluded verb form errors
Articles	Art	
Singular-plural	S/P	Referred to noun ending errors
Pronouns	PR	
Run-on	RO	Included comma splices
Fragment	FR	
Punctuation	PU	Comma splices, and fragments; excluded run-ons
Spelling	SP	
Sentence structure	SS	Included missing and unnecessary words and phrases and word order problems. Excluded run-ons, comma splices, and fragments
Informal	INF	Referred to register choices considered inappropriate for academic writing
Idiom	ID	Referred to errors in use of idiomatic expressions
Subject-verb agreement	SV	Did not include other singular-plural or verb form errors
Miscellaneous	N/A (category used for analysis only)	Errors that could not be otherwise classified

(e.g., Krashen, 1984; Zamel, 1985). After students submitted their initial drafts (draft A), teachers gave them written feedback dealing with their ideas and organization.[2] After students had revised and resubmitted their drafts (draft B), teachers gave them detailed feedback about their language errors (grammar, word choice, punctuation, spelling), with additional content feedback as deemed necessary by the instructor. The three instructors in our study agreed to provide error feedback in a consistent way by using a chart of 15 error categories, each designated by a code (Table 5.1). These categories were selected by the professor who supervised the course, in consultation with experienced LS 86 instructors, as representative of typical errors made by students in this specific context. The instructors were to mark errors in all 15 categories by attaching the appropriate error code. Students then completed final revisions and editing in the computer lab sessions and submitted a third and final draft (draft C) for grading on the 6-point LS 86 scale.

Subjects

The participants in this study were 92 ESL students and three teachers (two LS 86 sections per instructor). Most students were undergraduates; nearly half were first-semester freshmen. Eighty percent were immigrant students (long-term U.S. residents), while the other 20 percent were international (visa) students. Seventy-two percent of the students were from various Asian backgrounds (43% Southeast Asian). The subjects were split almost evenly between males and females. The three instructors were experienced ESL teachers with MAs, certificates in TESOL, or both; all three had taught the course previously.

Data collected

In collecting data, we took a longitudinal and triangulated approach. We gathered data throughout the semester, and our sources included student texts, background information about the students and the course, interviews, and survey data. Specifically, we obtained the following types of information:

- Student background questionnaires for all subjects. These questionnaires are used in all LS 86 classes and include items about students' first language, time in the U.S., English language education, and literacy levels in the L1 and L2.
- 146 student essay projects: All three drafts of the first and fourth out-of-class essay assignments for the semester, with the teacher corrections on the second (B) drafts. The total was 146 student essay projects. (We were not able to obtain complete sets of both essays for all 92 subjects.)
- Tapes, notes, and transcriptions of interviews with 25 student subjects and with all three teachers.
- Anonymous student surveys completed near the end of the semester by 65 of the subjects.[3]
- The LS 86 master syllabus and essay assignment sheets for essays 1 and 4.

Table 5.2. *Teacher marking categories*

Label	Description
Indirect, correct	Teacher made indirect, correct marking using codes included in log.
Indirect, incorrect	Teacher made indirect, incorrect marking using codes included in log.
Direct, correct	Teacher made direct correction of error.
Direct, incorrect	Teacher made direct marking but the change was incorrect.
Indirect, correct, not coded	Teacher correctly noted location of error by underlining or circling, but did not indicate type of error.
Indirect, incorrect, not coded	Teacher incorrectly underlined or circled location of "error."
Indirect, correct, non-log marking	Teacher correctly marked error but used a code not included in log.
Indirect, incorrect, non-log marking	Teacher incorrectly marked an error using a code not included in log.
Unnecessary; no grammar error but teacher indicated error	Teacher indicated a change should be made, although student had not made a grammatical error; may be feedback regarding style.

Data analysis

The data analysis stage was complicated by the fact that the three instructors did not adhere consistently to the error-marking scheme on which we had agreed. We had expected that they would do comprehensive correction of all errors, using indirect marking (underlining errors but not providing the target forms) and the standard codes shown in Table 5.1. However, during preliminary analysis of the feedback on the B drafts, it was immediately apparent that they had deviated from this plan in a variety of ways. Thus, we added "teacher marking strategy" as a variable for analysis and developed an original coding scheme for this purpose. Following the "constant comparative method" of analysis (Ferris, 1997; Glaser & Strauss, 1967; Lockhart & Ng, 1995), categories were developed and refined through several initial passes through a subset of the data sample. The final scheme is described in Table 5.2, and it includes categories such as direct versus indirect corrections, correct versus incorrect feedback, "unnecessary" markings, markings that had no codes attached, and markings with codes not included in the standard 15 categories.

After coding the teacher marks found on the essay draft Bs (5,707 marks in all), we turned to analysis of the students' revised draft Cs.

Table 5.3. *Student revision analysis categories*

Label	Description
Error corrected	Error corrected per teacher's marking.
Incorrect change	Change was made but incorrect.
No change	No response to the correction was apparent.
Deleted text	Student deleted marked text rather than attempting correction.
Substitution, correct	Student invented a correction that was not suggested by teacher's marking.
Substitution, incorrect	Student incorrectly made a change that was not suggested by teacher's marking.
Teacher-induced error	Incomplete or misleading teacher marking caused student error.
Averted erroneous teacher marking	Student corrected error despite incomplete or erroneous teacher marking.

Again, we developed an original analysis scheme based on what we found in the data sample. The scheme is shown in Table 5.3. It shows whether the student attempted to make the correction, whether the correction was successful or unsuccessful, whether the writer made a substitution or deleted the problematic portion of the text, and whether the student made or avoided a "teacher-induced error" (an error caused by an erroneous, misleading, or unclear teacher mark).

Each teacher mark that addressed a student's language errors was classified according to one of the 16 types shown in Table 5.1 (the 15 categories used by the teachers, plus a miscellaneous category used only in the analysis stage). If the teacher mark utilized one of the 15 error codes, we counted it as an instance of that category of error. If the teacher mark had no code attached (e.g., an underlining) or was marked with a code, word, or phrase not on our list of categories, we assigned the mark to one of the 16 error categories ourselves. In addition to determining the error type related to each teacher mark, we coded each mark according to the teacher marking categories scheme shown in Table 5.2. Once we had analyzed the teacher marks on the draft Bs for both error type and marking strategies, we examined the students' draft Cs and traced the effect of each teacher mark on the students' revisions, using the analytic scheme shown in Table 5.3.

For all three stages of coding reflected in Tables 5.1 through 5.3, four researchers spent substantial time validating and refining the analysis categories against a subset of the data. Then three of the researchers worked together intensively over a period of several months to code the remaining papers. All coding decisions were made by the three researchers together during a series of analysis sessions. Any questions or disagreements were brought to the lead researcher (the author) for resolution. Since the analysis was done collaboratively and not independently, no inter-rater reliabilities were calculated (i.e., agreement was ultimately 100 percent for all marked errors and revisions). The findings for each of the three analyses, stated as frequencies and percentages, are provided in the appendix.

Once the coding for the three analysis schemes was completed, a variety of descriptive and analytical statistical procedures were conducted. These included cross-tabulations undertaken to examine relationships and variation among teacher marking strategies and student revision actions, among error types and teacher marks, and among error types and student revision behaviors.

To assess the effects of error feedback over time (from the beginning to the end of the semester), two researchers also independently analyzed unmarked copies of 55 pairs of student essays (draft Bs of essays 1 and 4), marking all errors found in the five largest categories (verbs, noun endings, articles, word choice, and sentence structure) identified in the analysis of the entire sample (see the appendix). To assure inter-rater reliability, the two researchers independently marked a subset (20 of the 110 papers), achieving agreement on error totals for each category of about 95 percent. They then divided the rest of the papers and analyzed them separately. The resulting error counts were normalized to a standard of 750 words, using the procedure outlined in Biber, Conrad, and Reppen (1998).[4] The normalized counts for essays 1 and 4 were then compared by means of paired sample T-tests to assess student progress in accuracy from the first to the last essay assignment.

Study results and discussion

To structure the presentation of our findings, we return to the research questions outlined in the introduction to this paper. Each of the following sections is organized around one of the questions.

Research question 1: Improvement in accuracy

Does error feedback from instructors help L2 writers to improve their accuracy in the short run (from one draft of a paper to the next) and in the long run (from the beginning to the end of a writing course)?

The analysis of student revision behaviors between drafts B and C showed that in a substantial majority of cases (about 80%), the student writers were able to successfully edit errors marked by teachers. Students made no change in response to teacher markings in 9.3 percent of the

Table 5.4. *Summary of students' short-term revision behaviors*

"Error corrected" includes totals for the original categories "error corrected," "deleted problem," and "substitution correct." "Incorrect change" includes the original categories "incorrect change," "substitution incorrect," and "teacher-induced error." The totals and percentages for all original categories are shown in the appendix.

Revision outcome	Frequency and percentage
Error corrected	4,590 (80.4%)
Incorrect change	562 (9.9%)
No change	531 (9.3%)
Other	24 (0.4%)
Total	5,707 (100%)

cases and incorrect changes in slightly under 10 percent of the cases. The results are shown in Table 5.4.

This finding – that students in this study were able to make effective revisions in response to teachers' error markings – stands in contrast to Truscott's observation that "students may well fail to understand" teachers' grammar feedback. However, Truscott also goes on to point out that "A learner who understands a comment – well enough even to rewrite the composition correctly – may not grasp the general principle involved and therefore may repeat the error later in other contexts" (1996, pp. 350–351). In other words, demonstrating that a student can utilize teacher feedback to make a successful edit from one draft to the next of a particular paper is not equivalent to showing that the linguistic construct addressed has been successfully acquired by the learner. Thus, we turn to the longitudinal analysis of student improvement in accuracy. The results of this analysis are shown in Table 5.5.

The comparison of 55 pairs of student papers (essay 1 and essay 4) showed that students made statistically significant reductions in their total number of errors in five major categories (see also Table 5.2) over the semester. The reduction in verb errors was highly significant, and the reduction in lexical errors approached significance at the $p < .05$ confidence level, but results for the rest of the categories were not significant, and the scores for "articles" and "sentence structure" were slightly worse at the end of the semester. We will return to the issue of how different error categories respond to treatment in discussion of research question 4. At this point, however, we simply note that the students made significant progress in accuracy over the semester.

It is important to observe that the standard deviation for the "change score" (essay 1 normalized totals minus essay 4 normalized totals) was

Table 5.5. *Longitudinal comparisons: Essay 1 versus essay 4 (N=55)*

Category	Mean/std Dev	T	df	Significance
Total errors				
Essay 1	52.93 / 22.70	2.68	54	.01
Essay 4	46.25 / 17.03			
Verb errors				
Essay 1	12.93 / 8.95	3.69	54	.001
Essay 4	9.46 / 5.27			
Noun errors				
Essay 1	6.20 / 4.85	1.49	54	.14 (n.s.)
Essay 4	5.16 / 4.46			
Article errors				
Essay 1	5.82 / 5.46	−.75	54	.45 (n.s.)
Essay 4	6.29 / 5.13			
Lexical errors				
Essay 1	13.58 / 7.72	1.88	54	.07 (n.s.)
Essay 4	11.78 / 8.14			
Sentence errors				
Essay 1	13.34 / 8.14	−.04	54	.97 (n.s.)
Essay 4	13.39 / 8.00			

extremely large (over 18, which is three times larger than the mean score!), demonstrating that there was tremendous individual variation in the amount of progress among the 55 students examined in this phase of the study. This finding illustrates a comment made by Ferris and Hedgcock that "there is tremendous variability in students' ability to benefit from grammar instruction and feedback" (1998, p. 201). Individual variation in students' ability to utilize and process teacher feedback successfully (in the short or long term) has been a largely unexplored question in error correction research. The results shown here suggest that this may be an important area for future inquiry (see also Ferris, 1995c).

Research question 2: Adequacy of feedback

Do teachers give their students accurate and complete feedback on their errors?

Truscott (1996) contends that there are "serious problems regarding the quality of teachers' written responses to L2 compositions" and that research has also shown "many cases in which teachers failed to notice errors" (p. 350). In this study, we assessed the quality of the teacher feedback in two different ways. First, as already discussed, one of the parameters in the "teacher marking" coding scheme (see Table 5.2) was whether the individual mark was, in the estimation of the researchers,

Table 5.6. *Accuracy of teacher error correction*

Teacher marking category	Frequency and percentage
Correct marking	5,101 (89.4%)
Incorrect marking	206 (3.6%)
Unnecessary marking	400 (7%)
Totals	5,707 (100%)

correct, incorrect, or unnecessary (because no error had occurred). Table 5.6 shows the results of that analysis.

As shown in Table 5.6, the four researchers judged the teacher marks to be correct in 89.4 percent of the cases, incorrect in 3.6 percent of the instances, and unnecessary in the remaining 7 percent of the sample. We also compared the percentage of the errors marked by the three teachers with the comprehensive error marking done by two independent researchers in the longitudinal analysis described in Table 5.5, finding that the teachers had marked about 83 percent of the errors later identified separately by the two researchers.[5] Thus, we found that the three instructors in the study marked the overwhelming majority of the 5,707 errors accurately and that they left errors unmarked relatively rarely. Although a sample of corrections provided by only three teachers certainly cannot by itself refute the charge made by previous researchers that L2 writing teachers mark errors erratically and erroneously, we found in this study that the instructors' error feedback was by and large both comprehensive and accurate.

Research question 3: Strategies and their effects

What strategies do teachers use to give error feedback, and what is the effect of differing strategies on student writing?

As previously noted, the three instructors had originally agreed to give their students consistent and comprehensive feedback using a system of indirect marking and the 15 error codes shown in Table 5.1. However, as data collection and analysis proceeded, it became apparent that the teachers had not, in fact, adhered to the standard correction system we had discussed. Thus, we developed an analysis scheme (Table 5.2) that attempted to capture the range of marking options from which the teachers selected in practice. In our statistical analyses, we examined the relationship between the teachers' marking strategies and the students' actions in revision. Table 5.7 summarizes the major marking patterns used by the teachers and their relative frequency of occurrence (see the appendix also).

Table 5.7. *Summary of teacher marking patterns*

Teacher strategy	Frequency and percentage
Direct	2,586 (45.3%)
Indirect with standard code	2,346 (41.1%)
Indirect with no code	319 (5.6%)
Indirect with nonstandard code	250 (4.4%)
Unnecessary, no grammar error	206 (3.6%)
Totals	5,707 (100%)

The analysis of the teachers' marking patterns demonstrated that they used the 15 standard codes agreed on at the beginning of the study only 41.1 percent of the time in marking student errors. The teachers made direct corrections in which they provided the correct form to the student in more than 45 percent of the cases. In about 10 percent of the instances, the teachers either marked (underlined, circled, and so on) an error without attaching an error code or used a code, word, or phrase that was not one of the original 15 codes. This analysis illustrated for us not only the range of possible marking strategies but also the importance for researchers of double-checking what instructors actually do when providing feedback. Just as the analysis highlights the need to consider individual student variables in error correction studies, this finding suggests that it is critically important to include a "teacher" variable in the analysis.[6] For experimental research designs, there is also an argument to be made for having one teacher or researcher provide error feedback for all student subjects to ensure greater consistency in treatment and thus enable assessment of the effects of feedback without this potentially confounding variable.

Although it is interesting to observe the range of feedback types provided by teachers, it is even more valuable to relate the effects of the different marking strategies on the revisions made by students. The results of this analysis are shown in Table 5.8. It seems safe to assume that students would be most successful in incorporating direct feedback into their revisions, since it involves mere transcribing or copying of the teacher's suggestion into the next draft of their papers. In fact, students did utilize direct feedback more consistently and effectively than any other type.

The students were able to make correct changes in response to direct feedback in the vast majority (88%) of the cases. Surprisingly, the other, less explicit forms of feedback also led to accurate revisions most of the time. Indirect feedback, in which errors were underlined and marked with one of the 15 error codes, led to correct edits in 77 percent of the instances. More startling was the finding that indirect feedback, with either codes not on the standard list or no codes at all, could be traced to nearly as high

Table 5.8. *Teacher feedback and student revision*

Feedback type	Correct revision	Incorrect revision	No change
Direct	2,238 (88%)	107 (4%)	214 (8%)
Indirect	1,759 (77%)	305 (13%)	231 (10%)
Non-log	409 (75%)	86 (16%)	52 (9%)
Incorrect	38 (62%)	14 (23%)	9 (15%)
Unnecessary	164 (80%)	17 (8%)	25 (12%)

Note: Percentages reflect frequencies of each revision outcome within the feedback categories. For instance, for 88 percent of the errors marked directly, the revisions made were correct.

a percentage of accurate changes (75%) as the error markings with the codes. Even inaccurate error codes seemed to help students: They made correct edits in 62 percent of those instances as well! These observations are similar to the findings of Robb et al. (1986), who reported that subject groups who received less explicit error feedback progressed in accuracy at about the same rate as those who received very detailed feedback. Our findings also suggest that, at least for this (largely immigrant) ESL student population, indication and location of error, regardless of whether a code was attached or even accurate, provided adequate information for them to revise. This result ran directly counter to the intuitions of both instructors and students in this study, who strongly indicated in interviews that coded feedback was necessary for student writers at this level of L2 proficiency and that error location alone (e.g., underlining) would not provide enough information to them. However, the number of errors in this sample that were marked with nonstandard codes, no codes, or erroneous codes was relatively small (comprising about 10 percent of the total teacher marks; see the appendix), so this finding should be interpreted cautiously.[7]

Research question 4: Variations among error types

Are different types and categories of errors affected differently by error treatment?

The appendix shows the relative frequency with which the 15 categories identified at the beginning of this study were marked by the teachers. Table 5.9 shows how well students fared in revising the various error types after receiving feedback.

Since the overall number of successful student revisions was quite high (over 80%; see Table 5.4), it was not surprising to note that the percentage of successful revisions in most of the individual error categories was also fairly high, generally in the 70–85 percent range. Notable exceptions were the "idiom" and "subject-verb agreement" categories, which both

Table 5.9. *Student revision outcomes by error type*

Error type	Correct change	Incorrect change	No change	Total
Word choice	513 (78.8%)	75 (11.5%)	63 (9.7%)	651
Verb tense	492 (78.9%)	65 (10.4%)	67 (10.7%)	624
Verb form	319 (72.5%)	79 (18.0%)	42 (9.5%)	440
Word form	285 (77.0%)	52 (14.1%)	33 (8.9%)	370
Articles	314 (84.2%)	24 (6.4%)	35 (9.4%)	373
Singular-plural	428 (84.9%)	21 (4.2%)	55 (10.9%)	504
Pronouns	137 (82.5%)	17 (10.3%)	12 (7.2%)	166
Run-ons	144 (87.3%)	10 (6.0%)	11 (6.7%)	165
Fragments	81 (80.2%)	16 (15.8%)	4 (4.0%)	101
Punctuation	314 (80.9%)	16 (4.1%)	58 (15.0%)	388
Spelling	286 (85.4%)	13 (3.9%)	36 (10.7%)	335
Sentence structure	1,072 (84.4%)	111 (8.7%)	88 (6.9%)	1,271
Informal	16 (84.2%)	2 (10.5%)	1 (5.3%)	19
Idiom	27 (56.2%)	19 (39.6%)	2 (4.2%)	48
Subject-verb agreement	112 (68.3%)	33 (20.1%)	19 (11.6%)	164
Miscellaneous	42 (82.3%)	6 (11.8%)	3 (5.9%)	51
Total	4,584 (80.8%)	559 (9.9%)	530 (9.3%)	5,673

Percentages represent frequencies of revision categories within each error type. For instance, 78.8 percent of the "word choice" errors had a revision rating of "correct change."

had lower percentages of successful revisions than the other categories. However, those two error types combined accounted for less than 5 percent of the total sample of errors marked (see the appendix), so it is difficult to speculate on the causes of those differences.

Two further points can be made about the effects of error treatment on particular categories of error. First, students' short-term ability to edit certain types of errors did not always translate to long-term improvement. As shown in Table 5.5 above, over the course of the semester, the students made by far the most progress in the "verb" category (including errors in both tense and form), even though Table 5.9 shows that they were less successful in editing these error types (verb tense, verb form, and subject-verb agreement) from one draft to the next than they were with many other error types. In contrast, they were quite successful at revising sentence structure errors (84.3% in Table 5.9) in the short term but showed no progress at all (in fact, a slight regression) in avoiding those types of errors over time (Table 5.5). One possible explanation lies in an examination of how the instructors responded to the different types of errors; indeed, it was discovered that the teachers marked 75 percent of errors in verb tense and form indirectly but only 15 percent

Table 5.10. *"Treatable" and "untreatable" error types*

	Teacher feedback type*		
Error type	Direct	Indirect	Unnecessary
Treatable	36.7%	58.7%	4.6%
Untreatable	65.3%	33.6%	1.1%

Differences in teacher feedback type between treatable and untreatable error categories were significant at *p=.000.

of the sentence structure errors indirectly. In other words, the students' relative short-term success in correcting sentence structure errors may be attributed to the fact that the teachers provided them with the correct form in about 85 percent of the cases, but this direct intervention did not appear to have any lasting effect over time. In contrast, the indirect feedback that students received on verb errors may have helped them more over time because it consistently called this error to their attention, triggering the "guided learning and problem-solving" processes recommended by Lalande (1982, p. 140).

A second observation about the different categories of error is drawn from the anecdotal observations of Ferris (1999) in her response to Truscott (1996). Ferris suggested that, for pedagogical purposes, some errors could be considered "treatable," because they "occur in a patterned, rule-governed way," whereas other errors are "untreatable," meaning that "There is no handbook or set of rules students can consult to avoid or fix those types of errors" (1999, p. 6). In this study, the errors that could be argued to be "treatable" include problems with verb tense or form, subject-verb agreement, run-ons, fragments, noun endings, articles, pronouns, and possibly spelling (because a dictionary or computer spell-check could be consulted), whereas the others (the lexical error categories, such as word choice and idioms, and the sentence structure category) could be considered "untreatable." A statistical reanalysis of our data with attention to this dichotomy demonstrated that there were indeed substantial, statistically significant differences in how the teachers responded to these errors (Table 5.10).

Specifically, the error types in the "treatable" category received indirect correction nearly 59 percent of the time, whereas the "untreatable" errors received direct feedback in more than 65 percent of the cases. These findings were somewhat startling, given that we had expected *all* error types to receive the same type of feedback (indirect coded marks). As noted by Chaney (1999), the teachers may have intuitively given different types of feedback to treatable and untreatable errors because they believed that their students would not be able to self-correct untreatable errors marked indirectly. Teacher interviews completed after the semester confirmed this impression. However, teachers also indicated that their awareness of the students' relative ability levels also may have, at least unconsciously, affected the amounts and types of feedback they provided on different student papers. Further, one of the three teachers was heavily biased in favor of direct correction in almost all circumstances, following his instincts that students in this class would be unable to self-edit if the correct forms were not provided. Although he tried (at least initially) to adhere to the marking system agreed on for this study, he frequently reverted to his customary comprehensive direct correction methods.

Conclusion

The following sections summarize the study findings and suggest implications for further research and teaching.

Summary of findings

We found a strong relationship between teachers' error markings and successful student revisions on the subsequent drafts of their essays (Table 5.1). Students appeared to address the vast majority of their teachers' error markings. Only 9.3 percent of the corrections on students' draft Bs received "no change" ratings on draft C, and in over 80 percent of the cases, the revisions made in response to feedback were correct. We also found that students made statistically significant progress in reducing their numbers of errors in five major categories between the first and last essay assignments of the semester (Table 5.5). In addition, our data add to the substantial evidence from previous studies that students who receive error feedback show progress in written accuracy over time. We also found that the feedback given by the three instructors, as assessed by independent researchers, was overwhelmingly accurate (89.4%; see Table 5.6) and fairly comprehensive, covering 83 percent of the errors identified independently by the researchers. These findings, taken together, do not support the claims of previous researchers that teachers give incomplete and inaccurate error feedback and that students ignore teacher feedback or cannot utilize it effectively in revision (Cohen & Robbins, 1976; Truscott, 1996; Zamel, 1985).

We also examined the various marking strategies utilized by teachers, finding that the error corrections ranged from direct feedback (correct forms provided for the students), indirect feedback using 15 standard error codes, indirect feedback with nonstandard codes, indirect feedback with no codes, and corrections judged "unnecessary" (Table 5.7). The various correction patterns were compared with students' revision actions and the different error categories. It was found that students were able to utilize both direct and indirect feedback successfully in their revisions, even when the corrections had no code or an inaccurate code attached (Table 5.8). Also, the student writers were able to correct errors representing a wide range of linguistic categories (Table 5.9). However, there was a longitudinal difference in student achievement, based on whether errors were "treatable" or "untreatable" (Table 5.5; Table 5.10), and this distinction may possibly be attributed to widely disparate teacher feedback strategies (Table 5.10); "treatable" errors were most often marked indirectly, but "untreatable" errors were overwhelmingly marked directly. The findings shown in Tables 5.5, 5.8, and 5.10, therefore, make a strong case for the superiority of indirect feedback over direct feedback for facilitating student writing improvement over time, at least with this particular population of students. They appear to contradict the findings and recommendations of Robb et al. (1986), who found in their study that there was little difference in long-term achievement in accuracy related to the level of explicitness of error feedback.

Implications for further research

The discussion in the introduction to this paper should make it clear that there are many unexplored areas of error correction research. From the specific findings of this study, three research issues appear particularly salient: (1) the importance of individual student variability in responsiveness to error correction; (2) the significance of examining what teachers actually do when giving error feedback; and (3) the impact of different error types on student progress in accuracy.

Implications for teaching

For instructors who want to help students improve linguistic control in their writing and who spend quantities of time and energy providing error feedback on their students' papers, the findings of this study should be taken as encouraging. Our student subjects attended to teacher corrections on intermediate drafts of their essays and in most cases utilized them to make accurate changes in their texts. It is important to remember that these were highly motivated students in an academic context at relatively high levels of L2 proficiency and that they were operating in a multiple-draft, process-oriented context. It has been previously suggested that students attend to and process teacher feedback better when it occurs at intermediate, rather than final, stages of the drafting and revision process (Ferris, 1995b; Krashen, 1984; Zamel, 1985). Although final-draft feedback was not examined in this study, it seems safe to assume that in-process feedback had such a strong impact on students in part because they had the opportunity to revise their papers and immediately implement the corrections they had received, rather than just applying them to future writing assignments. Thus, under these specific conditions, it appears that error feedback helped students to edit their papers successfully and to make progress in overall accuracy over time. The implication is that error correction can help at least some student writers under certain circumstances and that teachers should consider provision of error feedback as a potentially valuable tool.

With the caveat that this study considered a specific population of L2 writers (mostly immigrant learners at intermediate to advanced levels of English L2 proficiency), the evidence suggests several possible feedback approaches for teachers:

• Provide primarily indirect feedback;
• Locate errors rather than labeling or coding them;
• Vary feedback approaches for treatable and untreatable error types;
• Use a relatively small number of error categories when providing feedback.

Final reflections

Error correction continues to be a source of great concern for L2 writing instructors and their students. Students know that the accuracy of their writing may affect how it is received and how their abilities are judged by academic and professional audiences. Teachers know that their students expect feedback on the linguistic form of their writing and believe that it is part of their role as language and writing experts to provide it for them. The findings of this study highlight pedagogical and research issues related to error correction in student writing, including the importance of the "teacher variable," the variation in individual student achievement, the effects of various teacher marking strategies, and the amenability of different types of linguistic structures to feedback treatments. Perhaps most important, our findings raise a number of issues and questions that can help teachers to reflect on and even reassess their error feedback practices. It is hoped that this study and others like it will help to shed light on an important instructional issue for L2 writing teachers and their students.

Notes

1. This paper is adapted from a presentation at the 2000 TESOL Convention in Vancouver, B.C. The author would like to acknowledge the substantial contributions in data collection and analysis for this project made by Sarah Chaney, Keiko Komura, Barrie Roberts, and Sue McKee.

2. It is program policy, explicitly stated by supervisors, that instructors give content-only feedback on initial student drafts and save grammar and editing feedback until the penultimate draft. However, in a previous study conducted at this institution, it was reported that not all instructors were adhering to the strict separation of content- and form-based feedback (Ferris, 1995b). It is possible that students received some language-specific feedback on draft As in this study as well.
3. In-depth analyses of the qualitative data are included in a separate paper (Komura, 1999). They are referred to in passing in this paper when they shed light on quantitative findings.
4. This procedure consists of dividing the error counts by the number of words in the text and then multiplying that result by a standard number that represents the average-length text in the sample. In this case, the standard number was set at 750 words after a mean was calculated on the word counts for all individual texts.
5. In the teacher interviews, one of the three instructors commented that she had not actually attempted comprehensive correction of all student errors but had instead marked selectively based on her assessment of the student/paper's most serious language problems. Thus, in at least some of the cases in which errors identified by the researchers were not marked by an instructor, the omission was the result of a pedagogical decision as opposed to an oversight.
6. There was indeed considerable variation among the three teachers in their proportions of direct and indirect feedback. In particular, one of the teachers gave almost entirely direct feedback (92%), whereas the other two instructors gave about two-thirds indirect coded feedback.
7. A follow-up experimental study in the same context directly examined the effects of coded versus uncoded feedback on student revision, finding no significant differences between treatment groups (Ferris & Roberts, 1991).

References

Bates, L., Lane, J., & Lange, E. (1993). *Writing clearly: Responding to ESL compositions*. Boston: Heinle & Heinle.

Biber, D., Conrad, S., & Reppen, R. (1998). *Corpus linguistics: Investigating language structure and use*. Cambridge, UK: Cambridge University Press.

Brown, J. D. (1988). *Understanding research in second language learning: A teacher's guide to statistics and research design*. Cambridge, UK: Cambridge University Press.

Brown, J. D. (1991). Statistics as a foreign language – Part 1: What to look for in reading statistical language studies. *TESOL Quarterly, 25*, 569–586.

Chandler, J. (2003). The efficacy of various kinds of error feedback for improvement in the accuracy and fluency of L2 student writing. *Journal of Second Language Writing, 12(3)*, 267–296.

Chaney, S. J. (1999). *The effect of error types on error correction and revision*. Sacramento, CA: California State University, Department of English, M.A. thesis.

Cohen, A. D., & Cavalcanti, M. C. (1990). Feedback on compositions: Teacher and student verbal reports. In B. Kroll (Ed.), *Second language writing: Research insights for the classroom* (pp. 155–177). Cambridge, UK: Cambridge University Press.

Cohen, A. D., & Robbins, M. (1976). Toward assessing interlanguage performance: The relationship between selected errors, learners' characteristics, and learners' expectations. *Language Learning, 26,* 45–66.

Cook, V. J. (1991). *Second language learning and language teaching.* London: Edward Arnold.

Corder, S. P. (1981). *Error analysis and interlanguage.* Oxford: Oxford University Press.

Fathman, A. & Whalley, E. (1990). Teacher response to student writing: Focus on form versus content. In B. Kroll (Ed.), *Second language writing: Research insights for the classroom* (pp. 178–190). Cambridge, UK: Cambridge University Press.

Ferris, D. R. (1995a). Can advanced ESL students be taught to correct their most serious and frequent errors? *CATESOL Journal, 8(1),* 41–62.

Ferris, D. R. (1995b). Student reactions to teacher response in multiple-draft composition classrooms, *TESOL Quarterly, 29,* 33–53.

Ferris, D. R. (1995c). Teaching ESL composition students to become independent self-editors. *TESOL Journal, 4(4),* 18–22.

Ferris, D. R. (1997). The influence of teacher commentary on student revision. *TESOL Quarterly, 31,* 315–339.

Ferris, D. R. (1999). The case for grammar correction in L2 writing classes: A response to Truscott (1996). *Journal of Second Language Writing, 8,* 1–10.

Ferris, D. R. (2002). *Treatment of error in second language writing classes.* Ann Arbor, MI: University of Michigan Press.

Ferris, D. R. (2003). *Response to student writing: Implications for second language students.* Mahwah, NJ: Lawrence Erlbaum.

Ferris, D. R. (2004). The "grammar correction" debate in L2 writing: Where are we, and where do we go from here? (and what do we do in the meantime . . . ?) *Journal of Second Language Writing, 13,* 49–62.

Ferris, D., & Hedgcock, J. S. (1998/2004). *Teaching ESL composition: Purpose, process, and practice.* Mahwah, NJ: Lawrence Erlbaum.

Ferris, D., & Roberts, B. (2001). Error feedback in L2 writing classes: How explicit does it need to be? *Journal of Second Language Writing, 10,* 161–184.

Frantzen, D. (1995). The effects of grammar supplementation on written accuracy in an intermediate Spanish content course. *Modern Language Journal, 79,* 329–344.

Frantzen, D., & Rissel, D. (1987). Learner self-correction of written compositions: What does it show us? In B. VanPatten, T. R. Dvorak, & J. F. Lee (Eds.), *Foreign language learning: A research perspective* (pp. 92–107). Cambridge: Newbury House.

Glaser, B. G., & Strauss, A. L. (1967). *The discovery of grounded theory: Strategies for quantitative research.* Chicago: Aldine.

Hedgcock, J., & Lefkowitz, N. (1994). Feedback on feedback: Assessing learner receptivity in second language writing. *Journal of Second Language Writing, 3,* 141–163.

Hendrickson, J. M. (1978). Error correction in foreign language teaching: Recent theory, research, and practice. *Modern Language Journal, 62,* 387–398.

Hendrickson, J. M. (1980). The treatment of error in written work. *The Modern Language Journal, 64*, 216–221.

Higgs, T., & Clifford, R. (1982). The push toward communication. In T. Higgs (Ed.), *Curriculum, competence, and the foreign language teacher* (pp. 57–79). Skokie, IL: National Textbook Company.

Horowitz, D. (1986). Process, not product: Less than meets the eye. *TESOL Quarterly, 20*, 141–144.

James, C. (1998). *Errors in language learning and use: Exploring error analysis.* London: Longman.

Johns, A. M. (1995). Genre and pedagogical purposes. *Journal of Second Language Writing, 4*, 181–190.

Kepner, C. G. (1991). An experiment in the relationship of types of written feedback to the development of second-language writing skills. *The Modern Language Journal, 75*, 305–313.

Krashen, S. D. (1984). *Writing: Research, theory, and application.* Oxford: Pergamon Press.

Lalande, J. F. II (1982). Reducing composition errors: An experiment. *The Modern Language Journal, 66*, 140–149.

Leki, I. (1991). The preferences of ESL students for error correction in college-level writing classes. *Foreign Language Annals, 24*, 203–218.

Lockhart, C., & Ng, P. (1995). Analyzing talk in ESL peer response groups: Stances, functions, and content. *Language Learning, 45*, 605–655.

Polio, C. (1997). Measures of linguistic accuracy in second language writing research. *Language Learning, 47*, 101–143.

Polio, C., Fleck, C., & Leder, N. (1998). "If only I had more time": ESL learners' changes in linguistic accuracy on essay revisions. *Journal of Second Language Writing, 7*, 43–68.

Robb, T., Ross, S., & Shortreed, I. (1986). Salience of feedback on error and its effect on EFL writing quality. *TESOL Quarterly, 20*, 83–93.

Selinker, L. (1992). *Rediscovering interlanguage.* London: Longman.

Semke, H. (1984). The effects of the red pen. *Foreign Language Annals, 17*, 195–202.

Silva, T., Brice, C., & Reichelt, M. (1999). *Annotated bibliography of scholarship in second language writing, 1993–1997.* Stamford, CT: Ablex.

Sheppard, K. (1992). Two feedback types: Do they make a difference? *RELC Journal, 23*, 103–110.

Truscott, J. (1996). The case against grammar correction in L2 writing classes. *Language Learning, 46*, 327–369.

Truscott, J. (1999). The case for "the case for grammar correction in L2 writing classes": A response to Ferris. *Journal of Second Language Writing, 8*, 111–122.

Zamel, V. (1985). Responding to student writing. *TESOL Quarterly, 19*, 79–102.

Appendix: Results for error and revision analyses

Table A.1. *Frequency of error types marked*

Error type	Frequency	Percent of total
Sentence structure	1,287	22.6
Word choice	654	11.5
Verb tense	624	10.9
Noun endings (singular/plural)	506	8.9
Verb form	443	7.8
Punctuation	391	6.8
Articles/determiners	376	6.6
Word form	371	6.5
Spelling	335	5.9
Run-ons	168	2.9
Pronouns	167	2.9
Subject-verb agreement	165	2.9
Fragments	102	1.8
Miscellaneous	51	.9
Idiom	48	.8
Informal	19	.3
Total	5,707	100

(Chaney, 1999, p. 20)

Table A.2. *Distribution of teacher feedback types*

Type of feedback	No.	Percent	Ranking
Direct, correct	2,559	45	1
Indirect, correct	2,295	40	2
Indirect, correct, not coded	318	6	3
Indirect, correct, non-log marking	229	4	4
Unnecessary; no grammar error	206	4	5
Indirect, incorrect	51	1	6
Direct, incorrect	47	1	7
Indirect, incorrect, non-log marking	21	0	8
Indirect, incorrect, not coded	1	0	9
Total	5,707		

(Chaney, 1999, p. 19)

Table A.3. *Types of student revision*

Type of student response	Number	Percent	Ranking
Error corrected	4,130	72	1
No change	531	9	2
Incorrect change	377	7	3
Deleted problem	313	6	4
Substitution, correct	147	3	5
Teacher-induced error	99	2	6
Substitution, incorrect	86	2	7
Averted teacher-induced error	24	0	8
Total	5,707		

(Chaney, 1999, p. 23)

6 Electronic feedback and second language writing

Paige D. Ware
Mark Warschauer

The rapid growth of educational technologies creates a broad spectrum of ways in which technology can be integrated into classroom instruction. These multiplying points of contact between technology and second language writing converge in the concept of electronic feedback. Writers who are linked to the screen are connected as well to the certainty of receiving some form of reply, whether that feedback comes as an e-mail note about favorite movies from a distant key pal, as an evaluation generated by an automated essay processing algorithm that performs high-stakes writing assessments, or as a compendium of comments from a class peer helping to make final revisions on an academic essay. Instructors can find it difficult, however, to choose from the variety of different pedagogical approaches and recommendations made by researchers. This chapter, by examining the latest developments in electronic feedback and the associated research, aims to help practitioners understand the issues and make a more focused and informed choice.

As we demonstrate, *electronic feedback* is a slippery term that covers a range of often dissimilar approaches to the teaching of writing. Just as the purposes of literacy take on different meanings and uses in a range of contexts, so do the uses of technology come to bear in a variety of ways depending on the research lens and pedagogical frame. For those who teach writing mainly as mastery of a compendium of subskills, electronic feedback often refers to automated feedback provided by a computer. Sophisticated software systems that can generate immediate evaluative feedback on student writing are readily available. For those who view writing as a social practice, the term *electronic* indicates the means by which human feedback is provided. Instructors might choose to integrate technology-mediated peer response groups into their classrooms or to match their students with native-speaking key pals using Internet-based communication platforms.

This variance can be misleading for practitioners. Uses of technology are borne out of locally and institutionally construed notions of what constitutes writing and what is considered quality feedback. As instructors turn to research-based evidence for answers about how best to use technology for providing feedback, they deserve a critically informed, empirically based inquiry that makes explicit how electronic feedback was used, and the criteria that were applied to evaluate its effectiveness. Justification for the new uses of technology must be based on empirical data matched to particular uses in specific contexts.

In the following sections, we traverse the realm of technology and writing instruction to map the ways in which the concept of electronic feedback plays out in different areas of research and instruction. We begin by addressing in turn three strands of research on electronic feedback for second language writing. First, we examine research on the potential usefulness and cost-effectiveness of software-generated feedback to replace or enhance direct human feedback. The second strand is comparative, evaluating the effect of computer-mediated human feedback on ESL writing when compared with more traditional face-to-face feedback, particularly in post-secondary composition classes. A third strand of research, often framed by sociocultural and socio-cognitive perspectives, examines differentiation within electronic modes, ranging from a specific focus on academic modes of second language writing to a notion of feedback that encompasses other communicative modalities, such as online chat, e-mail collaboration, and multimedia authoring. We conclude by summarizing lessons from the three strands of research for instruction and for future inquiry.

Strand One: Automated feedback and writing assessment

Interest in automated electronic feedback on essay writing has increased in the last 10 years. Much of the current research on automated feedback is undertaken by institutions developing commercial testing or teaching materials and tends to focus on the individual and performative aspects of writing. Although to date there is a paucity of research on the social and communicative dimensions of automated feedback, its proponents argue that over time automated feedback can help illuminate our understanding of the varied cognitive and social processes involved in writing (Kukich, 2000).

The impetus for creating automated essay evaluation tools is rooted in considerations of both human and monetary resources. Systems that generate feedback on written work through sophisticated computer-generated models have been promoted as cost-effective ways of replacing or enhancing direct human input. These programs provide a range of feedback from individualized reports on grammatical errors for ESL students (Bolt, 1992; Dalgish, 1991; Liou, 1994; Warden & Chen, 1995) to holistic evaluations that attend to many of the content, organizational, and mechanical aspects of essay writing for both first and second language writers (Brock, 1990, 1993; Burston, 2001; Ferris, 1993; Leacock,

2004). As class sizes continue to grow and as instructors are expected to provide more rigorous evaluations than multiple-choice tests can provide, automated essay evaluation is touted as a viable, economically feasible alternative to the expensive endeavor of hand-scored writing assessments.

Cost-effectiveness of replacing human raters with e-raters

A major justification for turning to automated feedback grows out of needs cited by large-scale educational testing organizations to test content knowledge and writing competence. For national and international language performance evaluation companies, large-scale testing that employs any form of written response entails a high cost. Teams of graders must be given inter-rater reliability training, and grading must be regulated with reliability checks. These necessary protocols are costly, which makes automated essay evaluation appear as an attractive, economically viable alternative. Replacing human raters with automated raters reduces the overall cost of evaluation.

One of the better-known automated evaluation systems is the Criterion e-rater (Burstein et al., 2003), developed by the Educational Testing Services (ETS). The e-rater is trained to look for lexical complexity, syntactical variety, topical content, and grammatical errors to provide both holistic scores and specific feedback in grammar, organization, style, and usage. Using a Web-based system, students can choose from a range of practice essay topics that are leveled by grade. The database also includes prompts that provide practice in such high-stakes tests as postsecondary writing placement essays and TOEFL exams. To develop a model for a single essay question, two human raters must score up to 500 essay responses, and the e-rater is then trained on this scoring model until it consistently arrives within one point of agreement with the human raters. Even in cases in which a third human rater must resolve the score, the agreement rate is typically 97 percent between e-raters and human raters. In a study conducted by Chodorow and Burnstein (2004) on a data set of approximately 10,000 essays from student responses to seven exam prompts on the TOEFL exam, e-raters differed little from human readers in achieving agreement on holistic scores.

Another automated electronic feedback program, MY Access!, developed by Vantage Learning (Eliot & Mikulas, 2004), has found its way into a growing number of public school classrooms. As with the e-rater, students can post multiple essays and receive holistic scores on their final drafts. MY Access! currently does not have as sophisticated a system as the e-rater for providing individualized feedback, although it does provide a potentially useful range of writing tools, including online portfolios, a writer's checklist, scoring rubrics, word banks, spell checkers, and graphic charts. In four studies, researchers have documented significant gains in performance on statewide writing assessments for fifth through eleventh grade students (Elliot & Mikulas, 2004). The findings remain preliminary at this time, because the subjects were not randomly assigned to participation in the use of the MY Access! program.

The impact of automated electronic feedback on writing instruction in the classroom

The sheer number of hours spent commenting on student papers is reduced dramatically when instructors can rely on automated electronic feedback systems. Without question, the speed with which a computer can provide individualized feedback outstrips even the fastest human reader. Arguably, by using such systems, instructors can free time to turn their attention to other aspects of teaching in the process writing approach (Chen, 1997; Yao & Warden, 1996). Questions surface, however, about the efficacy of the "more is better" and "faster is better" tenets in writing instruction. To date, we have not found any studies that directly examine the question of whether immediacy is more effective in strengthening student writing in the long term than the normal feedback turnaround provided by instructors.

Many developers of automated feedback software insist that computer-generated feedback should be considered only a supplement to classroom instruction (Burstein et al., 2003; Burstein & Marcu, 2003). Although they do not give a clear indication of what the core instruction might include, we would propose that the importance of social interaction not be underestimated. Many automated programs are theoretically grounded in a cognitive processing model of the human brain, which does not fully explain the learning that takes place on the social and interactional plane.

Accolades for automated feedback often carry a message with a subtext that makes many writing instructors uncomfortable. In the automated environment, writing is construed as primarily a performance piece designed to evaluate student mastery of grammar, usage, and organization. It has yet to be modeled on real interaction or on writing for a communicative purpose. Questions arise about the authenticity of the writing: Are students who post several revisions of their work, as in the case of high school students practicing for their statewide essay exams, actually becoming stronger writers, thinkers, and communicators? Or might they merely be applying the same kinds of test-taking strategy skills so often used to outwit multiple-choice exams?

A lesson learned in the 1990s in the fields of foreign and second language education adds credence to this cautionary perspective. In foregrounding software-generated approaches as the preferred path for teaching second languages and second language writing, the computer was viewed primarily as a *tutor* (Kern & Warschauer, 2000) that could offer an untiring source of practice opportunities for students by generating individualized error feedback and grammatical explanations. When technological developments later inspired a rush of software development, computers also became *tutees* (Kern & Warschauer, 2000). Using closed-system CD-rom technology, students could navigate through large data banks of culturally and linguistically rich material, such as video clips, translations, glosses, and quizzes. The shortcomings of such systems included the lack of meaning negotiation in real-world contexts and the emphasis on highly individualized learning at the expense of attention to social processes.

Summarizing issues of automated electronic feedback

Programs like the Criterion e-rater and MY Access! are relative newcomers to the field of second language writing, and their impact has yet to be systematically evaluated across a range of contexts, particularly those in which second language learners receive instruction. Past studies in the field of second language learning examined the impact of automated software systems that provide grammatical feedback and reported quite mixed, inconclusive results on the improvement of student writing (Dalgish, 1991; Healey, 1992; Liou, 1994; Nutta, 1998; Warden & Chen, 1995). It remains unclear what specific advantages these new products will offer. Ultimately, though, the potential of automated essay evaluation for improving student writing is an empirical question, and virtually no peer-reviewed research has yet been published that examines students' use of these programs or the outcomes. With the certain growth of such software in coming years, this will be a prime area of research related to electronic feedback.

Strand Two: Technology-enhanced peer response and writing instruction

In this strand, electronic feedback refers to the means by which human feedback, particularly peer response, can be provided through technology. In the studies we highlight here, technology is explored as a way to promote interaction about writing through peer response groups. The central question is how computer-mediated peer response might mimic or even enhance the positive outcomes cited by research on face-to-face peer review. Many of these studies have a comparative design to examine the viability of transferring familiar classroom practices of peer response groups into an electronic medium. Teachers often conduct research in their own classrooms and use as their evaluative measures both holistic evaluations of essay writing and qualitative analyses of student attitudes.

Matching technology to second language writing pedagogy

Technology-enhanced environments provide resources for promoting student peer response online in a range of useful ways. Student papers can be made more widely available, and such collaborative effort can foster a sense of community in the classroom (Kahmi-Stein, 2000; Plass & Chun, 1996). Electronic discourse provides an audience of peers beyond the instructor, which helps heighten awareness of audience and of communicative purpose (Ware, 2004). Online discussions also provide spaces for students to practice their literacy skills in a nonthreatening environment (Colomb & Simutis, 1996). Nonnative speakers, in particular, have been found to participate more actively and with greater motivation when provided the opportunity to share their writing through online discussions (Greenfield, 2003; Sullivan & Pratt, 1996; Warschauer, 1996a, 1996c). From an instructional perspective, the use of technology makes the exchange of student drafts more efficient (Palmquist, 1993), and teachers are better poised to monitor peer feedback on the screen than in a large number of face-to-face small-group clusters (DiGiovanni & Nagaswami, 2001).

In a study examining how e-mail writing might help enhance students' academic writing, Biesenbach-Lucas and Weasenforth (2001) used a functional-analytical approach to compare the variation found between e-mail writing and word-processing writing. Because of the assertion that e-mail writing has both oral and written features, they examined what kind of linguistic transfer might occur between e-mail writing and formal academic writing. They analyzed ESL student writing for how cohesive features were used, how much text was produced, and how students contextualized their writing. Their findings indicated that students tended to write shorter texts in their e-mails and to provide more contextualization in their word processing documents. In another study of the impact of word processing on ESL student writing, Pennington (1993) found that successful implementation relies on assessing many factors, including the students, the context of use, and the software chosen.

Another body of research examines more specifically the linguistic advantages of computer-mediated discussion formats in second and foreign language classes. Although these studies do not focus specifically on improvement of writing through direct feedback, they attempt to identify how peer interaction online might enhance the overall accuracy and complexity of second language writing. Research in this area has produced mixed results when comparing technology-enhanced to face-to-face contexts of instruction (for extended reviews, see Ortega,

1997; Warschauer, 1996b). Kern (1995), for example, found that there were a higher proportion of simple rather than complex sentences in online discussions, whereas Warschauer (1996a) found that students wrote with greater complexity and a higher lexical range in their online writing. Pellettieri (2000) gave evidence of greater attention to form, to negotiation of meaning, and to linguistic modification in online writing. Sotillo (2000) compared synchronous with asynchronous modes and found that ESL students tended to write with greater syntactic complexity when writing in asynchronous discussions, which she attributed to the increased amount of composing time students had available.

Up to this point, we have reviewed only those studies in which researchers perform post-hoc analyses of the downloaded transcripts of computer-mediated peer reviews and peer interactions. Another substantial advantage of this form of electronic feedback, however, includes the large database of student writing that computers can store. Many instructors actively use these transcripts for in-class discussion and analysis. They print out transcripts of student writing and work with them to build students' metacognitive awareness of particular linguistic, interactional, organizational, and rhetorical features (Sengupta, 2001; Swaffar et al., 1998). Asynchronous discussion formats, in particular, are believed to combine the interactive aspect of written conversations with the reflective nature of composing. Lamy and Goodfellow (1999) call this "reflective conversation" (p. 43) and cite its strength in instructional contexts for drawing students' conscious attention to linguistic function and form.

In a small case study designed to examine the effectiveness of working with students' own writing to develop metalinguistic awareness, Yuan (2003) showed how two students actively analyzed transcripts of their own writing and thereby became more attentive to the errors they produced when writing. For a 10-week period, Yuan met with both students on a weekly basis. In their face-to-face discussions with the instructor, the students discussed the errors found in their transcripts and over the semester became more effective at monitoring and self-correcting their own writing. In this case, students provided their own feedback on their writing; the electronic mode was simply a useful way to store their writing for analysis during in-class sessions.

Revising essays: Peer feedback and technology

Another group of comparative studies examines how well peer response groups, popular in traditional face-to-face environments, can be transferred to computer-mediated interaction. Using a control group experimental design, Schultz (2000) compared face-to-face with computer-mediated peer feedback by examining the revisions that intermediate and upper-intermediate French students made across their writing in a classroom with a process-oriented approach. She used the Daedalus Interchange package, which allows for real-time interaction on a local area network (LAN). Students wrote comments about one another's essays in real time, and they also received a written transcript of these online sessions so that they could more easily draw upon their peers' comments. She then analyzed essays from a pool of 54 students and conducted attitude surveys across 106 students. Her unit of analysis was the number and type of changes that students made between their rough drafts and their final essays following two types of feedback, that provided in face-to-face discussion and that provided in online real-time discussion. She found that students made more specific, *local* changes in the online mode, as writers were able to save and follow the detailed suggestions made in writing. However, students made more global changes in the face-to-face mode, which seemed to facilitate more rapid interaction and thus a better exploration of the writer's intentions and goals. Students who received feedback in both modes made the most productive overall use of feedback.

Schultz's findings were to some extent replicated in a study by Tuzi (2004), who examined how electronic feedback impacted the revisions that first-year university second language writers made to their academic compositions. Although Tuzi found in interviews with the student participants that they preferred oral feedback, they actually made more revisions in response to electronic feedback than to either oral feedback or feedback provided at the writing center. He suggests that this preference for oral feedback might stem from the familiarity of oral feedback as a classroom practice, or from students' beliefs that there was a substantial difference between oral and written feedback. Nonetheless, he found that the changes made in response to electronic feedback were more frequent and that they tended to be at the clause, sentence, and paragraph levels, rather than at overall global organization.

DiGiovanni and Nagaswami (2001) showed that students were more focused when providing feedback during real-time electronic interaction. In a brief questionnaire that asked about students' perceptions of both oral and electronic feedback, reactions were generally evenly divided between the two modes as useful. Instructors, however, indicated that advantages to the electronic medium included the ability to monitor peer response conversations and to utilize printouts of transcripts. They suggest an indirect positive impact for students who may feel that this kind of teacher oversight is appropriate (see also Sengupta, 2001).

Braine (1997, 2001) and van der Geest and Remmers (1994) point out potential negative features of using technology for peer response groups. Braine, for example, found that several features of the medium made peer response groups less effective than they could be. In studies designed to compare writing instruction for EFL students in LAN-mediated and face-to-face classrooms, he argued that the use of a LAN has not been shown to improve the quality of students' final essays. For three consecutive semesters on three separate cohorts of students, he consistently found that students in the face-to-face classroom condition produced better quality essays by the end of the semester than students in the LAN-mediated class. He attributes this finding in part to the difficulty students faced in navigating the multiple, simultaneous discussion threads of a large quantity of online writing. Van der Geest and Remmers (1994) also indicated that the system of computer-mediated peer review was made difficult because of technical difficulties and because of student dissatisfaction with a distance learning environment. Although they are illustrative of potential barriers, these studies are inconclusive, because many of the difficulties cited can be resolved through better navigation software and instructional design.

Summarizing computer-mediated peer response

Judgments about good writing are locally influenced, which makes the results of studies somewhat difficult to compare across contexts. Similarly, results in studies of student attitudes and of pedagogical integration differ, depending both on how instructors integrate the face-to-face and electronic forms of feedback into the class assignments and on how familiar students are with technology (Greenleaf, 1994; Hyland, 1993; Phinney & Khouri, 1993; Ware, 2004; Warschauer, 1999).

Strand Three: Differentiation among forms of electronic feedback

The tools of technology, as with many instructional strategies and innovations, provide the most beneficial results when integrated into a strong curriculum and when clearly matched to instructional purposes. There is a great deal of variety in what constitutes purposeful writing, and as Warschauer (1999, 2002) has demonstrated, the underlying assumptions that teachers hold about literacy are integral players in how they choose to integrate technology as a resource into their writing classrooms. As the studies that follow show, many instructors are using technology in novel ways to engage second language learners in writing for a wide range of communicative purposes.

One size does not fit all: Differing notions of technology in academic writing

In the study cited above, Warschauer (1999, 2002) embarked on an ethnographic action research project that examined how three different writing teachers integrated technology into their second language writing classrooms. Each of the teachers took a different theoretical stance on what constitutes academic writing: formalist, constructivist, and social constructivist. In the formalist approach, academic writing was seen as mastery of a set of subskills that led to a grammatically correct product, usually in the form of a traditional five-paragraph essay. In this classroom, computers merely provided the means to meet a singular end of training students to produce this type of writing. Students used the computer to complete grammar exercises and formulaic writing tasks common to many basic writing classrooms. In the constructivist approach, writing was viewed as not just an academic task but also as one with personal meaning and practical applications. The instructor in this classroom used computers to engage her students in genres such as multimedia authoring that opened up a range of literacies, not just formal academic writing.

In the classroom with a social constructionist approach, Warschauer (1999, 2002) documented an important shift away from viewing technology as the means by which conventional beliefs about writing and the teaching of writing could be made more efficient and toward a vision of technology as driving new approaches to literacy instruction. The instructor saw in technology unique opportunities for students to collaborate with one another and to engage in a tutor-tutee apprenticeship with the instructor. By requiring the creation of professional Web pages and participation in academic listservs, she also helped them connect to the academic communities relevant to their studies. Drawing on a similar view of literacy, Kasper (2000) demonstrated how new technologies could be used in focus discipline research to engage students in multiple literacies in ESL writing instruction as well as in professional, social, and personal realms beyond the classroom.

Electronic feedback in two languages: Online language and culture exchanges

The Internet allows for the creation of meaningful, rich contexts of interaction that enable students to engage in personal communication (Kern & Warschauer, 2000; Warschauer, 1999). These electronically mediated interactions provide them with peer feedback from native-speaking peers; through this form of electronic feedback, they gain experience as writers who use language not just to perform a skill but also to communicate across linguistic and cultural lines. Findings have consistently reported that students produce more output and report being more motivated to write when communicating in the target language with native language partners on the Internet (Kern, 1996; Meagher & Castaños, 1996;

Ware, 2003; Warschauer, 1996c). Students have access to resources and materials that provide insight into the issues and controversies that are relevant in the country of study. "Key pals," or one-to-one e-mail partners who communicate in their respective target languages through writing, offer personalized feedback and meaningful communication in the online medium (Brammerts, 1996). In her ethnographic study of high school students in Finland and England communicating over e-mail, Tella (1992) showed that having real-world native-speaking peers as their audiences made a positive impact on student writing (see also Barson et al., 1993). Students wrote in a wider range of genres, and they focused more on content, which allowed them to utilize a larger vocabulary and more idiomatic expressions. Classroom instruction was no longer teacher-directed, and class time was used for more individualized, learner-centered workshops.

Using a sociocultural lens in foreign language research (Lantolf, 1994; van Lier, 2000), many researchers have begun to address the complex interplay of language and culture in the online context in which peers provide one another feedback on writing (Belz, 2002; Furstenberg et al., 2001; Kramsch & Thorne, 2002; Ware, 2004; Warschauer, 1999). Kramsch and Thorne (2002), based on findings from a joint French-American writing exchange, suggest attending to genre and discourse in the online context. Belz (2002) addresses issues relating to social and institutional constraints in an international e-mail exchange. Through one-to-one writing over e-mail (O'Dowd, 2003) and asynchronous discussion groups (Belz, 2002, 2003; Thorne, 2003; Ware, 2003), students writing and responding over the Internet can gain intercultural understanding. These studies have in common the call, echoed across an array of disciplinary fields, for more research that examines online social interaction in its cultural, historical, and social dimensions (Belz & Müller-Hartmann, 2003; Chapelle, 1997).

Summarizing differences among forms of electronic feedback

Feedback in many foreign language education contexts does not always refer in the strictest sense to writing instruction that has a primary focus on academic writing development. Instead, electronic feedback is often construed as human interaction between native and target language speakers. The feedback that peers provide serves purposes such as fostering overall communicative competence and second language development. Researchers and instructors have just begun to explore ways that online interaction can provide a form of electronic feedback that allows students to write in a second language to accomplish a wide range of interactionally meaningful purposes (for an extensive review, see Liu et al., 2002).

Conclusion

As the research findings from all three strands have shown, the task of evaluating writing and providing quality feedback is complex. In the strand of research, which examined computer-generated feedback, such complexity is largely dealt with by creating large-scale systems that provide efficient, automated individualized feedback loops. In the second strand, evidence points strongly to the advantages of combining both oral and computer-mediated feedback when using peer response groups in the writing classroom. The research agenda in the third strand is in many ways still in its early stages. As researchers and educators look for new ways to use computers in the classroom, second language writers will actively help shape new genres, and educators will need to develop innovative approaches to meet the demands of these new areas.

Instructors interested in integrating electronic feedback into their writing classrooms can draw on the findings synthesized in this chapter as they choose from the variety of pedagogical approaches and recommendations presented by researchers. As we have shown, certain uses of technology and certain technology-mediated contexts appear more favorable than others, as summarized here:

- Automated feedback programs help instructors save large amounts of time that can be used for other types of writing instruction.
- Automated feedback systems tend to emphasize formulaic writing, because it lends itself to systematic codification. Therefore, automated feedback is recommended as a supplement to, but not a substitute for, other forms of classroom instruction that include both social interaction and writing for a variety of audiences and communicative purposes.
- Writing performance improves when students receive detailed comments across several iterations of their writing, either in the form of electronic feedback provided by automated scoring systems or by peer response. Long-term effects of electronic feedback on student writing development are still under investigation.
- Electronic feedback through peer response increases student writing output, enhances student motivation, provides a nonthreatening environment, makes papers more readily available for sharing, and allows instructors greater opportunity to monitor peer response.
- Electronic feedback in the form of peer response results in specific, local changes at the clause, sentence, or paragraph level. It is most effective when combined with some form of oral feedback, because students prefer oral discussion for generating ideas and exploring arguments.

The dynamics of oral interaction allow for more free-flowing discussion and thereby result in more global changes to writing, such as a general refocusing of direction, purpose, or organization.

- The database of student writing produced through electronic feedback can be used during in-class discussions to increase students' metacognitive awareness of linguistic form and function, audience, and communicative purpose. Teachers can use this database to increase students' autonomy in correcting errors and in reflecting on their writing.
- The type of electronic interface used for electronic feedback strongly influences successful outcomes. Interfaces with multiple strands are difficult to navigate and tend to result in less interaction.
- Notions about conventional forms of literacy and feedback are expanding as second language writers shift their audiences from a single classroom teacher to peers and professionals across contexts. Cultural aspects of second language writing are also increasingly foregrounded in research, particularly in projects that examine written interactions between native and target language writers across international lines. In this time of change, instructors need to examine their own beliefs about the goals of writing instruction and about how best to meet those goals.
- Instructors must play a central role in technology-enhanced classrooms. Pedagogical framing and instructional guidance are powerful tools that help shape the success of online learning. Suggestions include providing opportunities and support for multiple types of writing; utilizing electronic databases of student writing for developing metacognitive and metalinguistic awareness; combining automated feedback with electronic peer review and face-to-face discussions; making expectations for electronic writing explicit; discussing the criteria used for evaluating student performance in tasks such as electronic peer review; and attending to local and institutional needs when making decisions about how best to integrate technology into the writing classroom.

Research is sure to continue in all three strands we have discussed, particularly as instructors continue to integrate technology into their writing classrooms. As researchers further examine the areas we have outlined in this chapter, we will gradually increase our understanding of how educators might enhance conventional forms of writing, and how students might become more autonomous learners through increasingly sophisticated computer-generated feedback software. In the near future, we will most likely explore questions related to novel forms of writing and to new ways of teaching and conducting research. These new forms of electronic literacy (Warschauer, 2002 and 2004) are certain to push the boundaries of computer-mediated and computer-generated feedback in ways that pose new areas for inquiry.

References

Barson, J., Frommer, J., & Schwartz, M. (1993). Foreign language learning using e-mail in a task-oriented perspective: Interuniversity experiments in communication and collaboration. *Journal of Science Education and Technology, 4(2)*, 565–584.

Belz, J. A. (2002). Social dimensions of telecollaborative language study. *Language Learning and Technology, 6(1)*, 60–81.

Belz, J. A. (2003). Linguistic perspectives on the development of intercultural competence in telecollaboration. *Language Learning & Technology, 7(2)*, 68–99.

Belz, J. A., & Müller-Hartmann, A. (2003). Teachers as intercultural learners: Negotiating German-American telecollaboration along the institutional faultline. *The Modern Language Journal, 87(1)*, 71–89.

Biesenbach-Lucas, S., & Weasenforth, D. (2001). E-mail and word processing in the ESL classroom: How the medium affects the message. *Language Learning & Technology, 5(1)*, 135–165.

Bolt, P. (1992). An evaluation of grammar-checking programs as self-help learning aids for learners of English as a foreign language. *Computer Assisted Language Learning, 5(1–2)*, 49–91.

Braine, G. (1997). Beyond word processing: Networked computers in ESL writing classes. *Computers and Composition, 14(1)*, 45–58.

Braine, G. (2001). A study of English as a foreign language (EFL) writers on a local-area network (LAN) and in traditional classes. *Computers and Composition, 18*, 275–292.

Brammerts, H. (1996). Language learning in tandem using the Internet. In M. Warschauer (Ed.), *Telecollaboration in foreign language learning* (pp. 121–130). Honolulu, HI: University of Hawaii Press.

Brock, M. (1990). Customizing a computerized text analyzer for ESL writers: Cost versus gain. *CALICO Journal, 8(2)*, 51–60.

Brock, M. (1993). Three disk-based text analyzers and the ESL writer. *Journal of Second Language Writing, 2(1)*, 19–40.

Burstein, J., Chodorow, M., & Leacock, C. (2003, August). Criterion[SM]: Online essay evaluation: An application for automated evaluation of student essays. *Proceedings of the Fifteenth Annual Conference on Innovative Applications of Artificial Intelligence*. Acapulco, Mexico.

Burstein, J., & Marcu, D. (2003). Developing technology for automated evaluation of discourse structure in student essays. In M. D. Shermis & J. Burstein (Eds.), *Automated essay scoring: A cross-disciplinary perspective*. Hillsdale, NJ: Lawrence Erlbaum.

Burston, J. (2001). Computer-mediated feedback in composition correction. *CALICO Journal, 19(1)*, 37–50.

Chapelle, C. (1997). CALL in the year 2000: Still in search of research paradigms? *Language Learning & Technology, 1(1)*, 19–43.

Chen, J. (1997). Computer generated error feedback and writing process: A link. *TESL-EJ, 2(3)*. Available at www.kyoto-su.ac.jp/information/tesl-ej/ej07/a1.html. Retrieved on February 3, 2004.

Chodorow, M., & Burnstein, J. (2004). Beyond essay length: Evaluating e-rater's performance on TOEFL essays. Educational Testing Service Research, Report 73. Educational Testing Services. Available at ftp://ftp.ets.org/pub/toefl/990112.pdf. Retrieved on May 21, 2004.

Chun, D., & Plass, J. (2000). Networked multimedia environments for second language acquisition. In M. Warschauer & R. Kern (Eds.), *Network-based language teaching: Concepts and practice* (pp. 151–170). Cambridge, UK: Cambridge University Press.

Colomb, G., & Simutis, J. A. (1996). Visible conversation and academic inquiry: CMC in a culturally diverse classroom. In S. C. Herring (Ed.), *Computer-mediated communication: Linguistic, social, and cross-cultural perspectives* (pp. 203–224). Amsterdam: John Benjamins.

Dalgish, G. (1991). Computer-assisted error analysis and courseware design: Applications for ESL in the Swedish context. *CALICO Journal, 9(2)*, 39–56.

DiGiovanni, E., & Nagaswami, G. (2001). Online peer review: An alternative to face-to-face? *ELT Journal, 55(3)*, 263–272.

Eliot, S., & Mikulas, C. (2004, April). *The impact of MY Access! use on student writing performance: A technology overview and four studies.* Paper presented at the Annual Meeting of the American Educational Research Association. San Diego, CA.

Ferris, D. (1993). The design of an automatic analysis program for L2 text research: Necessity and feasibility. *Journal of Second Language Writing, 2(2)*, 119–129.

Furstenberg, G., Levet, S., English, K., & Maillet, K. (2001). Giving a virtual voice to the silent language of culture: The Culture Project. *Language Learning & Technology, 5(1)*, 55–102.

Greenfield, R. (2003). Collaborative e-mail exchange for teaching secondary ESL: A case study in Hong Kong. *Language Learning & Technology, 7(1)*, 46–70.

Greenleaf, C. (1994). Technological indeterminacy: The role of classroom writing practices and pedagogy in shaping student use of the computer. *Written Communication, 11*, 85–130.

Healey, D. (1992). Where's the beef? Grammar practice with computers. *CAELL Journal, 3(1)*, 10–16.

Hyland, K. (1993). ESL computer writers: What can we do to help? *System, 21(1)*, 21–30.

Kahmi-Stein, L. D. (2000). Looking to the future of TESOL teacher education: Web-based bulletin board discussions in a methods course. *TESOL Quarterly, 34*, 423–455.

Kasper, L. (2000). New technologies, new literacies: Focus discipline research and ESL learning communities. *Language Learning & Technology, 4(2)*, 105–128.

Kern, R. (1995). Restructuring classroom interaction with networked computers: Effects on quantity and characteristics of language production. *The Modern Language Journal, 79(4)*, 457–476.

Kern, R. (1996). Computer-mediated communication: Using email exchanges to explore personal histories in two cultures. In M. Warschauer (Ed.), *Telecollaboration in foreign language learning* (pp. 105–119). Honolulu, HI: University of Hawaii Press.

Kern, R., & Warschauer, M. (Eds.). (2000). Introduction. In M. Warschauer & R. Kern (Eds.), *Network-based language teaching: Concepts and practice* (pp. 1–19). Cambridge, UK: Cambridge University Press.

Kramsch, C., & Thorne, S. (2002). Foreign language learning as global communicative practice. In D. Block and D. Cameron (Eds.), *Globalization and language teaching* (pp. 83–100). London: Routledge.

Kukich, K. (2000). Beyond automated essay scoring. *IEEE Intelligent Systems, 15(5)*, 22–27. Available online at www.knowledgetechnologies.com/papers/IEEEdebate.pdf. Retrieved May 20, 2004.

Lamy, M-N., & Goodfellow, R. (1999). "Reflective conversation" in the virtual language classroom. *Language Learning & Technology, 2(2)*, 43–61.

Landauer, T., Laham, D., & Foltz, P. (2000). The intelligent essay assessor. *IEEE Intelligent Systems, 15(5)*, 27–31. Available online at www.knowledge-technologies.com/papers/IEEEdebate.pdf. Retrieved May 20, 2004.

Lantolf, J. P. (2000). Introducing sociocultural theory. In *Sociocultural theory and second language learning* (pp. 1–26). Oxford: Oxford University Press.

Leacock, C. (2004). Scoring free-responses automatically: A case study of a large-scale assessment. *Examens, 1(3)*.

Liou, H.-C. (1994). Practical considerations for multimedia courseware development: An EFL IVD experience. *CALICO Journal, 11(3)*, 47–74.

Liu, M., Moore, Z., Graham, L., & Lee, S. (2002). A look at the research on computer-based technology use in second language learning: A review of the literature from 1990–2000. *Journal of Research on Technology in Education, 34(3)*, 250–273.

Meagher, M. E., and Castaños, F. (1996). Perceptions of American culture: The impact of an electronically-mediated cultural exchange program on Mexican high school students. In S. Herring (Ed.), *Computer-mediated communication: Linguistic, social, and cross-cultural perspectives* (pp. 187–201). Amsterdam: John Benjamins.

Nutta, J. (1998). Is computer-based grammar instruction as effective as teacher-directed grammar instruction for teaching L2 structures? *CALICO Journal, 16(1)*, 49–62.

O'Dowd, R. (2003). Understanding the "other side": Intercultural learning in a Spanish-English e-mail exchange. *Language Learning & Technology, 7(2)*, 118–144.

Ortega, L. (1997). Processes and outcomes in networked classroom interaction: Defining the research agenda for L2 computer-assisted classroom discussion. *Language Learning & Technology, 1(1)*, 82–93.

Palmquist, M. (1993). Network-supported interaction in two writing classrooms. *Computers and Composition, 10(4)*, 25–57.

Pellettieri, J. (2000). Negotiation in cyberspace: The role of *chatting* in the development of grammatical competence. In M. Warschauer & R. Kern (Eds.), *Network-based language teaching: Concepts and practice* (pp. 59–86). Cambridge: Cambridge University Press.

Pennington, M. (1993). A critical examination of word processing effects in relation to L2 writers. *Journal of Second Language Writing, 2(3)*, 227–255.

Phinney, M., & Khouri, S. (1993). Computers, revision, and ESL writers: The role of experience. *Journal of Second Language Writing, 2(3)*, 257–277.

Plass, J., & Chun, D. (1996). A hypermedia system for CALL in a networked environment. In M. Warschauer (Ed.), *Telecollaboration in foreign language learning* (pp. 83–103). Honolulu, HI: University of Hawaii Press.

Schultz, J. M. (2000). Computers and collaborative writing in the foreign language curriculum. In M. Warschauer & R. Kern (Eds.), *Network-based language learning: Concepts and practice* (pp. 121–150). Cambridge, UK: Cambridge University Press.

Sengupta, S. (2001). Exchanging ideas with peers in network-based classrooms: An aid or a pain? *Language Learning & Technology, 5(1)*, 103–134.

Sotillo, Susana M. (2000). Discourse functions and syntactic complexity in synchronous and asynchronous communication. *Language Learning & Technology, 4*, 82–119.

Sullivan N., & Pratt, E. (1996). A comparative study of two ESL writing environments: A computer-assisted classroom and a traditional oral classroom. *System, 29(4)*, 491–501.

Swaffar, J., Romano, S., Arens, K., & Markley, P. (Eds.) (1998). *Language learning online: Research and pedagogy in the ESL and L2 computer classroom.* Austin, TX: Labyrinth Publications.

Tella, S. (1992). *Talking shop via email: A thematic and linguistic analysis of electronic mail communication* (Research report 99). Helsinki: University of Helsinki, Department of Teacher Education.

Thorne, S. L. (2003). Artifacts and cultures-of-use in intercultural communication. *Language Learning & Technology, 7(2)*, 38–67.

Tuzi, F. (2005). The impact of e-feedback on the revisions of L2 writers in an academic writing course. *Computers and Composition, 21(2)*, 217–235.

van der Geest, T., & Remmers, T. (1994). The computer as means of communication for peer-review groups. *Computers and Composition, 11*, 237–250.

van Lier, L. (2000). From input to affordance: Social-interactive learning from an ecological perspective. In J. P. Lantolf (Ed.), *Sociocultural theory and second language learning* (pp. 245–260). Oxford: Oxford University Press.

Warden, C., and Chen, J. (1995). Improving feedback while decreasing teacher burden in R.O.C. ESL business English writing classes, In P. Bruthiaux, T. Boswood & B. Du-Babcock (Eds.), *Explorations in English for professional communications* (pp. 125–137). Hong Kong: City University of Hong Kong.

Ware, P. D. (2003). *From involvement to engagement in online communication: Promoting intercultural competence in foreign language education.* Unpublished doctoral dissertation, University of California, Berkeley.

Ware, P. D. (2004). Confidence and competition online: ESL student perspectives on web-based discussions in the classroom. *Computers and Composition, 21(4)*, 451–468.

Warschauer, M. (1996a). Comparing face-to-face and electronic discussion in the second language classroom. *CALICO Journal, 13(2)*, 7–26.

Warschauer, M. (1996b). *Computer-mediated collaborative learning: Theory and practice.* Honolulu, HI: University of Hawaii, Second Language Teaching and Curriculum Center.

Warschauer, M. (1996c). Motivational aspects of using computers for writing and communication. In *Telecollaboration in foreign language learning* (pp. 29–48). Honolulu, HI: University of Hawaii Press.

Warschauer, M. (1997). Computer-mediated collaborative learning: Theory and practice. *The Modern Language Journal, 81(4)*, 470–481.

Warschauer, M. (1999). Electronic literacies: Language, culture, and power in online education. Mahwah, NJ: Lawrence Erlbaum.

Warschauer, M. (2002). Networking into academic discourse. *Journal of English for Academic Purposes, 1(1)*, 45–58.

Warschauer, M. (2004). Technology and writing. In J. Cummins and C. Davison (Eds.), *The Kluwer international handbook of English language education.* Dordrecht, Netherlands: Kluwer.

Yao, Y., and Warden, C. (1996). Process writing and computer correction: Happy wedding or shotgun marriage? *CALL Electronic Journal [online journal], 1(1).* Available at www.lc.tut.ac.jp/callej/callej.htm. Retrieved January 22, 2004.

Yuan, Y. (2003). The use of chat rooms in an ESL setting. *Computers and Composition, 20*, 194–206.

7 Resource-rich Web-based feedback: Helping learners become independent writers

John Milton

This chapter reviews some of the problems in manual and automatic feedback to student writing and describes software tools I have developed to address some of these problems. The purpose of these tools is to encourage learners to look up language patterns and other information in online resources as they write and revise and to help teachers guide their students in using these resources effectively as writing aids.

The wider goal of this approach is to provide novice writers the means to access comprehensive and targeted input and to assist teachers to guide students in exploring appropriate resources and thus to become less dependent on their teachers' support. The tools are designed to improve students' linguistic performance and competence in the EFL context of Hong Kong, but the methodology may be helpful for novice writers in general and for teachers of other languages and subjects when responding to student texts.

Theoretical issues and practical constraints in form-focused feedback

In spite of criticisms of form-focused feedback, (e.g., Krashen, 1982; Truscott, 1996), second language acquisition (SLA) researchers increasingly appear to recognize that language acquisition is optimized when learners attend to both meaning and form (e.g., Doughty & Varela, 1998; Ellis, 2002). However, the drive to provide form-focused feedback is discouraging to many language teachers, especially in foreign language (FL) contexts, who are compelled by educational and social pressures to spend the greater part of their time in what often seems a fruitless attempt to eradicate interlanguage errors at the sentence level (Tsui, 1996). Several strategies have been suggested to help teachers cope with these demands (e.g., Cogie et al., 1999; Ferris, 2002 and 2003) and to make feedback more effective. However, teachers are often under extreme pressures of time and student numbers, and frequently fail adequately to describe the constructs of the target language, or to understand sources of interference from the students' L1. Various studies have criticized written teacher feedback as hasty, generic, inconsistent, unclear, and discouraging to students (e.g., Cohen & Cavalcanti, 1990; Straub, 1997). Even positive remarks can be unhelpful or misleading (Hyland & Hyland, 2001). Unsatisfactory feedback is compounded by constraints in instruction, insufficient access to the target language in FL contexts, and widespread pressure to write error-free examination copy. Such factors can lead learners to adopt short-term avoidance strategies at the expense of acquiring broad lexico-grammatical and communicative competence in the target language (Milton, 2001).

The dilemma of appropriation

Individual feedback from the most competent and well-intentioned teacher, even if available, may be inadequate and not necessarily appropriate in helping novices to become independent and effective writers. In the process of giving feedback on student writing, particularly in commenting on and correcting errors in FL learners' texts, teachers often lose sight of the goal of making their students independent of our guidance. Written teacher feedback, or even individual teacher conferences, cannot adequately provide students with techniques that increase their control over future revisions (Cogie et al., 1999). Reid (1994) argues that second language (SL) and FL teachers should be benign editors, but in the attempt to be helpful, they often take over the learner's language and writing process (Brannon & Knoblauch, 1982). Although Ferris (2002) concedes that SL/FL students need editorial help, she, along with most other commentators, warns against giving direct feedback on errors (i.e., against reformulating the student's text) except as a final resort.

In spite of such injunctions against direct intervention, many FL instructors are expected, or feel compelled, to correct errors explicitly, and, indeed, it is often difficult to provide useful advice without doing so. An FL learner who suspects that a language structure is nonstandard is often at a loss as how to confirm the suspicion or how to amend the structure. Thus, the conscientious teacher more often than not intervenes to make decisions for the learner by identifying selected usage as nonstandard and by imposing a reformulation. Such appropriation, besides depending on the teacher's fallible intuition, may do little in the long term for students' linguistic competence, since the learner is often required to do no more than copy the teacher's correction into a rewrite. Chen (1999) found that Hong Kong students are inured to this vicious circle and by secondary school have become resistant to encouragement to reformulate for themselves: They dislike commentary in question form, preferring explicit correction and advice. It is telling that this does not appear to be true for all student populations (see Leki, 1990). What seems to be missing is a mechanism to help students self-edit and to enable teachers to facilitate rather than to dictate. Ideally, such a mechanism would turn the notion of appropriation around and point learners to resources where, as in Bakhtin's (1981) concept, they would be the ones appropriating the usage of more experienced writers of the L2.

Limitations of current text analysis software

It is a common presumption that the technological fix for FL writers' nonstandard English is the development of reliable software that will automatically detect and correct error. There are two major problems with this expectation. The first is that it is a very difficult computational goal. In the past decade, text analysis software has not had significant improvements in supporting FL novice writers, largely because of the difficulties in parsing natural language – especially interlanguage (see Schneider & McCoy, 1998). Research on automated response to writing continues, with large testing corporations claiming to be able automatically to rank content-restricted essays (see Valenti et al., 2003), but whether the statistical techniques they use can provide useful feedback to L2 writers is unclear (see Hearst, 2000).

A second problem is that reliance on a deus ex machina for correction is not necessarily a better alternative than dependence on a teacher. From its first introduction through its current versions, grammar-checking software has been criticized for unreliability (Krishnamurthy, 2005), for giving narrow and prescriptive advice (Pennington, 1992), for compounding the already constrained nature of L2 production (Chapelle, 2001), and for otherwise abusing the tenets of good pedagogy (McGee & Ericsson, 2002).

Helping students become independent writers

The approach outlined below provides students with the means to check and improve their language by referring to copious, authentic, and comprehensible resources during the writing process. This access, combined with resource-rich feedback from their teachers, can greatly increase the amount of positive and negative evidence available to students. Many researchers believe such evidence promotes acquisition (Doughty & Varela, 1998; Trahey & White, 1993), and if this approach can help students become more confident, responsible, and independent in selecting forms and patterns that are accurate and appropriate, it can also help relieve teachers of the need to act as proofreading slaves.

Providing students with context-sensitive online resources

Given the unreliability and questionable pedagogy of current text analysis software, I suggested in Milton (1999) a method for turning necessity into a virtue through a discovery-based approach to writing that integrates concordancing software into the writing process. This method gives EFL novice writers a cognitive support tool with which to check their evolving language hypotheses. I elaborate on this approach here by describing two tools, one that links novice writers to a wide web of lexico-grammatical and semantic resources and a companion program that helps teachers guide their students through the sticky bits.

Check My Words (http://webtools.ust.hk/mmw/downloadcmw/) helps learners access language in online resources as they compose and proof-read. Mark My Words (http://webtools.ust.hk/mmw/Mark_My_Words.htm) enables teachers to point to the same online resources when giving feedback. These companion programs install as word processor toolbars from which students can open dialogue boxes to search and teachers can assist in selecting appropriate responses and online resources. There are a growing number of such online resources that can be exploited to help students self-edit and to help teachers provide feedback. Dynamic Web sites, such as Google and its search functions, can cater to inductive modes of language learning (Joyce & Weil 2000). Targeted text-retrieval sites can help students clarify the strong selectional restrictions of specific words. These include Word Neighbors (access from the Mark My Words site) (Milton, 2004), an online concordancer that displays a specified number of words to the left, right, or within a target lexeme in specialized corpora, and JustTheWord (Whitelock, 2004), which displays collocates identified statistically and clustered by word class and sense from the British National Corpus. The twin programs, Check My Words and Mark My Words, also link to didactic references, including online dictionaries, thesauruses, encyclopedias, and an online English grammar guide directed at the needs of Chinese speakers (Milton, 2004).

I recently introduced Check My Words to students at my university and since then have logged all search requests made by the students. For a short reflective journal entry written half-way through a 28-week, first-year university course in academic English, 323 students performed about 800 searches using these resources. In most cases, these searches helped to resolve inaccurate usage; relatively few new errors resulted from students' misunderstanding the evidence. The students saw their teachers for one 50-minute class each week. They were guided in using the resources by having to complete a number of online proof-reading activities that focused on noticing common interlanguage patterns. These in-class and online prewriting activities required students to identify errors that had been abstracted from their own and other students' previous written assignments and to use appropriate resources to reformulate the errors. The students were required to write two drafts of each journal entry, one in which they concentrated on meaning and a second in which they focused on form by using the proofing technique.

Helping L2 students learn to self-edit interlanguage patterns

Many interlanguage structures tend to fossilize in the writing of Chinese-speaking intermediate-level learners of English, especially when L2 input is impoverished, as is the case in Hong Kong. The degree and manner in which these errors breach standard English are often difficult to reconcile and to explain to the student. Ferris (2002) calls them "untreatable," and the standard English variants are variously considered "unlearnable" (Yip, 1995) and "unteachable" (Pienemann, 1998). One of the patterns, which was drawn to students' attention in the prewriting online activity, stems partly from the fact that the English verbs *have* and *be* are expressed by one Chinese word.

Figure 7.1 lists the steps one student followed in using the Check My Words toolbar to self-edit an error of this type. I tracked these steps by comparing the first and second drafts of the student's assignment and by reviewing the server log. The student had written "You both have the same age." When he was asked to edit his document, he decided, out of class and without specific prompting, to check this structure. After highlighting it, he selected "Google Search" from the Check My Words toolbar, which opened a dialogue box. He highlighted the suspect word *have* and clicked "Search." Check My Words created the appropriate search syntax (i.e., it searched for any word to replace *have* in the string – in case that word were incorrect – and searched for the string without a word in this slot, in case the word were redundant). It then directed the student to the Google Web search site, which suggested that the most likely verb was *are* and the next most likely was *look*. This process took the student less than a minute.

The Google search site is not necessarily the most appropriate resource for students to investigate interlanguage patterns. Because the Web search is unrestricted, they may very well encounter the nonstandard usage ("have the same age") they are investigating. Such possibilities make it necessary that students be taught to be thoughtful researchers (e.g., to discount infrequent matches and evidence from suspicious sites). On the other hand, the benefit of an unrestricted search is that it requires students to exercise judgment and to experience language as a spectrum of possibilities rather than the simple "right" and "wrong" choices they may be exposed to in conventional instruction. The evidence from an unrestricted Web search will almost always favor standard usage. If the

Step 1: The student highlighted the expression "You both have the same age" in Microsoft Word.

Step 2: The student selected Google Search from the options in the Check My Words drop-down menu.

Check My Words generated a dialogue.

Step 3: In the dialogue, the student selected the query text, then clicked Search.

Check My Words generated the appropriate search syntax: "*You both * the same age,*" then Google Search displayed the results.

The first three highlighted results were

You both are about the same age
... even though you look the same age
... you both have boys the same age

Figure 7.1. Steps a student took to investigate the interlanguage pattern "you both have the same age" using the Check My Words *word-processor toolbar to query Google Search.*

student had dropped the familiar pronoun *you* from his search, he could, with somewhat more confidence in the results, have successfully queried edited texts, for example Google News (newspaper text), instead of the Web in general. The student might also have queried the specific collocational properties of the noun *age*, using the more structured search engines described below (Word Neighbors or JustTheWord), and found that the verb *have* does not govern nouns such as *age*. Each of these resources opens the way to discoveries of the ways in which words can, and cannot, combine.

Another example of a common error successfully self-edited was *It will benefit to them*. Here, the properties of the noun and verb forms are confused. The student who produced this sentence corrected it in his second draft by using the Google News function in the Check My Words toolbar. The result was a display of standard usage (e.g., "It will benefit them"). Searching further, he would have discovered that this clause normally occurs after *because, (understand) how, find out if, feel,* and *think* and in the company (at least in the newspaper text corpus he searched) of such idioms as *down the road*. On encountering this idiom, the student looked it up in the online Cambridge dictionary and rewrote his original sentence to "I feel it will benefit them down the road."

Other students used Check My Words to look up the word *benefit* in Word Neighbors, which allows the user to display up to four words on either side of the target word and to see what words can be used in a span of up to 10 words (e.g., to determine whether a particular phrasal verb is separable and what elements occur within the span). The user can choose to see all forms of the words, the word class of each word in each context, all sentences containing the target expression, and the surrounding sentences. In this case, the student would have seen that *benefit*, when used as an intransitive verb (the typical case), is not followed by the preposition *to* but rather by *from*. He would also have seen that the word occurs overwhelmingly as a noun. Some students apparently realized this because they modified their sentences to produce forms such as "The benefits are clear" and "The benefits will outweigh the costs."

Students can query a range of text types on the Word Neighbors site. My colleagues and I have collected 50 million words representing about 20 distinct text types, including academic and technical reports, business articles, and legal texts. The collection and part-of-speech tagging of representative and relevant corpora is challenging but ongoing. The Word Neighbors site also allows students to hear any highlighted stretch of text read by a text-to-speech simulated voice and to open glosses from other online resources, such as dictionaries and encyclopedias.

Together, the nearly 800 searches conducted in the resources already mentioned resulted in about 500 revisions in the 323 journal entries. About 70 of the revisions misinterpreted the evidence or contained what appeared to be careless mistakes. However, most of the others resulted in more natural, effective, and accurate usage. Many of the successful corrections were of lexical patterns not singled out in the prewriting activities. It appears that such resources can partly compensate for FL writers' lack of L2 intuition and for their limited exposure to the target language and its cultural contexts. Because the students not only had access to the resources but were also taught how to use them and held responsible for doing so, it was also possible to give feedback that drew students' attention to patterns they had not managed to self-correct and to suggest resources they could use in further revisions.

Providing resource-rich feedback through computer-assisted comments

Computer-assisted commenting software designed to help teachers insert prewritten comments in students' electronic documents has been available for some time (see Robb, 1997). These programs help teachers insert consistent explanations and avoid the overly cryptic comments and symbols associated with "minimal marking" (Haswell, 1983) and feedback forms. Prewritten comments can be useful for responding to repetitive, easily explained errors, although most comments need to be modified by the teacher to be made specific and helpful. There are several shortcomings to this approach: Sorting through long lists of comments can be time consuming; the method does little to help learners develop autonomous writing skills; and the grammar explanations are didactic. Moreover, there is no evidence that this approach makes students more likely to use the feedback to improve future revisions.

I designed Mark My Words to overcome those shortcomings, i.e., to help teachers insert customizable comments in any language in a student's electronic document and to link the comments to the same online resources that are available to students. The commenting toolbar lists approximately 100 recurrent lexico-grammatical and style errors common in the writing of Chinese speakers, with suggested links to resources. Crucially, teachers who must respond to a wide range of sentence-level errors do not need to scroll through this long list. The program can identify word classes and lexical patterns and automatically shortlist suggested comments. When the teacher right-clicks or enters a keyboard shortcut, only the errors associated with the corresponding word class are displayed. This feature minimizes the time it takes a teacher to insert comments and guides teachers who are unsure of grammatical terminology in selecting appropriate comments.

This tool differs from other commenting software by assisting teachers to guide students to reformulate their own texts. In doing so, it helps resolve the dilemma of giving directive vs. facilitative feedback (see Straub, 1996). Because teachers can provide authentic language data in lieu of usage examples derived by intuition, students are not compelled to accept particular and possibly idiosyncratic reformulations. Teachers can by stages relinquish control over their students' texts and allow students to make their own editing decisions.

This approach also helps teachers to give feedback on content, a process that can encounter problems similar to those found with feedback on form (Cohen & Cavalcanti, 1990; Fathman & Walley, 1990; Leki, 1990). The Mark My Words toolbar contains comments addressing persistent errors in logic, content, style, organization, and so on. Comments can be created or edited easily and can be linked to resources identified by the teacher. When the teacher has finished giving feedback on a document, the Mark My Words program uploads the student's document (saved as a Web page) to a server, and the student is sent an e-mail, prompting him or her to retrieve it. As the student moves the mouse, the teacher's comments and linked resources (e.g., collocational resources or static reference pages containing explanations, such as grammar advice) are displayed. Crucially, teachers can decide what type of feedback to provide, and students can choose whether to attend to inductive or deductive resources and which of these strategies to use in future revisions.

Recently, a student sent me a 10-page document, asking if I would "correct all the grammar mistakes" in it the same day (!) for a proposal competition deadline. There were many sentence-level errors in the document, although he claimed to have done his best to edit the text using the Check My Words toolbar. The document's organization was not at issue, and the student's meaning in most cases was clear, but he realized that many of his constructions might annoy the judges. I agreed to help, and rather than impose my own corrections, commented on the 100 errors I spotted in about 15 minutes of using Mark My Words. The student had to consult the resources and reformulate the text for himself. The student sent me the final draft showing the tracked changes. He had modified all the language I had commented on and similar structures that I hadn't. Almost all of the modifications were more effectively expressed than in the original. It seemed highly unlikely that he would have been able to improve the text to the degree he did if I had merely highlighted the errors, and he certainly would not have learned any editorial skills had I reformulated his language for him.

One of the sentences the student was not at first able to self-edit was "It enhances the controlling and decision-making of general management." Using standard practices, I would either have had to "correct" this sentence myself or explain specific properties of the lexis (i.e., that *enhance* is a transitive verb tending to collocate with the noun *ability*). However, neither would have helped the student to acquire the means and confidence to self-edit in the future. Instead, I referred the student to JustTheWord, which informed him that *ability* is often *enhanced*. I was thus able to avoid taking time to reformulate his text explicitly, and to demonstrate how he could access such information himself in the future. The student's rewrite ("It enhances the controlling and decision-making abilities of general management") was still awkward. A little more exploration of the corpora might have shown him that a long participial noun clause is uncommon in comparison to a possessive *of* structure followed by infinitives (e.g., "It enhances the ability of general management to maintain control and to make decisions"). Clearly, these tools do not obviate the need for instruction in matters of style and general composition, but the student was able to take a step forward in his mastery of the language and his development as a writer.

The Mark My Words commenting toolbar allows a teacher to generate a summary of the comments on each assignment. Oxford (1990) suggests that such error logs help draw students' attention to recurrent problems. The log can act as a marking guide, or the teacher can turn off marks if they are felt to be a hindrance or distraction. The logs are uploaded to a database when the teacher returns the students' scripts and can be accessed by the student for reference in future assignments and by teachers to track the student's progress from one semester to another.

In trials of these programs by a dozen teachers and several hundred students, it has become apparent that some EFL teachers are not easily moved to adopt a computer-assisted commenting approach. Many teachers expect a computer-based approach to be capable of automatic error detection, believing that only in this way can the tedium of error correction be reduced. This expectation parallels the sometimes unrealistic desire of FL students for reliable error identification and correction.

Automatic error detection revisited

The examples of Chinese interlanguage errors already mentioned (and most others) are not flagged by current grammar-checking software, so students must rely on instruction and their own vigilance and motivation in the identification of potential error. As already suggested, it is difficult to build a reliable and comprehensive error-flagging mechanism for FL text. Many users implicitly trust these programs, regardless of the limitations in current natural language processing techniques, whereas others recognize the limitations but believe that they are simply the result of bad engineering (e.g., Krishnamurthy, 2005). Both attitudes exhibit a remarkable faith in the ability of technology to achieve near-complete sensitivity in flagging nonstandard usage, as well as near-perfect specificity in recognizing and *not* flagging standard usage. In reality, current grammar-checking software makes a trade-off between displaying false positives (flagging standard usage) and displaying false negatives (failing to flag nonstandard usage). In the case of the Microsoft Word grammar checker, greater recall (the attempt to flag all nonstandard language) has been suppressed for the sake of greater precision (the attempt not to flag acceptable standard usage). The result is that many nonstandard usages – errors – go unflagged by this program.

Among methods of automatic response that are being actively researched is the identification of nonstandard collocational patterns, independent of grammatical parsing (Gao, 2004). Another approach has been to augment probabilistic parsers with rules that account for observed interlanguage patterns. I have recently incorporated a simple, preliminary application of these techniques into Check My Words. A rule editor allows teachers to add and modify rules to flag a subset of common interlanguage errors by identifying nonstandard lexical patterns with the aid of a part-of-speech tagger (see Garside, 1996). One example of such a pattern is the Chinese interlanguage structure that blends noun and verb properties mentioned previously ("This will benefit to you"). This structure is not flagged by the Microsoft® Word grammar checker, and unfortunately the program cannot be readily tweaked to make it more sensitive to this type of pattern. The part-of-speech tagger component of Check My Words reliably identifies the word class of such polysyntactic words as *benefit*. The following rule flags this usage:

If *benefit*=verb and is followed by a preposition other than *from*, then flag it as suspicious.

When an error of this type is identified by the program, the student is alerted to a possible problem and directed to both a collocational resource, such as Word Neighbors or JustTheWord, depending on the context, and a grammar guide.

Constructing rules that reliably alert students to possible nonstandard usage in a text is time-consuming, but the rule editor has been designed so that rules added by collaborating teachers can be uploaded to a server and reused by other teachers. The result is an ongoing collaborative project to build a useful bank of error-flagging rules. This approach is not likely to provide the high recall in flagging nonstandard language expected by some users, but it may enable teachers to focus students' attention on a subset of recurrent sentence-level errors.

Teacher conferencing and student reflection on feedback

The type of computer-assisted feedback I describe here does not preclude, and indeed can assist, teacher conferencing. My own experience suggests that writing conferences are very productive when held after students have received and reviewed documents containing embedded comments linked to resources. Students also react well to a whole-class review of selected comments, which can be an opportunity for further instruction in exploring the advantages of various resources for developing writing skills.

As with the reflection and introspection that ideally accompanies a conference, teachers can encourage students to query anything they do not understand in their feedback. Providing relevant resources at appropriate points in the writing and revision process may further encourage such reflection. The error logs generated by Mark My Words are archived on the server and can be referred to in face-to-face or online conferences.

Peer response

This method of response need not be restricted to tagging sentence-level error: A potential danger in exclusively focusing on error is that both teacher and student may undervalue the dialogic nature of the writing process. Various studies (e.g., Mendonça & Johnson, 1994) claim that peer review improves the communicative aspects of learner texts. However, in EFL contexts, students need particular support and encouragement in overcoming reluctance to respond to each others' texts (Sengupta, 1998). I asked a class of third-year students to use the Mark My Words commenting tool to respond to an assignment each had written analyzing a business case study. They were asked to work in pairs and critique their partner's analysis by inserting comments relevant to the content and then linking their comments to online resources, which they had to locate themselves. Several of them found issue-related Web logs (blogs) that they passed on to their partners. Others located and linked to relevant online company prospectuses, and one student found and linked to the transcript of a related court case. In a brief discussion after this exercise, most of the students felt that the process of critiquing another student's analysis by referring to online resources was useful. These students, after receiving resource-rich comments from both their peers and their teacher, all said that they had learned more in this way than from previous feedback they had received.

Unresolved issues

To be successful, resource-assisted instruction and response must be integrated into the curriculum. Many students have difficulty using conventional dictionaries productively, and the effective use of the discovery-based resources described in this chapter makes even greater cognitive demands by requiring learners to generalize for themselves. Whether students are able to use this method effectively when composing and revising depends partly on the learning climate (e.g., affective factors, the quality of instruction, the communicative opportunities available, and their readers' expectations). It especially requires that students be taught how and when to use the resources (e.g., when a text-retrieval engine is more useful than a bilingual dictionary) and that students be held responsible for using available resources.

Thus far, Mark My Words has been used by about a dozen teachers over a two-year period to give feedback on about 1,000 assignments. Surveys of the teachers suggest that the rate of successful follow-up revisions by students, based on the explanatory comments and the linked resources, is high. The teachers observed rates of student revision similar to situations in which students were given overt corrections and explicit advice. This observation is promising, because Hong Kong students usually want comprehensive reformulation of their errors and are resistant to feedback that requires them to use paper dictionaries or to rephrase without explicit advice. When asked to do so, they make few appropriate corrections (Chen, 1999).

The program has evolved considerably, based on suggestions from the teachers who have used it. However, there are a number of obstacles to its universal adoption. Although computers and broadband Internet connections are ubiquitous in schools and at teachers' and students' homes in Hong Kong, many teachers appear resistant to respond to students' electronic documents online, or even to encourage students in using the Check My Words toolbar to edit their writing. Their reluctance seems partly a matter of habit (e.g., preferring to handle paper, discomfort at reading online, unease at introducing a new methodology into a heavy schedule), as well as skepticism about adopting a discovery-based approach to instruction and feedback. A more persuasive case needs to be made for the underlying philosophy, as some teachers see no advantage in pointing students to resources over the expediency of correcting on paper or just circling and underlining errors. Some of those who have tried the program briefly used it mainly to reformulate students' errors, rather than to point the students to online resources, perhaps because of unfamiliarity with the resources. I have compiled context-sensitive help files, self-running tutorials, and quizzes to introduce the tools and resources, but it may require a critical mass of users, especially students, before many teachers see the benefit of the approach.

Another methodological issue that makes the programs a hard sell is that writing in Hong Kong schools and universities tends to focus on product, which is at odds with a discovery- and process-based approach. Many students and teachers resent the idea of reviewing recursive drafts of the same assignment: The goal of maximum efficiency and swift reward is sometimes taken as a cultural trait of Hong Kong. Still another obstacle is that, although most teachers in local secondary schools are compelled to give copious form-focused feedback, many tertiary teachers of EFL have abandoned the practice, reasoning that if years of such feedback have had little effect, there is no point in giving more.

One teacher objected that he would not encourage his students to use a tool that made it easy to browse the Internet, since this would increase the incidence of plagiarism. But, if we are to encourage a constructivist learner-centered approach (i.e., one that allows learners to construct, interpret, and modify language through investigation, reflection, and analysis), then we must allow learners to appropriate from many sources – and what better mechanism for doing so than the Web? The danger of plagiarism does not necessarily increase with the number of sources, and in any event, Mark My Words makes it possible for the teacher to check suspicious text easily. We need to make it possible for learners to appropriate language to their own ends by, for example, providing them with the language that makes this kind of appropriation productive (e.g., "*This is what X means when she says*..."). We also need to teach them how to do it.

The ultimate test of this feedback method is whether it extends learning opportunities and it affects students' subsequent drafts. Will students become better writers when they have easy access to relevant resources, are taught how to use them, and are guided when they go wrong? It may take some time to test this, but one way I hope to enhance the companion programs is to provide "automatic" reminders to students during the writing process of comments on their previously submitted work. Ideally, comments made by peers and teachers across the curriculum and over a period of time will be available to the student, along with an automatically generated lexical profile of his or her writing over the same period. We might reasonably expect such information to increase learner sensitivity to input and encourage reflection. Bull (2004) cites evidence that providing learners with such an evolving model of their performance increases the use they make of feedback in subsequent drafts.

Conclusion

This chapter has described a method for giving students access to online resources while they write and for assisting teachers to provide resource-rich feedback on lexico-grammatical error and other developmental aspects of learner text. Teachers can make language or discipline-specific resources dynamically available to students while they are composing or revising. Such an approach can help put feedback in the context of instruction when the same resources are integrated into teaching materials. It is based on the premise that learners can acquire more language by being given the means, and the responsibility, for reformulating their own developing interlanguage, rather than by just being told how to do it in theory or by having a teacher do it for them.

These programs are not intended to take precedence over face-to-face interaction and make no attempt to replace the teacher or the students' peers as sympathetic readers. I have focused on feedback to sentence-level error in this chapter because this is perhaps the most problematic aspect of response to the writing of FL students. However, the need of these students for error correction does not diminish our responsibility for responding to their ideas.

Early advocates of computer-generated feedback made what are in hindsight naïve projections of the imminent liberation of writing teachers from the slavery of proofreading student papers:

Teachers of writing may soon rely on computers to help in the mind-numbing task of editing and evaluating student essays, and teachers of the future, perhaps in four or five years, may expect programs that will, almost entirely, free them from editing so that they can focus on those matters of greater moment – organization, logic, ideas. (Smith & Kiefer, 1982)

It may be a long time before computers can embody human judgment reliably enough to edit and evaluate learner language. However, I hope to have shown that we can build tools and provide resources to guide learners through the difficult processes of language acquisition and composition and thereby make them more independent learners and at the same time relieve teachers of the need to carry the burden of reformulating students' texts.

Acknowledgments

I gratefully acknowledge funding support from the Hong Kong University of Science and Technology's Center for Enhanced Learning and Teaching and the Office of the Vice-President for Academic Affairs. I am also indebted to staff from those organizations, as well as to staff from its College of LifeLong Learning and Language Centre, who have helped to evaluate and otherwise supported the development described in this chapter.

References

Bakhtin, M. M. (1981). *The dialogical imagination*. C. Emerson and M. Holquist. (Trans.), M. Holquist (Ed.). Austin: University of Texas Press.

Brannon L., & Knoblauch, C. (1982). On students' rights to their own texts: A model of teacher response. *College Composition and Communication, 33*, 157–166.

Bull, S. (2004). Supporting learning with open learner models. *Proceedings of the 4th Hellenic Conference with International Participation: Information and Communication Technologies in Education*. Athens, Greece. 47–61. Available online at www.eee.bham.ac.uk/bull/papers-pdf/ICTE04.pdf.

Chapelle, C. (2001). *Computer applications in second language acquisition: Foundations for teaching, testing, and research*. Cambridge, UK: Cambridge University Press.

Chen, J. (1999). Effective feedback on student writing. Talk given at the Action Learning Project Conference on English Language Teaching, City University of Hong Kong.

Cogie, J., Strain, K., & Lorinskas, S. (1999). Avoiding the proofreading trap: The value of the error correction process. *The Writing Center Journal, 19(2)*, 7–32.

Cohen A. D., & Cavalcanti, M. C. (1990). Feedback on compositions: Teacher and student verbal reports. In B. Krall (Ed.), *Second language writing: Research insights for the classroom* (pp. 155–177). Cambridge, UK: Cambridge University Press.

Doughty, C., & Varela, E. (1998). Communicative focus on form. In C. Doughty, & J. Williams (Eds.), *Focus on form in classroom second language acquisition* (pp. 114–138). New York: Cambridge University Press.

Ellis, R. (2002). The place of grammar instruction in the second/foreign language curriculum. In S. Fotos & E. Hinkel (Eds.), *New perspectives on grammar teaching in second language classrooms* (pp. 17–34). Mahwah, NJ: Lawrence Erlbaum.

Fathman, A. K., & Whalley, E. (1990). Teacher response to student writing: Focus on form versus content. In B. Kroll (Ed.), *Second language writing* (pp. 178–185). Cambridge, UK: Cambridge University Press.

Ferris, D. R. (2002). *Treatment of error in second-language student writing*. Ann Arbor, MI: The University of Michigan Press.

Ferris, D. R. (2003). *Response to student writing: Implications for second language students*. Mahwah, NJ: Lawrence Erlbaum.

Gao, J. (2004). The English writing wizard. Talk delivered at the Hong Kong University of Science and Technology, November 15.

Garside, R. (1996). The robust tagging of unrestricted text: The BNC experience. In J. Thomas and M. Short (Eds.), *Using corpora for language research: Studies in the honour of Geoffrey Leech* (pp. 167–180). London: Longman.

Haswell, R. H. 1983 Minimal marking. *College English, 45*, 166–70.

Hearst, M. A. (2000). The debate on automated essay grading. *Intelligent Systems, 15(5)*, 22–37.

Hyland, F., & Hyland, K. (2001). Sugaring the pill: Praise and criticism in written feedback. *Journal of Second Language Writing, 10(3)*, 185–212.

Joyce, B. & Weil, M. (2000). *Models of teaching*. Upper Saddle River, NJ: Prentice-Hall.

Krashen, S. (1982). *Principles and practice in second language acquisition*. Oxford: Pergamon.

Krishnamurthy, S. (2005). A demonstration of the futility of using Microsoft Word's spelling and grammar check. faculty.washington.edu/sandeep/check/. Retrieved September 4, 2005.

Leki, I. (1990). Coaching from the margins: Issues in written response. In B. Kroll (Ed.), *Second language writing* (pp. 57–68). Cambridge, UK: Cambridge University Press.

McGee, T., & Ericsson, P. (2002). The politics of the program: MS Word as the invisible grammarian. *Computers and Composition, 19*, 453–470.

Mendonça, C., & Johnson, K. (1994). Peer review negotiations: Revision activities in ESL writing instruction. *TESOL Quarterly, 28*, 745–769.

Milton, J. (1999). Lexical thickets and electronic gateways: Making text accessible by novice writers. In C. Candlin & K. Hyland (Eds.), *Writing: Texts, Processes & Practices* (pp. 221–243). Harlow, UK: Longman.

Milton, J. (2001). *Elements of a written interlanguage: A computational and corpus-based study of institutional influences on the acquisition of English by Hong Kong Chinese students*. Research Reports, Vol. 2, Hong Kong: Hong Kong University of Science and Technology.

Milton, J. (2004). From parrots to puppet masters: Fostering creative and authentic language use with online tools. In B. Holmberg, M. Shelly, & C. White (Eds.), *Distance education and language: Evolution and change* (pp. 242–257). Clevedon, UK: Multilingual Matters.

Oxford, R. L. (1990). *Language learning strategies: What every teacher should know*. Boston: Heinle and Heinle.

Pienemann, M. (1998). *Language processing and second language development: Processability theory*. Amsterdam: John Benjamins.

Pennington, M. C. (1992). Beyond off-the-shelf computer remedies for student writers: Alternatives to canned feedback. *System, 20(4)*, 423–447.

Reid, J. (1994). Responding to ESL students' texts: The myth of appropriation. *TESOL Quarterly, 28*, 273–292.

Robb, T. (1997). The paperless classroom? *TESL-EJ, 3(1)*. www.kyoto-su.ac.jp/information/tesl-ej/ej09/int.html. Retrieved on September 20, 2004.

Schneider, D., & McCoy, K. F. (1998). Recognizing syntactic errors in the writing of second language learners. *Proceedings of the 36th Conference on Association for Computational Linguistics, Vol. 2*. Montreal, Quebec.

Sengupta, S. (1998). Peer evaluation: I am not the teacher. *ELT Journal, 52*, 19–28.

Smith, C., & Kiefer, K. (1982). Writer's workbench: Computers and writing instruction. In *Proceedings of the Future of Literacy Conference*. Baltimore, MD: University of Maryland.

Straub, R. (1996). The concept of control in teacher response: Defining the varieties of directive and facilitative commentary. *College Composition and Communication, 47(2)*, 223–251.

Straub, R. (1997). Students' reactions to teacher comments: An exploratory study. *Research in the Teaching of English, 31*, 91–119.

Trahey, M., & White, L. (1993). Positive evidence and preemption in the L2 classroom. *Studies in Second Language Acquisition, 15*, 181–204.

Truscott, J. (1996). The case against grammar correction in L2 writing classes. *Language Learning, 46(2)*, 327–369.

Tsui, A. B. M. (1996). Learning how to teach ESL writing. In D. Freeman & J. C. Richards (Eds.), *Teacher learning and language teaching* (pp. 97–119). Cambridge Language Teaching Library. Cambridge: Cambridge University Press.

Valenti, S., Neri, F., & Cucchiarelli, A. (2003). An overview of current research on automated essay grading. *Journal of Information Technology Education, 2*, 319–330.

Whitelock, P. (2004). Personal e-mail communication, September 2.

Yip, V. (1995). *Interlanguage and learnability: From Chinese to English*. Amsterdam & Philadelphia: Benjamins.

8 Feedback in portfolio-based writing courses

Liz Hamp-Lyons

Process approaches to the teaching and learning of writing remain popular and convincing. At the same time, portfolios are becoming an accepted tool for demonstrating abilities and performances in key skill areas; portfolio-based assessment of writing is one of the most researched forms of alternative assessment and is now accepted in many different teaching contexts. Writing courses that use a portfolio-based approach to assessment appear to provide a fertile environment in which teachers and learners can engage in feedback on writing and thus mesh well with process approaches.

However, concerns have been raised that a portfolio-based writing course puts assessment at the top of the agenda and therefore colors feedback exchanges with the awareness that this text will be formally assessed (Roehmer et al., 1991). This chapter looks at the effects of a methodology for the teaching and learning of writing that values process approaches, specifically feedback and revision, and that also incorporates assessment by portfolio. By focusing on one case study, I try to understand whether multiple drafting, stimulated by a feedback-privileging teaching and learning environment, results in work that is judged to be better post-revision; and I ask whether teacher-judges working in a portfolio-based assessment at the end of a course oriented to process writing recognize and reward the student's multiple revisions stimulated by the feedback.

Portfolios for assessment and beyond

Portfolio assessment is the best-known and now most popular form of alternative writing assessment (Belanoff & Dickson, 1991; Hamp-Lyons, & Condon, 2000; Yancey & Weiser, 1997). A portfolio is a collection of the writer's work over a period of time, usually a semester or school year. The writer, perhaps aided by classmates or the teacher, makes a selection from the collected work through a process of reflection on what she or he has done and what it shows about what has been learned. These three elements – collection, selection, and reflection – are the core of a portfolio. Typically, a student's portfolio will include some elements of the processes the learner went through to arrive at a final text. These process elements become visible and can be evaluated in a portfolio assessment. However, early portfolio assessment programs did not recognize that the requirements of good assessment practice apply to performance assessments also, and a number of studies uncovered problems with portfolio assessments in practice (Callahan, 1995; Despain & Hilgers, 1992; Hamp-Lyons & Condon, 1993; Hamp-Lyons, 1996). Others proposed means of remedying or reconciling the difficulties (Calfee & Perfumo, 1996; Elbow & Belanoff, 1997; Herman et al., 1996).

However, all commentators on portfolio assessment agree that it is an excellent form of professional development activity for teachers. Smith and Murphy (1992) make this point strongly in the case of school-level staff development programs within the United States. In Hong Kong, in a professional development program on portfolios, working with mainly nonnative writing teachers and focusing on college preparatory and college freshman EFL students, I (Hamp-Lyons, 1999) found the same benefits and the same enthusiasm. Perhaps the most interesting area of professional development in working with portfolios is helping teachers learn to give feedback on writing.

The opportunities for feedback are greatly expanded in teaching with portfolios. First, there is the opportunity for several drafts of each piece of writing – the *process writing* approach that is so fruitful for feedback – enhanced by the possibility of revisiting and revising the paper further during the semester. Second, there is the *cyclical learning* process that is available to students when they work to build a portfolio that represents a semester or year of work and progress. And third, there is the opportunity, in some portfolio programs, for *accessible evidence*, that is, for evidence of these dual processes to be made visible to teachers, as judges in a formal portfolio evaluation.

There is now a large literature on the use of portfolios in first language writing. There is far less literature about the use of portfolios for second language users in either teaching and learning or assessment (although work has been done by Freeman & Freeman, 1992; Pierce & O'Malley, 1992; and Song & August, 2002). In earlier work (Condon & Hamp-Lyons, 1991) I argued strongly for the benefits of portfolio assessment with second language learners, but as I have carried out empirical studies over the years I have come to understand that this is a complex educational question with no simple answer.

Although portfolio-based writing assessment can be used with any of the theories and models of writing instruction (Hamp-Lyons & Condon, 2000), the greatest strength and power of portfolios in teaching and learning comes when the potential for a focus on process is capitalized on in learners' development of their portfolios (Roehmer et al.,

1991). The writing and the collection of a portfolio must be done over time, and with developing writers time and practice mean change. It is not then surprising that portfolios are most usually (and happily) found in process writing classrooms; the development of a portfolio, over time, allows students to revise papers based on feedback and incorporate the final draft or a sequence of drafts in the portfolio. Further, feedback in various forms is an essential part of the learning opportunity of each student, and when portfolio-based writing assessment is combined with a process approach to writing instruction, windows of possibility are opened for teachers (and portfolio judges) to look closely into students' portfolios and learn about the effectiveness of those learning opportunities.

Effectiveness, effect, and affect of feedback

The most fundamental things that we do not know about feedback are how effective it is and how circumstances and conditions affect it. We always hope that in process writing classes there will be plenty of feedback, that much of it will focus on areas other than error, and that the feedback will be effective in helping learners to improve their writing. We have an expectation that the process writing teacher will look at *all* dimensions of students' learning and writing during the span of a semester. However, studies in many contexts – I am most familiar with the United States and Hong Kong – have shown that the concept of process writing often becomes sadly distorted and diluted when inadequately introduced to teachers in training and when used in hostile educational environments. In encouraging the introduction of portfolios as a teaching tool in a variety of teaching and learning contexts around the world, we aim to seed ground that will become fertile for positive educational practices such as process writing and its components, especially formative feedback. We hope that the incorporation of humanistic handling of feedback opportunities will bring about better and closer relationships between the teacher and each learner, and between learners – that the "affect" in the classroom will be positively affected.

The other side of this coin is assessment. We hope that by assessing writing in portfolios, instead of through one or more snapshot essays written in 50 or even 30 minutes, we will allow learners to show what they can do and have done and allow teachers to reward a wider range of writing-related elements and performances. With portfolios though, things get complicated. Although teachers may be happy to have each student collect all work into a writing folder, this practice does not work as an assessment. Although assessment portfolios *do* look at multiple texts, the amount of text that teachers can read and assess is necessarily limited. Teachers therefore ask students to *select* from their writing for the assessment portfolio. A number of issues immediately arise. Can students make good choices about which pieces of their writing to select? Should the teacher help or advise the students about which writing would be best placed into an assessment portfolio? Should *all* the writing around one final text be included in the portfolio, including all (written) feedback whether positive or negative? We hope that effective feedback and positive affect will lead to portfolios that in formal assessment can reveal to teachers and judges the best qualities of each writer.

In the final analysis, portfolios, like snapshot essays, are *evidence*. Therefore, the second focus of this chapter concerns whether evidence of the feedback the student has received, and how it has been used, should be included in the assessment portfolio. If so, should it be assessed in its own right? How? For many classroom teachers, the answers come down to two things: (1) the value the individual teacher places on the feedback components of the course and (2) the teacher's sense of whether the feedback evidence will help or harm the student's assessment result. Answers to the second concern will probably vary student by student, so the decision needs to be a programmatic one. I cannot claim that this chapter will provide an answer; my intention is to use a single case study drawn from a much larger study to clarify some of these questions and concerns and to investigate some of the hopes in detail.

Background to the study

A portfolio-based writing course

The data I use in this chapter are drawn from a larger study of the relationships between student learning and assessment of student writing in a portfolio-based composition course in the United States. I focus only on those aspects of the data that illuminate questions about the interactions between the incorporation of frequent and varied feedback opportunities and the conscious positioning of the student's work toward fairly formal assessment in a portfolio. In the study as a whole, I looked at two composition classes in a U.S. university; the classes were the first level of the mainstream college composition program that is almost universal in U.S. tertiary education. As is frequently the case, many students in this lowest level course were foreign students or recent immigrants whose first language is not English. As is also frequently – even usually – the case, their instructors are not trained in teaching to the particular needs of nonnative users of English.

I followed two such classes for a full semester (14 weeks), attending more than half the class meetings and most extra activities, such as teacher-initiated group meetings. In each of the classes, I focused on the students and their learning and coping strategies, but because I was also a senior staff member overseeing the teachers, I was able to closely observe the teachers as well. I collected all the writing from six students in each class and spent some time working with each of them during class time (classes were often run in workshop mode) to understand them as learners and to get closer to their feedback behavior and the reasons for the ways they responded to feedback.

The empirical data

In the following discussion, I focus on a single nonnative English speaker. Research into writing assessment involves large data sets; once one moves beyond relatively uninteresting, uninformative scores into learner and teacher response, the data quickly become unruly. This is very much more the case in looking at empirical data from portfolios! I observed the student, Esing, and her class for a semester, attending more than half the classes and all the extra sessions Esing was involved in. I collected all the writing she printed out, more than 100 pages. I spoke to Esing individually in or after class on almost all those occasions and discussed her with her teacher on four occasions. I attended the final formal evaluation where her work was judged by a second teacher in the program and then discussed for a final decision by the team teaching that particular course. Data collection was primarily in the forms of field notes on class observations and teacher-student meetings; recording equipment would have been intrusive and intimidating in the class, altered the tone of the one-to-one meetings between teacher and student, and constrained the student when talking to me in my dual role of researcher and insider to the composition community.

At the time of this data collection, Esing was a first-year undergraduate in the United States, newly arrived from Taiwan for the purpose of getting a degree. Esing's English standard was typical of Taiwan high school graduates – in the region of 5.5 IELTS[1], a little lower for writing. Like almost all second language users of English entering U.S. colleges, Esing was placed into the lowest level of freshman composition. The course was pre-freshman composition, sometimes unkindly referred to as "remedial comp." The course was not restricted to L2 writers but was designed for any learner who placed at that level on an in-class essay test during the first class period (two hours). In fact, this course usually caught in its net almost all nonnative writers, as well as many second-generation immigrants from homes where another language was used.

The data from Esing's case raise and illustrate many of the principal issues of the intersection between feedback and portfolio assessment, allowing us to address some important points of both practice and theory. In what follows I show how Esing used feedback as she had been

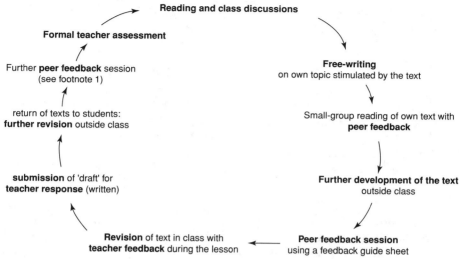

Figure 8.1. Teaching cycle

taught and encouraged to do by her instructor to revise her writing for improvement over a whole semester. Esing did between five and nine revisions of each of her essays, most following some form of feedback. Text analysis of each version has shown me what changes she made and what feedback she received if the feedback was written. In addition, I noted some parts of the oral feedback.

At the institution where Esing was studying, students in the lowest level course prepare a portfolio of their writing that includes evidence of the processes by which each completed text was created and the kinds of feedback that the writer received along the way. The use of portfolios in a class opens the way for a wide range of feedback types and for differing participation types in giving and receiving feedback. Many of these were found in the course, but I will confine myself to those that arise in the discussion of the case study from which these data have been taken. The teaching cycle looked like the model in Figure 8.1. When the cycle was completed, it began again with a new topic area and possibly a new genre.

Esing's participation

Esing started the course with a very enthusiastic, serious, positive attitude. She went willingly into the feedback groups that were a regular feature of each class period, and she was always prepared with a draft or

> *"Esing why don't you just give it a try?" a voice from my heart asked.*
> *"I can't." I answered.*
> *"Why?"*
> *"How, then. . . . ?"*
>   *It always ended as a BLANK. This kind of dialogue had been performed inside of myself millions of times. Maybe we could be friends first, but how should I do? And what would gonna happen if I did? Scary, anger, worries, struggle were filled in my mind, and so did grant disappointment of myself.*

Figure 8.2.   First draft (Portfolio pp. 36–37)

a revision to share with her peers. After each peer feedback session, she revised her writing, based (she believed) on the input she had received. She paid careful attention to the teacher's verbal feedback during the class times when students composed or revised on the computer and the teacher went around the room. In speaking to Esing at the end of class as I often did, I learned that whenever opportunities were offered for people to go to the teacher for additional feedback, Esing took the opportunity. She also submitted some of these further drafts for written feedback from the teacher, which she received. All Esing's behavior, then, suggested that she was a very motivated learner.

The first and second drafts

At the end of the third week of the 14-week course, when she handed in her first writing sequence (which, confusingly, was also called a "portfolio," with the final portfolio called the "show portfolio"), Esing already had several drafts of her essay, "Promise." She continued to work on this essay throughout the semester, ultimately producing seven versions. Esing willingly gave me copies of her work at each stage, as well as a copy of her final portfolio.

Esing's first draft of "Promise" (originally titled "Andy") contained the closing text shown in Figure 8.2[2]:

The peer group discussion on Esing's first draft was appreciative and encouraging, focusing on wanting more detail and wanting to know what happened next. In her second draft Esing responded to this feedback, adding two paragraphs, one of them quite substantial, and picking up on the romantic interest she had perceived in her peer group members. Figure 8.3 shows the same paragraph as Figure 8.2, together with the added material. (The title has been changed to "Promise.") Figure 8.3

also suggests that Esing added some handwritten ideas just before sharing her second draft with her peer group. Comparing the first and second drafts, we can clearly see that Esing has worked hard on the content and detail in her essay.

A look at the third and fourth drafts

Esing received verbal and written feedback from her classmates on the second draft (Figure 8.3) and as a result she developed her essay further, as shown in Figure 8.4. Esing received further feedback from each member of her peer group on this draft, her third. In accordance with what was happening in the instructional cycle at that time, this was in written form, and classmates used a peer feedback sheet prepared and provided by the teacher. Appendix 1 is an example of the peer feedback sheet.

Esing also received more feedback from the teacher on this draft than on any other. The teacher gave her very detailed feedback, much of it grammar-focused and direct rather than indirect. The feedback did not include any evaluative comments at all: If she gave these, it was verbally as she moved around the classroom. As Ferris (2002) suggests, given feedback like this Esing had only to transfer the teacher's corrections directly into her next draft to eliminate a significant proportion of the errors. Esing could then have stopped working on this paper; the class instruction and use of class time had moved on to another writing cycle. However, Esing was motivated by the input she had received from teacher and peers on her third draft and captivated by the new notion that a text is dynamic and always open to change (and, she may have hoped, improvement). Esing volunteered another revision, her fourth draft. After she gave her teacher this draft, the teacher asked her, as an alternate form of feedback, to write an explanation of what she was doing in each paragraph and add it into her text, which she did. The teacher then added notes of her own to the essay. An example is shown in Figure 8.5.

It is only with the help of the detailed text analysis, indicated by the highlighting, that we can see the thought and work Esing must have put into this fourth draft, as she had done to all the previous drafts. Esing had had input from her peer group both in a workshop-style group feedback session and in the form of response sheets into which they had written comments, and it was this feedback that encouraged her to add the explanations about cities XX and YY being far apart and the pressures of the Taiwanese exam system. However, her teacher did not, it seems, see the positive side – the purposefulness – of these additions. Nor did she comment on the gradual improvements in punctuation Esing was

"Esing, why don't you just give it a try?" a voice from my heart asked.

"I can't." I answered.

"Why?"

"How, then . . . . ?"

"hun . . . ."

It always ended as a BLANK. This kind of dialogue had been performed inside of myself millions of times. Maybe we could be friends first, but how should I do? And what would ~~gonna~~ happen if I
γ ^Why he couldn't do a something besides look at me? did? Scary, anger, worries, struggle were filled in my mind, and so did grant disappointment of myself.

Aug 28 1992, the day right before the ~~our~~ departure day leaving for Taiwan, also the Chinese Valentine's Day, ~~We~~ ^we held a farewell party in the auditorium of the language school. He went up to the stage and held the ^microphone.

Kevin, a friend of Andy, was playing the guitar next to him. The foreword music was soft and tender, but when he started to sin g, his funny accent ~~which~~ made people want to laugh, including me. (to tell the truth) But I could tell he was serious and sincere about this song. I didn't exactly hear what was the words were, except: "wherever you go, whatever you do, I will be right here waiting for you. . . ." Which put me in a . Still, I could notice that every one below the stage was trying not to laugh. My heart moved, but also embarrassed. He didn't give me much time to prepare or tell me what exactually his thought ~~in person~~, and this song just gave me more confusion.

I went home by the execuse of headache. ~~I was regretted after I came home for not telling Andy what I felt.~~ Again, I ran away. Now two years after that, I am 18 and he is 22. During those two years we have never seen each other ~~ever since~~. However, this promise has become one sweetest thing of my 16-year-old memory box ~~every offered well this~~. Every time when I heard this song, it reminds me of him and this ambivalent promise. T ~~I wanna say Thank You for~~ used to love me.
        To me, it really doesn't
the promise will come true or not
    wish   can find   just
I even ~~hoping~~ he ~~found~~ someone ~~who~~ right for him.
and I am T thankful for he
        very

Figure 8.3.   Second draft (Portfolio pp. 39–40)

"Esing, why don't you just give it a try?" a voice from my heart asked.
"I can't." I answered.
"Why?"
"How, then....?"
"hun............"
It always ended as a BLANK. This kind of dialogue had been performed inside of myself millions of times. Maybe we could be friends first, but how should I do? And what would happen if I did?**I was still in high school, and he was in college, so we couldn't be together back in Taiwan, anyway. Besides, we lived quite far away, and I knew a long-distance relationship doesn't work. The most important thing: I even didn't know him well enough even as a friend.** Scary, anger, worries, struggle were filled in my mind, and so did grant disappointment of myself.

Aug 28 1992, the day right before the our departure day leaving for Taiwan, also the Chinese Valentine's Day. ~~We held~~ a farewell party in the auditorium of the language school. The students were voluntary for performing the show, and all the students and their host families were invited. He went up to the stage and held the microphone. Kevin, a friend of Andy, started to play the guitar next to him. The foreword music was soft and tender, but when he started to sing, his funny accent ~~which~~ made people want to laugh, including me (to tell the truth) But I could tell he was serious and sincere about this song. I didn't exactly hear what was the words were, except: "wherever you go, whatever you do, I will be right here waiting for you....". ***. Still, I could notice that every one below the stage was trying not to laugh. My heart moved, but also embarrassed. He didn't give me much time to prepare or tell me what exactually his thought <u>in person,</u>and this song just gave me more confusion.

I went home by the execuse of headache. Again, I ran away

Now two years after that, I am 18 and he is 22. During those two years we have never seen each other. *** However, this promise has become one sweetest thing of my 6-year-old memory box. —Every time when I heard this song, it reminds me of him and this ambivalent promise **—which, of course, has not been proved yet,and probably won't have a chance in the future, either. I have decided** to **let this perfect thought stays there forever as long as I live.**

Key to draft markings
Italic: Material from second draft (figure 8.3)
Bold: Material added
Shadow: Change confirmed from draft 2
Plain text: New change
∗∗∗ New deletion
Underline: Change made on draft 2, representing a return to earlier version

Figure 8.4.   *Esing's third draft (Portfolio pp. 26–27)*

> *It always ended as a BLANK. This kind of dialogue had been performed inside of me millions of times. Maybe Andy and I could be friends first, but how should I let him know this? And what would happen if I did? I was still in high school* **in XX, (high school is an important step for entrance to colleges, because we have College Entrance Exam to decided),** *and he was in college* **in YY (those two cities are far away), either the personal or the environmental reasons** *didn't allow us to be together, anyway. The most important thing: I even didn't know him well enough even as a friend. Fear, anger, worries, struggle* ********filled in my mind, and so did great disappointment with myself* **that I wouldn't do such a small thing – talk to him.**
>
> Esing: I started to think the difficulties in the future which I guess I
>   tried to convince another part of me to give it up. [Explanation of
>   changes in preceding paragraph]
> Teacher: I don't think you need the parenthetical explanations. This
>   sentence confused me

Figure 8.5.   Example of Esing's explanation and teacher's response (Portfolio pp. 33–34)

making, nor the appearance at last of an articulation of a specific regret that Esing felt when she relived this romantic high point of her life.

Esing's continuing work

My in-class observations showed that Esing made two more drafts, using the last part of each computer lab lesson – when students had control of their own time – before she completed and submitted her seventh version as the final one. I have numbered these as drafts because they were versions that Esing submitted to the teacher. In fact, she made at least some small changes to this paper during every computer lab class (one per week) through the semester. Esing did not get any peer feedback on these later drafts, and as the semester progressed she became less willing to take an active part in peer group-work on the papers that came along later in the course. Instead, by her choice, she spent all the time she could working alone at the computer.

However, as she continued to work on "Promise," Esing proved unable to identify problems in her writing, whether at the grammatical, mechanical, organizational, or ideational levels. Even when problems

> Now two years after that, I am 18 and he is 22. During those two years we have never seen each other. **Maybe both of us were hiding from each other, even though I truly was thinking about him all the time.** However, this promise has become one sweetest event in my 16-year-old's memory box. Every time when I hear this song, it reminds me of him and this *** promise which, of course, has not been fulfilled yet, and probably won't have a chance in the future, either. I have decided to let this beautiful thought stay there forever as long as I live.

Figure 8.6. Esing's final paper (Portfolio, p. 24)

were pointed out and discussed with her in some detail, she seemed to lack the capacity to implement the kinds of changes suggested by the feedback, that is, to self-correct. Esing received some verbal feedback from her class teacher on each successive version, as she circulated in the lab classroom, although the teacher's feedback became less detailed, and the teacher told me that she felt the paper should have been set aside after the third version so that Esing could focus on her other writing.

A typical exchange went something like the following (from my observation notes):

T: So you're working on this one again?
E: Yeah.
T: OK... (reading over her shoulder)... (pointing) the tense is not right there – you want a perfect form
E: OK (teacher moves on; Esing pauses, then continues what she was doing)

During the second half of the semester, Esing also went once to the Writing Center for guidance with "Promise" but came away disheartened by the weight of the errors that were pointed out to her. Esing's final version showed few differences from the fourth draft, but the final paragraph had some small but (to Esing) important changes, as shown in Figure 8.6.

My notes from my interview with Esing after she completed her final paper indicate that she remained unaware that she was in a negative loop: Her writing was not improving, and the feedback she was getting was increasingly unhelpful.

L: ...so, do you think your paper is better now than when (T) last saw it?
E: Yes, I'm sure.
L: In what way?
E: I feel happy now about the conclusion. I tried to make it seem a bit stronger but not to write too many words.
L: Why did you want to work on the end?

E: [Teacher] told me she have a feeling about my story, if he came back or I
went or what happened.
L: And do you think that now it will be clearer for her?
E: I think.
L: What about the language; what did she tell you?
E: She didn't tell me much.... only... some parts weren't clear.
L: I think I remember she told you that before...?
E: yeah... yes
L: Well?
E: Mmm... I changed some words... not much... er...
L: Did you want to ask (her) some questions, when you were doing it this
last time?
E: (pause)...not really... it's my thing to clear it

Our detailed look at just one paper by one writer gives us a close look
at a problem that is by no means unique to her but that in my experience is a relatively common pattern for L2 writers: experiencing a
feedback-rich writing environment in which teachers themselves may be
less than fully skilled in the use of feedback as an instructional tool.
My research has shown this to be a particular problem when using
portfolio-based assessment in process-based, feedback-rich writing classrooms. Like many other nonnative writers, Esing seemed to have internalized a view of all feedback as leading compulsorily to revision. At
first embracing feedback, she became trapped by and in it and ended
by avoiding it. She was not taught, and did not acquire, any strategies
for making decisions about whether to use feedback or which feedback
to use.

Esing's portfolio and judgments about it

Although the portfolio instructions specified that students need put
only two of their formal papers into their portfolios, Esing put at
least one version of each essay into her portfolio and all versions of
"Promise." The final portfolio was 40 pages long; by comparison,
most portfolios are between 15 and 22 pages long. She also, curiously,
put the various drafts of the Promise paper not in their chronolog-
ical order but in the following order: final, third draft, sixth draft,
fourth draft, fifth draft, peer response, first draft, second draft. This
made for a puzzling and unrewarding reading experience – and for
19 pages of text. Unfortunately, I had not predicted that I would
need to observe readers actually reading the portfolios and so did not
observe teachers reading portfolios for judgment purposes in real time.
I could only depend on the comments they made and the ways they
flipped through pages during the face-to-face discussion of a particular
portfolio.

In this program, each portfolio was judged by the class teacher and by a second rater, the teacher of another class in the program. Teachers then met in teams of three or four, composed of teachers who had read the same subsets of portfolios, and the assessments were discussed and, where needed, adjusted for closer agreement. Esing's portfolio received a B- from her class teacher, and a C+ from the second reader. This gap of one score-step between class teacher and outside reader is normal in portfolio assessment and has been documented (e.g., Hamp-Lyons & Condon, 1993).

Appendix 2, which shows Esing's self-reflective letter written following the guidelines given to all students, also shows the second reader's memo to her (really, just a few comments at the foot of the page) with the grade this reader gave. (Writing such memos was the normal practice in this program.) Students had the final class session of the semester – 50 minutes long – to compose this letter on the computer, but they had known that it was required since the first day of the course and had in various ways prepared themselves for the task.

As we can see in Appendix 2, the outside reader was puzzled by "Promise," and I think we are not surprised; the reader may even have been unaware of the actual sequence in which drafts had been composed, since the order was shown only on the contents page but not at the top of each draft. We should also remember that most of the feedback was given in peer group discussion or in class orally with the teacher and was therefore not visible in the portfolio. For any reader to be able to extricate the changes made by Esing, as I have done for some parts of some of the drafts in this chapter, and to relate those to feedback she may have received, would take much more time and attention than we can expect in this (and most other) contexts. Reading the "Promise" drafts as presented gives the portfolio judge no sense of improvement overall and no opportunity to see specific changes such as the enrichment of content or the gradual move toward correct formatting of punctuation. The concept of evidence of response to feedback, then, becomes a very problematic one in practice. But another of Esing's essays, "Windmill," was rather better laid out and rather more obviously revised from one draft to the next; yet the second reader seems not to be particularly aware or appreciative of the significant changes in this paper either. This reader summarizes her response to the whole portfolio with a comment about "adhering to the assignment(s)" and "language problems," which once we are sensitive to Esing's struggle to compose a paper that truly captured her real memory and feelings seems a disappointingly trivial response.

Looking again at the self-reflective letter in Appendix 2, I think we see that it is itself a source for the reader's comments about both language problems and lack of clarity. In the portfolio literature, this genre of public reflection has been much studied and both feted and criticized. Esing's reflection reveals again an immature writer who has learned to value the writing process but is painfully aware of her weaknesses. Esing states in her reflection that she received "bad grades" on two papers, which in itself is poor psychology for positively influencing a reader! Her closing comment that "tomorrow is another new day with no mistakes yet" by no means reflects the positive affect we would hope a learner to take from a writing course. Feedback seems to have become, for Esing, a negative rather than a positive element of learning to write.

In this portfolio-based assessment program, the class teacher is not expected to provide further feedback to students as part of the portfolio review and scoring process. However, in my own discussion with the teacher of Esing's progress in her course, she expressed concern that Esing's grammar had not improved; however, she gave her credit for her hard and persistent work and her ideas. But she felt that, having given credit for the ideas early on, Esing would have needed significant expansion and clarification of ideas before she, the teacher, "could give more credit."

How feedback and revision worked for Esing

Esing was able to respond to the early feedback she got from her peers, and she was able to generate new detail that would answer the kinds of questions they had raised. On the occasions when I spent time closely observing Esing write, and when I spoke to her about what she was doing and why, she each time showed me the written feedback she had received, or referred to something said in her peer group, and related these comments to what she would like to be able to say in her text. Esing appeared to have developed a very strong sense of the meaning of process writing and the opportunities it offered her to revise her work, but I had to conclude that she had acquired a faith in it that was unjustified. But also, she was much less able to work with the teacher's feedback, whether oral or written, corrective or would-be inspirational. She seemed not to be able to work out whether any particular feedback was directive or advisory. Similarly, Esing's teacher was unable to understand the educational and cultural background that Esing brought to her studies; she was unaware of how unusual the whole concept of feedback and opportunities to make changes without penalty were for Esing and therefore was unable to understand why Esing could not draw a line between reasonable feedback and revision and a kind of fruitless perpetual motion. It was also perhaps unfortunate that Esing was both so young and so immature for her years; the older woman teacher was not able to respond to the emotional load Esing's essays carried and did not provide any feedback that might have led Esing to take her writing and thinking outside her own feelings and make them interesting to a wider audience than her age peers.

The role of feedback in portfolios for assessment

In this chapter I have dealt with only one case and only a small part of the information in the data in it. Portfolios are not only complex but also large, and writing portfolios dauntingly so. This chapter can hardly pretend to answer big questions about the role and value of feedback – of any kind – in portfolio-based writing classes. My data have instead caused me to raise more questions about how well process-based writing – especially its vital feedback element – sits with portfolio-based writing assessment. Esing's assessment anxiety, coupled with an overgeneralization of the value of feedback and revision, led her to focus on more and more reworking. Feedback became of less and less use to her. Close observation of Esing and examination of this single process writing sequence and readers' responses to it has also caused me to wonder if there are upper limits to the benefits of feedback as a teaching and learning strategy. Do (some) students need more extensive or intensive learner training in the use of feedback? Are there ways to balance the positive role of rich feedback with the summative demands of portfolios when used in assessment conditions? These questions are important for teachers who use process approaches and portfolios in their teaching.

Implications for teaching

Should the portfolio include evidence of process? Like the views of most people in the composition and second language writing community, my views are evolving all the time. My current view is that in a portfolio for assessment at least one paper should bring with it the full process evidence. My reason for this is based less on a belief that this makes the portfolio more valid (because this study of Esing has made me question that claim) than on my practical experience that skeptical bureaucracies often question the reliability of portfolios containing only final work that may have been through unknown numbers of drafts and unknown amounts of support. Some writing programs have faced the inclusion of a mandatory test essay, supposedly to counter the unduly rosy impression given by a portfolio. Including one full process set is a way to head off such a bureaucratic intrusion.

What additional skills do teachers need? Given a cautious "yes" to the preceding question, what skills do teachers need if they are to successfully combine a feedback-rich writing classroom and a portfolio-based assessment at the end of the course?

- Grounding in process writing principles and practice, preferably as part of in-service professional development
- Understanding of the relationship between methodology and curriculum, so that they can incorporate a coherent feedback plan into their teaching plan for the course
- Experience in classroom-based assessment principles and practice, to enable them to carry out real-time judgements of individual problems and needs and establish a plan of support to help each student meet those needs and solve their composition problems
- Clear understanding of the objectives, criteria, and standards (in other words, the expectations) of the portfolio-based assessment, so that they provide appropriate and clear feedback

What additional skills do students need? If students are to learn to write in a portfolio-based writing course that also uses the student's portfolio as an assessment tool, what additional skills do they need to be taught? The core elements of the writing teacher's toolkit must be actively applied so that students understand how purpose, audience, and voice can drive and help them to decide the structure of the portfolio. This clearer sense of where the end point should be, in turn, helps students to do the following:

- Manage their time across the various tasks and drafts that may become the material for the portfolio
- Learn how teacher feedback can be used productively for linguistic and rhetorical revision
- Learn to see the self-reflection genre as both reflection and revelation – as addressing the dual audience of self and other
- Plan the sequence of materials in the portfolio to illuminate the writer's journey for the reader
- Understand the importance of physical presentation, such as typing quality and neatness

How should we train readers of assessment portfolios? One of the problems in portfolio-based classroom assessment that this study revealed to me is the need for most teachers to learn more about classroom-based assessment. It cannot be dealt with in this paper due to length considerations, but without such knowledge teachers are unprepared to think about, let alone decide, some of the complex issues that surround the use of portfolios as assessments. Detailed discussion and advice on the training of reader-judges for portfolio assessment can be found in Hamp-Lyons and Condon (2000), which discusses the importance of reader-judges' discussion of key issues affecting decision making and the need for training in focusing on only those dimensions of every portfolio that it has been decided are salient. For example, there is a need to focus on the following dimensions:

- Are we looking at the teacher's or the student's work? How can we know? Does it matter?
- Do we give more credit to a student who has revised substantially on his or her own or one whose revisions follow only feedback?
- Do we focus on students' final products or do we take into account process evidence?
- Do we believe that strong evidence of revision based on feedback must always be rewarded, even if the final version is not strong?

Conclusion

The current attention to feedback in education as a whole, and in the writing classroom in particular, is a positive development. But it is also the case that here, as in all areas of instructional innovation I have studied, the need for effective teacher professional development is greater than generally recognized and certainly greater than is currently available. Effective giving of feedback is a highly skilled teaching process, and we need to develop strategies and materials for helping teachers to acquire this skill. The powerful contribution to teachers' professional development that comes with participation in a portfolio-based assessment program has been well argued already in the literature on writing portfolios (Condon & Hamp-Lyons, 1991; Ford, 1994; Stern, 1991). Learners can and do benefit in many ways from portfolios in terms of their potential as instruction tools, but whether learners benefit from portfolio-based assessment is unclear. Portfolio-based assessment still has unresolved issues of fairness and validity, and much more empirical research is needed.

This chapter and the case I have described are not meant to argue against the value of feedback, but this study has made me question whether all the feedback that the students receive during the writing and rewriting process will necessarily have a positive effect on the writing and the writer's development. Nor do I think we can make the simplistic claim that more feedback is a good thing, because giving – and receiving and using – feedback is a skilled activity, and teachers and students need help in acquiring these skills.

Portfolios are messy. Portfolio assessment is complex. Teaching with feedback is a skill and so is learning from feedback. When these two complex processes are brought together, the need to understand more about how they affect summative judgments about writing quality is very great.

Notes

1. IELTS: International English Language Testing Service, owned and administered by the University of Cambridge Local Examinations Syndicate, the British Council, and IDP Australia.
2. All examples of Esing's writing are verbatim. No corrections have been made other than those made by Esing herself.

References

Belanoff, P., & Dickson, M. (Eds.). (1991). *Portfolios: Process and product*. Portsmouth, NH: Boynton/Cook.

Calfee, R., & Perfumo, P. (1996). *Writing portfolios in the classroom: Policy and practice, promise and peril*. Hillsdale, NJ: Lawrence Erlbaum.

Callahan, S. (1995). Portfolio expectations: Possibilities and limits. *Assessing Writing 2*, 117–151.

Condon, W., & Hamp-Lyons, L. (1991). Introducing a portfolio-based writing assessment: Progress through problems. In P. Belanoff and M. Dickson (Eds.), *Portfolios: Process and product* (pp. 231–247). Portsmouth, NH: Boynton/Cook.

Despain, L., & Hilgers, T. L. (1992). Readers' responses to the rating of non-uniform portfolios: Are there limits on portfolios' utility? *WPA: Writing Program Administration 16* (1), 24–37.

Elbow, P., & Belanoff, P. (1997). Reflections on an explosion: Portfolios in the 90's and beyond. In K. Yancey & I. Weiser (Eds.), *Situating portfolios: Four perspectives*, (pp. 21–33). Logan, UT: Utah State University Press.

Ferris, D. (2002). *Responding to writing*. Mahwah, NJ: Lawrence Erlbaum.

Ford, M. F. (1994). *Portfolios and rubrics: Teachers' close encounters with self-evaluation as learners in teacher education courses*. ERIC, ED 379 628.

Freeman, Y. S., & Freeman, D. E. (1992). *Portfolio assessment for bilingual learners*. Alexandria, VA: TESOL.

Hamp-Lyons, L. (1999). *Efficacy and ethical issues of portfolios as assessments of nonnative students' writing*. Research Project Report, June 1999. Hong Kong: The Hong Kong Polytechnic University, Research and Postgraduate Studies Office.

Hamp-Lyons, L. (1996). Applying ethical standards to portfolio assessment of writing in English as second language. In M. Milanovich and N. Saville (Eds.), *Performance testing and assessment: Selected papers from the 15th Language Testing Research Colloquium* (pp. 151–164). Cambridge, UK: Cambridge University Press.

Hamp-Lyons, L., & Condon, W. (1993). Questioning assumptions about portfolio-based writing assessment. *College Composition and Communication, 44,* 176–190.

Hamp-Lyons, L., & Condon, W. (2000). *Assessing the portfolio: Practice, theory and research.* Cresskill, NJ: Hampton Press.

Herman, J. L., Gearhart, M., & Aschbacher, P. R. (1996). Portfolios for classroom assessment: Design and implementation issues. In R. Calfee & P. Perfumo (Eds.), *Writing portfolios in the classroom: Policy and practice, promise and peril,* (pp. 27–59). Mahwah, NJ: Lawrence Erlbaum.

Pierce, L. V., & O'Malley, J. M. (1992). *Performance and portfolio assessment for language minority students.* Washington, DC: George Washington University, Center for Applied Linguistics.

Roehmer, M., Schultz, L. M., & Durst, R. K. (1991). Portfolios and the process of change. *College Composition and Communication, 42,* 455–469.

Smith, M., & Murphy, S. (1992). Could you please come and do portfolio assessment for us? *The Quarterly, 14(1),* 14–17. Berkeley, CA: Center for the Study of Writing/National Writing Project.

Song, B., & August, B. (2002). Using portfolios to assess the writing of ESL students: A powerful alternative? *Journal of Second Language Writing, 11,* 49–72.

Stern, C. (1991). *Writing portfolios: A resource for teaching and assessment.* ERIC, ED 336–757.

Yancey, K. B., & Weiser, I. (Eds.). (1997). *Situating portfolios: Four perspectives.* Logan, UT: Utah State University Press.

Appendix 1: Sample peer feedback sheet

The following excerpt is from Esing's portfolio, page 35.

"Elsie" 35

Remembering Events workshop 1
Meaning

1. Read through the essay quickly and then summarize in one sentence the main point this author is making. Is the significance of this event for the writer clear? If it's not clear, what more do you need to be told or shown?

~~Th~~ When Esing & Andy ~~were~~ together.
In some parts, she needs more details.

2. Is there conflict and tension in the story? What is it? How does the writer report his/her thoughts or feelings about this?

   She couldn't express when, she talked with Andy. She always ended with blanks. Her thoughts are very honest with emotion.

3. How does the writer use description of people and scenes to depict the significance of the event? Give three examples that work.

   A. *"mg already – locked door of heart."*
   B. *"spontaneously into my mind"*
   C. *"I will be here waiting for."*

   Is there any piece of description that doesn't seem to pertain?

Appendix 2: Esing's self-reflective letter

This excerpt is from page 1 of Esing's portfolio.

"ELSIE" 35

Dear it may concerns
   From "The Windmill He Made", "Promise", to "The Junior Broken Dream is Part of Senior Growth", I found out writing itself is pretty interesting for it let me translate my 18-year phonetic memories into the language so that everyone can share it with me.
   Of course, in the middle of the writing I used to hate "English" very much, because I couldn't write well enough for readers to understand it. (English is my second language) And ever since my roommate criticized the paper "Promise" was too "simple and "oral". I became very depressed and the third paper I changed the way I used to write – Childlike, as she said. However, getting bad grades on the past two papers did make me feel any better.
   It was very nice of to ask me about what happened. I told her my roommate's influence upon me on my writing, and she told me not to listen to her opinion. DO IT AS MYSELF. She like the way I wrote, and she can follow my thought very smoothly. I am really thankful for her to say so. She taught me not only to be a more decent writer, but also a own-good happy writer.
   Well, It's kind of too late to realize how important it is to be personal writer for time is nearly the end of the semester now. But, on the other hand, I will still have 3 or 4 eighteen years to go in the future. (and I will turn 19 this Christmas) After all, isn't it nice to think that tomorrow is another new day with no mistakes yet?

   Merry Christmas, and Happy winter break!

A lot of hard work has gone into your Writing. Each paper adheres to the assignment. There are some language problems & parts that are unclear, however. I wasn't sure about "Promise" though – the "event" was a trip to the US, but the story was about Andy, and there are parts in the comparison that should be explained . . .   C+

9 Students and research: Reflective feedback for I-Search papers

Ann M. Johns

Teacher intervention in students' writing processes and peer and instructor feedback, often combined with student self-evaluation and reflection, have been central to the teaching and learning of writing for many years. Beginning with the Writing Process Movement in the 1970s, teachers have intervened while assisting students to develop more expert writing processes (Silva, 1990). Studies of expert processing indicated that "writing is not a straightforward plan-outline-write process" (Taylor, 1981). Instead, it is a "complex, recursive, and creative process or set of behaviors. . . ." (Silva, 1990, pp. 15–16). Encouraged by textbooks and this research, instructors scaffolded student work, providing intervention and feedback activities as students attempted to acquire the necessarily "complex, recursive . . . sets of behaviors." And as students prepared their texts, instructors offered opportunities to develop meta-awareness and autonomy by reflecting on their writing processes.

More recently, genre theorists and practitioners have shown how text structure and content, context, audience, writer purposes, and writer and discourse community ideologies influence the processing of written texts among expert writers. In this paradigm, writers need a sophisticated meta-knowledge of a variety of contextual and personal factors as they plan and execute their drafts and revisions, working toward a successful written product (Bawarshi, 2003; Hyland, 2002; Johns, 1997). Thus, teacher intervention, teacher and peer feedback, and student reflection should become even more important to novice writers as they develop increasing awareness of the need to balance their purposes, processes, target genre, audience, and context.

What can writing teachers do to encourage the writer autonomy and rhetorical flexibility essential to success in the genres our students will attempt to produce during their university and professional lives? In the short time permitted for classroom instruction, how can we help students to develop the motivation, confidence, self-reflection, and meta-awareness that will enable them to ask the right questions, make the right observations, select the appropriate genres, and take the necessary routes to task completion? No doubt there are many answers to these questions. Here, I will suggest one that I, and others, have found to be successful: the I-Search paper, which requires extensive student reflection after the completion of a demanding research writing task. The "I" in I-Search refers to the writer/researcher – the student who is searching for sources as well as for ways to wade through the process of writing the text. The I-Search paper describes the research and writing processes and is written by the student in the first-person "I."

The I-Search paper

In 1980, Ken Macrorie, a prominent North American composition expert, designed the I-Search to encourage student reflection and auton-omy as his class completed research paper assignments – projects that often make complex, varied, and perplexing demands on novice writ-ers. Macrorie's approach continues to be popular in North Ameri-can secondary schools and universities. (See, for example, TeachersNet Lesson 80, *I-Search paper* at http://teachers.net/lessons/posts/80.html and Seagrave's I-Search paper format guide from Gallaudet University at http://depts.gallaudet.edu/englishworks/writing/formatsheet.html.) The approach allows for multiple student opportunities to reflect upon their research and writing processes. In a typical I-Search paper, students are guided in assessing their prior knowledge of the research topic; record-ing their efforts to find sources; identifying their planning, note-taking, and revising strategies; and on remarking on what went well and what did not as they completed their work. While preparing this reflective text, students are involved in important self-evaluative feedback that can lead to increased meta-awareness and autonomy. Students may also be encouraged to provide feedback to the instructor about improving assign-ments and activity scaffolding. The I-Search paper has become a popular focus for post-research assignments because it encourages students' deep reflections upon their strategies for invention, reading and exploiting sources, drafting, revising, editing, and other activities related to research tasks.

The instructional context

The diverse group of American students discussed in this chapter was experiencing its first semester on the San Diego State University campus, the largest of 23 campuses in the California State University (CSU) sys-tem. The students were enrolled in a remedial class (Rhetoric & Writing Studies 101), designed for those who had come within a few points of passing the English Placement Test, a CSU system-wide expository read-ing, writing, and grammar examination that is designed to determine whether students are prepared for university work. The class curriculum is identical to the required freshman level (non-remedial) writing classes; however, it also provides weekly tutoring for the students as they complete their assignments, an advantage the non-remedial students do not enjoy. Students who pass the 101 class meet both the campus remedial requirement and the requirements for completion of the freshman-level writing course.

This 101 writing class consisted of 20 students, all U.S. citizens who had experienced most of their schooling in the United States. Of the three monolingual English speakers, all were African-American. The other students were bilingual. Eleven were native Spanish speakers, all born in Mexico. Two were Chaldean, speakers of Aramaic and Arabic born in Iraq, and four were born in Vietnam. In recent years, bilingual students like these, educated principally in the United States and speaking native-like English but lacking in academic literacy in any language, have been referred to as "Generation 1.5." Harklau, Losey, and Siegal (1999) first used this term in the ESL literature, and since that time it has become common in North American teacher parlance. Harklau (2003) describes this student population in the following way:

An increasing number of U.S. high school graduates enter college while still in the process of learning English. Referred to as Generation 1.5 because they share characteristics of both first- and second-generation immigrants (Rumbaut & Ima, 1988), they do not fit into any of the traditional categories of nonnative English speakers enrolled in college writing courses, nor have they been the focus of much research on students learning to write in English as a second language. Familiar with U.S. culture and schooling, Generation 1.5 students have different learning needs from other English language learners, such as immigrants with limited English proficiency or international students. . . . Equipped with social skills in English, Generation 1.5 students often appear in conversation to be native English speakers. However, they are usually less skilled in the academic language associated with achievement, especially in the area of writing.

Task design

Three papers were integral to the project cluster assigned to this 101 class. Paper 1 was an information competence assignment during which student groups located and evaluated Web sites; Paper 2 was a research-driven position paper into which students were to integrate the sources located while completing the Paper 1 assignment; and Paper 3, the I-Search paper, was an opportunity for students to use their collected notes to provide self-feedback and reflection based on Papers 1 and 2. In the following sections, I will describe the instructional decisions I made to optimize student learning and autonomy while students were completing these papers.

The research paper topic and question(s)

In their useful discussion of scaffolding writing tasks, Cotterall and Cohen (2003) point out that a teacher must make a number of curricular decisions before giving assignments, the first of which relates to the task topic. Rather than selecting a typical textbook topic for research (e.g., school uniforms, drug testing for athletes), I chose a contemporary one that might interest broader audiences. During the semester discussed here, the Bush administration was planning to invade Iraq. The French, among others, opposed these plans, a matter of considerable discussion in the North American media. Based on this international tension, the students' assignment involved researching French-American relations and suggesting to President Bush, Secretary of State Colin Powell, or President Jacques Chirac ways in which relations between France and the United States could be improved. Because the students were, for the most part, uninformed about much of American history despite their American educations, I gave them five research question alternatives to guide their search for sources and argumentation. I also planned extensive scaffolding of students' knowledge development in two major ways. The first was through a collaborative information competence and summary paper that required groups of students to search for relevant sources, evaluate those sources, and integrate their findings in a summary (Paper 1: Information competence). This experience was scaffolded through library instruction for analyzing Web sites (information competence) and my classroom read-alouds of summary paper models. Students were further introduced to the topic through a classroom presentation by a French-born professor who discussed current French-American relations.

Throughout the topic development process and throughout the entire project cluster, students were guided in taking reflective notes for the I-Search paper.

Genre

Another instructional decision, according to Cotterall and Cohen (2003), relates to genre. Although these writing instructors and many others (e.g., Dudley-Evans, 2002) focus on the academic essay for writing classrooms, I have found that introducing students to other genres helps them to explore additional possibilities for audience, context, text purposes, and structures and assists them to develop the necessary rhetorical flexibility for future writing tasks. Therefore, I assigned a position paper, to be written in memo form. The position paper genre is used by both business and government in the United States. According to the University of Hawaii Web site (http://homepages.uhwo.hawaii.edu/~writing/position.htm), a position paper presents an arguable opinion about an issue.

- The goal of a position paper is to convince the audience that your opinion is valid and worth listening to. ... Your job is to persuade your audience that you have well-founded knowledge about the topic presented and that you support your argument with appropriate evidence. (p. 1)

Students would therefore be challenged by at least two sets of new textual demands: the position paper as genre and the conventions of a memo.

Pre-teaching decisions must also be made about what information is to be made a "given" for students performing a writing task. There are two, related, purposes for providing givens in instruction. One, certainly, is that novice students cannot juggle the many demands made by complex writing tasks. The other relates to the principal objectives for the assignment: the skills, strategies, and knowledge that are to be the focus of instruction.

One of the givens for this project was the memo form. Using the students' handbook, *Keys for Writers* (Raimes, 2005, p. 265), I introduced them to the structure of typical memos, pointing out features such as headings, paragraphing, and other conventions like reference initials and attachment notations. The students and I examined a number of memos, noting that though the formats are conventional, memo macro structures and content are context-dependent.

Because this was a genre-based curriculum (see, for example, Hyland, 2002; Hyland, 2004; Johns, 1997), the context and audience were also central to the plan. Context was established through Paper 1 and the French professor's presentation, as well as through considerable reading of *Newsweek* magazine, their required text. Their choice for audience was one of three: Bush, Powell, or Chirac. I assisted students in researching how the person they had selected as audience should be addressed and the register appropriate for their position paper.

After considerable discussion of audience and context, I developed a model structure for the body of the position paper (Paper 2), to be written in memo form. This text structure, shown in Table 9.1, was presented as a given. The students' handbook also introduced them to APA style, again unfamiliar, since their secondary school research was conducted using MLA style.

Table 9.1. *Structure of the memo: A position paper*

Section	Comments and questions
A. Introduction	Why are you writing this paper? [Don't say that your instructor made you do it!] Play a role. Make up an appropriate title for yourself, e.g., "Assistant Director, European Desk, Department of State."
B. Problem	What is the issue being discussed? [Use your research questions to guide you.]
C. Historical background	What is the history of this problem? Here, you can cite your sources from paper 1.
D. Relevance today	Why is this problem still relevant? Again cite your sources.
E. Suggested solutions	Here, you make your argument(s) about what you think should be done about the problem. Defend your case knowledgeably.

After students recorded their reflective notes on the givens and we discussed them in class, I felt obligated to also provide a model position paper, in memo format. It is difficult to describe to those who do not teach U.S.-educated students how programmed they have become for one genre, the five-paragraph essay. For years, their teachers and the schools have assigned and assessed almost nothing else (see Johns, 2002). As a result of the students' limited experience, I prepared a position paper model and I asked them to work in groups to analyze and write about the functions and language of each section (those described in Table 9.1). I also asked them to consider how the research questions might be presented and solutions argued in their own texts.

Assistance in finding texts and data

Another decision that must be made when designing a complex writing task is whether and how to assist students in finding their "texts and data" (Cotterall & Cohen, 2003). When novice students are given a topic and asked to find sources, they tend to devote most of their research time to searching for sources rather than to writing the paper itself. Since I had established goals other than source searches for students in this class, I gave them a list of Web sites to consult in addition to texts that we read together in class. For Paper 1, groups of students located and evaluated a few additional Web sites; however, most of the data for the paper, including the faculty interview, were givens.

Staged instruction

Essential to research paper writing is scaffolding, or "procedural facilitation" (Bereiter & Scardamalia, 1987). Throughout the writing process, instructors need to assist novice students in completing the task, but more important, in developing self-regulatory mechanisms for writing to enable them to become more effective, flexible, and autonomous writers. Here are the steps that Bereiter and Scardamalia suggest for procedural facilitation:

1. Identify a self-regulatory function [for writers] that is characteristic of expert performance but that does not go on or goes on in an attenuated form in student performance, e.g., complex invention, revision from the top down.
2. Describe the self-regulatory function as explicitly as possible in terms of mental operations.
3. Design a way of cuing or routinizing the onset and offset of the process that makes minimal demands upon student mental resources.
4. Design external supports or teachable routines for reducing the information-processing burden of the mental operations and facilitate those operations. (pp. 254–255).

In accordance with these suggestions, I asked students to draft individual sections of the paper, such as the introduction, to make the writing more manageable, a self-regulatory function often employed by skilled writers. As they drafted each section, I conducted a classroom reading and commentary on my own model paper, asking students to take notes. In this process, we discussed making choices about discourse structure, vocabulary, syntax, and coherence. I also asked students to underline some of the rhetorical strategies I had employed, such as the use of textual metadiscourse, to bring coherence to the text. Throughout, students also took notes for their I-Search papers, reflecting on their own responses, texts, and processes.

The first section drafted by the students was a statement of the problem, since this section framed the entire paper. This section was then peer and instructor-reviewed, as were all sections, using criteria designed for the section and genre. The second section was about the history, which was constructed in the form of a narrative. Third was the current relevance section. Then the students drafted the solutions they had developed, based on the drafts of the other sections, again experiencing peer feedback. Finally, the students developed the introduction, which required additional discussion of audience and writer roles. After the entire paper was completed in draft form, students peer-reviewed and redrafted, working on coherence, editing, and appropriate register for the audience.

As we know, providing a model paper and detailed discussions and feedback on text development is criticized by some teachers of writing, who contend that students who echo another text may plagiarize or obliterate their creativity and personal voice. However, with students who have had little experience with writing in academic register, this approach works quite well and still allows for text variation and voice. Cotterall and Cohen (2003, p. 164) argue that learners need to be instructed in general conventions and registers of academic discourse. They note that "What . . . learners are demonstrating is the ability to master functional form of what are, after all, widely used and fairly formulaic signals of written discourse." Their argument, then, is that good academic writing can, and should, be modeled.

The I-Search paper assignment

After completing Papers 1 and 2 (the group-organized information competence paper for which they collected and evaluated additional sources and the research-based position paper written in memo format), the students were ready to apply their reflective notes to the I-Search paper that, as mentioned earlier, assisted them in evaluating their successes and problems when attempting to locate and evaluate sources (Paper 1) and when preparing the position paper requiring research (Paper 2). After working very hard and becoming increasingly frustrated with papers 1 and 2, the students were pleased to be able to write about themselves and their work in the I-Search paper, using the notes they had recorded during the research experience. Figure 9.1 shows the model for paper 3, "Search paper assignment." Three points must be made before examining a few typical student reflections that appeared in these papers. First, and perhaps most important, the I-Search assignment traditionally requires scripted student comments, not the open-ended ones (e.g., "What did you do well in this paper?") common to many process-based classrooms. The questions to be used for structuring the paper were posed to students while they were writing papers 1 and 2, and their notes reflected their responses. The second point relates to my curricular planning: The students in my class completed their I-Search papers before they were given their grades for papers 1 and 2, so they were not influenced by teacher evaluation. The third point relates directly to the purposes of this volume on feedback: It was my hope that students would develop a meta-awareness of their processes through self-evaluation and feedback and, as a result, become more autonomous and rhetorically flexible as writers.

Paper 3: The I-Search

For Papers 1 & 2, you searched the Web and completed a position paper based upon your sources. In Paper 3, you will be using your reflective notes to discuss the experiences, processes, strategies, frustrations, and learning that resulted from your earlier papers. This is an opportunity to be yourself: to use your personal voice and tell it like it was. You'll enjoy writing this, I hope!

Instructions:

Organize your papers under the following headings and answer the questions under each heading about your research experiences. Be yourself, but please edit your work.

1) *The opening:*

   a) Have you ever completed papers like Paper 1 and 2 before? If so, how is this research and writing experience alike, or different from, your previous experiences?

   b) What was the research question you selected? Did you revise it as you completed your search?

   c) Why did you choose this question? What interested you about it?

2) *The search:*

   a) What steps did you take in completing your research? Be specific and as detailed as possible.

   b) What roadblocks did you encounter as you searched the Web or completed other research tasks? What dead ends did you confront?

   c) What successes did you experience?

   d) Whom did you ask for help? What help did you get?

   e) Was the classroom feedback from peers and the instructor helpful? When? Why?

3) *My growth as a researcher:*

   a) How do you feel about your Paper 2? Do you think it is well-written? Thoughtful? Worthy of a good grade? Why?

   b) Are you satisfied with your writing and search processes? What went well? What would you change?

Figure 9.1. Paper 3: The I-Search paper.

[handwritten marginal note: Questions that foster reflection on the two previous writing experiences ...]

4) *My growth as a writer:*

   a) How did you grow as a writer, if at all, while completing Papers 1 & 2? That is, what can you do better as a result of these assignments?

   b) What will you do differently when you are assigned a research paper? What questions will you ask of your instructor? How will you plan your time? What other changes will you make in your research processes?

5) *My suggestions for future assignments:*

   a) In addition to what you have discussed before, what else helped you to complete this assignment?

   b) What might your instructors have done to enhance your writing processes and improve your written product?

Figure 9.1. (continued)

Student responses[1]

For the most part, the students' I-Search papers were quite complete. The students felt freed by their use of "I" and narrative responses. Response length varied, but it was not unusual for students to devote one or two pages to answering questions, using their notes, for a single section. One reason for the success of these papers, of course, is that the students were able to discuss themselves and their own processes. Though their secondary school writing experiences were limited, reflection on reading and writing was common to many of their previous classrooms. In this section, I include a few typical comments from their I-Search papers.

About source selecting and reading

In addition to the Internet sources that I had suggested to the class, students were to work together for Paper 1 to find a few additional Web sites that related to their research questions and supported their arguments. As experienced teachers know, selecting, evaluating, and then integrating sources into texts involve some of the most difficult expert routines to teach and to learn. Student handbooks for writing inevitably include a section on selecting and integrating sources (e.g., Raimes, 2005, pp. 130ff). Even highly selective post-secondary institutions, like Harvard University, offer assistance for students in source selection and integration (www.fas.harvard.edu/~expos/sources/chap1.html). For the linguistically diverse student, issues can be more complicated, as indicated by

Braine and May (1996). After selecting and evaluating sources, students must make decisions about what to cite, how to cite (paraphrase, summary, direct quotation), and how to frame the citation within their arguments. Diverse students can also be confused by first-culture practices of copying the words of great writers or with the problems of comprehending a reading in the second language to transform a citation into their own words. Some of the most articulate discussions of these cultural practices, often called "plagiarism" in the West, are by Pennycook (1996), who points out that many factors come into play when students copy from sources.

Not surprisingly, students had a great deal to say about their source searches. For one of the most diligent students, finding the right Internet sites to use as sources, as well as discovering what the sources actually said, was challenging:

> I found many blocks and dead ends [when searching the Internet]. I would research on my topic and I would click on the link, but when I red the article, it had nothing to do with my research question. Sometimes I would find a source that I think is good, but when I read it I am not sure what the article is talking about and I sit and read for 10 minutes trying to figure out whether it focused on my research questions. [Eventually, he consulted 11 sites.]

In class discussion, this student pointed out that when a reader knows very little about a topic, It may be necessary to consult a large number of sources and to attempt to interpret texts that are difficult to understand. He commented on the fact that if he were looking for sites and readings on biology (his major), for which he had background knowledge, he might have had much better luck. As he noted, what he learned from this experience is that if he is given a writing task that deals with topics unfamiliar to him, he had better begin early and find a reliable method for evaluating and reading sites.

About academic vocabulary

Most students' challenges in the discovery and reading-to-write processes were related at least in part to lack of familiarity with academic vocabulary. Although, as noted, all of the students were proficient in spoken American English, the academic vocabulary found on the more reliable sites and in the class readings was often new to them. Grabe and Stoller, in their review of second language reading research (2002), and Scarcella (e3.uci.edu/01s/34225/3000words.html) and Scarcella & Zimmerman (2004), in their recent studies of Generation 1.5 and other linguistically diverse students in California, have noted that control of academic vocabulary is central to literacy and student success in post-secondary education. It is not surprising, then, to find direct references to vocabulary in the students' I-Search responses. One student developed a strategy for dealing with difficult words and phrases.

A lot of vocabulary words in some of the articles make it difficult to understand. With the vocabulary, I still don't really know what they mean, but what I did was skip them and if I really didn't need that info. Then I figured that the vocabulary words weren't all that relevant to my topic and I don't need to spend hours of my research time looking up words.

In class discussion of these notes, she pointed out that she was learning to predict which vocabulary is important in a text, an important skill for any academic student.

looking at Student experiences of doing parts 1+2.

About source organization

In addition to making decisions about vocabulary, students had to organize their sources to marshal an argument in their position papers. One student had had considerable experience with integrating sources into texts and made these comments about the sites she selected and their value in terms of the arguments in her research paper:

The Embassy of France site gave me the current reasons why there is tension between France and the United States: France said they would fight by our side after September 11, but when the war came, France gave no support. The *Moscow Times* site had great evidence about whether there was proof for weapons of mass destruction. A quote on this site gave me lots of ideas about why France did not help. And finally, the Washington Files [from the U.S. Department of State] gave me two sites. The first one was defending France from not joining war, and this was the only article I found stating that France has a high Muslim population. And the second one defended the Americans. All of these sites helped me to argue the points I was trying to make.

It appears that this experience may have taught her that readers and researchers need to plan before they read to write. They need to know what they are looking for in a text and which elements of the argumentation or evidence will be useful for the research being conducted.

Because of this student's comments (and those of several others), I developed a scaffolding scheme that assisted students to develop notes from readings that were relevant to their papers. The example in Table 9.2 is based on the student's reflection just cited. Students are asked to first record the complete bibliographical information for their sources; then they number each of the sources and record information that might help them in a table.

This table represents another attempt on my part to assist students to select information relevant to the research question from their sources. I have not yet designed the appropriate scaffolding for note taking from different sources, but I do know from their comments that students need assistance in this area.

Table 9.2. *Taking notes from different sources*

Research question: Why does France object to the American invasion of Iraq?

Source #	Content
1: Site for the Embassy of France	Causes for tension between the two countries; response to September 11.
2: The *Moscow Times* site	Proof for weapons of mass destruction? Why did France object to the war?
3: Washington Files (site 1)	France has a large Muslim population who are anti-war.
4: Washington Files (site 2)	Defends the view propounded by the Bush administration.

Another student reflected on her strategies for finding material relevant to the question she had selected for the required paper:

It wasn't difficult finding articles or websites; it was difficult finding detailed and relevant information from the articles to answer my question. I wanted to make my paper as detailed and focused as possible. This meant cutting out unnecessary information, even though it might have sounded relevant (at first).

I had a few frustrations. The most exhausting one was finding things that the French did not like about America. I needed to write my problem section but was unable to with the more positive sources. But then I turned to the [Simon] Schama reading [assigned in class] where I found a lot of juicy negativity towards America!

What these comments seem to tell us about a central goal for the project, the selection and organization of sources, is that for diverse students whose academic English and reading skills are in the developmental stage, processes related to source discovery, evaluation, and citation selection are complex and often require the rethinking of their plans for reading. Strategies for selecting and reading sites that deal directly with their selected research question and argument are discussed at length in their I-Search reflections. Other students developed approaches to reading and evaluating the texts, particularly by working through the vocabulary. Even the most adept students needed to rethink their approaches to locating the detail necessary for their argumentation. In all of these cases, students benefited from the reflection encouraged by the note taking for the I-Search paper.

About integration of sources

How, then, did the students attempt to use their sources in their papers? How did they decide what to quote and what to paraphrase? Raimes

(2005) in the *Keys for Writers* handbook purchased by my students has the following to say about using direct quotations:

> Quote when you use the words of a well-known authority or when the words are particularly striking. Quote only when the original words express the exact point you want to make and express it succinctly and well. Otherwise, paraphrase. (p. 132)

Did the students follow Raimes's advice? As usual, they were honest about their work in their reflective feedback in the I-Search papers. Their comments indicate that they needed to explore additional strategies to integrate the citations they found in the readings into their texts. Here is a typical reflection:

> From the sources I finally selected, I decided to quote directly when there were phrases that I couldn't put into better words myself.

For another student, quoting and paraphrasing depended on what was new or striking for her.

> I decided to directly quote the messages that really stood out from the rest on the websites and that it also had a great argument. I paraphrased the sentences that I already knew.

A related approach was taken by a student who made his decisions based on whether the sites he was using quoted an authority directly or presented an important idea:

> In this paper, I used a total of eleven sources. I had the options of paraphrasing or direct quoting. I decided to directly quote when the website directly quoted a person or when it was an idea. Otherwise, I just paraphrase what points that I found useful towards my paper.

One student decided that the instinctual approach was best.

> To determine when I should directly quote the writer or to paraphrase, I just listened to my gut instinct. Sometimes, I would feel that I could rearrange the wording and use synonyms to describe what had been said. I often went to my (native English-speaking) roommate for reassurance for what I did.

Another decided that she needed direct quotes for both sides of the argument that related to her research question.

> When in-text citing my information, I made sure that I had a strong quote that would support each side. If I didn't have a strong quote or support, I would paraphrase the information to make it easier to read.

What about the demands of the writing itself? One student made every effort to paraphrase to make the paper her own.

> When I had the right sources, I had to start writing. I was very frustrated because when I started writing, I could not find the right words to match what

I wanted to say. It is hard to find different words that express the same meaning as my sources. I did not want to quote everything that I had because that would not be my research paper any more.

As can be seen from these approaches to quotation and paraphrase, the students' developing strategies relied upon a variety of factors. Some students quoted those who spoke in the classroom presentation or were quoted directly on Web sites and attempted to paraphrase other relevant parts of the texts. Others quoted what "stood out" or followed their "gut instincts." Several others developed strategies for putting the language of the texts into their own words without changing the meaning. Each of these strategies is viable, although some were more successful in terms of the final grade than others.

After deciding whether to quote or paraphrase selected text, the students had to decide how to insert the source material into their papers. Most students were challenged as they framed their citations; they had to make effective use of the sources within the text, relating them to their own arguments. This framing issue is one faced by writers at all levels, and most will be developing additional strategies for source integration throughout their academic lives.

About students' growth as researchers and writers

Another cluster of questions in the students' I-Search assignment dealt with their assessments of their own writing and research processes. The student who achieved the highest grade on the project, for example, discussed how his drafts improved as he wrote. He had devoted considerable time to a paper, and he learned to revise from the top down, even changing the structure. No doubt most writing instructors would consider top-down revision (in contrast to editing for sentence-level errors) an important expert strategy that students need to develop. This student did, and he was proud of his final product.[2]

As I begin writing my final draft, I looked back at the first and second draft to compare and see where I needed to work on. As I compare my first draft to my final draft, I am very happy with the completed paper. My first draft was unclear, the structure was very poor, and the lack of good evidence to prove my points. My final draft was very well research and the evidence was very well put together. I had trouble with my structure and transitions, but I looked over the drafts and fixed whatever I could. When I was done with the final draft I reread the paper and worked on word choices. I am very satisfied with my progress.

At the opposite end of the grading (and reflection) scale was a student who "hated the whole project" and said, "I do not think I developed any skills or knowledge that I have not had before." Unfortunately, he said no more, either in class or in his I-Search paper about why he felt this way. I can only hypothesize that he was one of several students who had received top grades in high school and was resentful about being placed in a remedial class.

Between these two in terms of response were the students who voiced frustration but felt that they grew as researchers or writers in a number of ways. For example, one said:

After completing Paper 2 I feel that I have grown. I have learned how to research more effectively and how to cite sources better. I did four drafts of the same paper and each time I would change the paragraphs or find more information. This was the hardest paper I've done and I'm confident that I did excellent.

Some students learned more about planning strategies as they conducted their research, noting that as they found sources, each draft became more detailed.

I am satisfied with my research process. I found more research with each draft and also each draft became more detailed. Throughout this process, I took my time and made sure not to rush. If I did [rush], the quality of my findings would not be good.

Throughout this section of the I-Search papers, students commented on their planning, drafting, editing – and on the differences between writing the typical English class essay and the type of research, in memo form, that was required for this position paper. What they did not discuss, but what was central to the process, were the instructor and tutor conferences, student peer reviews, and frequent in-process reflections, all of which may have contributed to the final paper.

Why didn't they discuss the scaffolding and conferencing in more detail? Perhaps because they viewed peer review and conferencing with the instructor and tutor about their papers as normal, a routine part of any assignment. Whatever the reasons, the tutor and I certainly hope that our extensive conferencing contributed to their strategy development and to the quality of their final papers.

About student learning

Students also reflected on what they believed they had learned from the experience. As with all of their reflections, these student comments will assist me and my colleagues to revise the assignment sequence, the interventions and feedback, and perhaps the objectives for the class, in the coming years.

One of my stated goals in selecting the topic for research was for students to separate themselves somewhat from their Southern California environments and consider other cultures and viewpoints. Three students mentioned this goal, and their discoveries, in their comments. Here is one:

> The things that I discovered in research for my papers were surprising. I found out a lot about the culture of a country (France) that I have never paid much attention to ... in fact, I never paid much attention to any other culture besides my own [Latino culture].
> I find that researching an unfamiliar topic is much more vivid and exciting than researching something I know. I wish I could have an interview with a French teenager, or even visit France.

Another student, whose research question dealt more directly with the war in Iraq, noted that she was finally paying more attention to current events.

> To be honest, I really never kept up with the whole issue about the war and everything related to it because I simply did not want to know about war. So during my research, I had to learn about what was going on and actually look up the historical background for myself.

How the students reflected on their learning depended, of course, on their prior knowledge and their willingness to plan and devote time to the project. What the reflections seem to have in common is the students' efforts to improve their strategies for a variety of necessary research skills. Thinking and writing about these strategies for the I-Search paper gave them an opportunity to provide self-feedback on their attempts to grow and to write a satisfactory product in the required genre.

Conclusion and suggestions for teachers

In this paper, I have discussed both the scaffolding of a cluster of research tasks and student self-evaluatory feedback in an I-Search paper. I have discovered after many years of teaching Generation 1.5 and diverse students that it is very important to predetermine givens so that students can focus upon specific objectives when a complex task is assigned. Because goals for students in the tasks discussed here related to source discovery, reading and evaluation, source integration, and text coherence, I made decisions about a number of "givens" in the assignments. In this way, I attempted to provide students with the following:

> ... supportive conditions in which the novice can participate in, and extend, current skills and knowledge to higher levels of competence (Donato [1994], cited in Cotterall & Cohen, 2003, p. 158).

Student success and developing autonomy depend at least in part on an instructor's ability to carefully scaffold activities for the development of strategies and skills in the classroom, providing sufficient modeling, feedback, and student practice.

The second main section of this chapter looks at the I-Search paper, which I have found to be an excellent tool for encouraging continuous reflection, self-evaluation, and commentary. As can be seen from their comments, the I-Search assignment encouraged students to record, discuss, and develop strategies for success and, I hope, to consider how they might approach future writing tasks. A second benefit of the I-Search feedback relates to improved instruction. In this and all my other writing classes, I request formative feedback from students throughout the course, attempting to improve both my teaching and their learning as the semester progresses. I also benefit from the richer student feedback that the I-Search process affords. It is more useful to me than the institutional end-of-term teacher evaluation forms with questions such as "Did the teacher understand his/her subject?" required by American universities.

When asked what worked in the research cluster and what did not, the students made these recommendations in the final section of the I-Search paper:

- Continue to provide background information in the form of readings and speakers before the research begins
- Select a more interesting research topic
- Help us more with reading and note taking
- I learned patience and management – but please help us to plan
- Continue to conference one-on-one with us about our drafts[3]

There was nothing in the comments about how overtly taught procedural facilitations, such as Jigsaw reading, summarizing and modeling of texts, and vocabulary work, assisted students to complete their work. Perhaps when I next assign an I-Search paper, I will ask more direct questions about procedural facilitations.

In this action research, my questions were:

- Did the students show evidence of having learned to reflect deeply upon the class and their research and writing processes by the time they had completed the assigned papers?
- Was the I-Search process useful in improving my efforts to assist students in producing complex research papers in a new genre?

It appears that the answer to both questions is a qualified yes. Students appeared to benefit from the experience and become more self-analytical and meta-aware. They identified and sometimes analyzed their strategies, particularly those they used to find, evaluate, and integrate sources into their texts. They recognized some of the strategies that they have yet to develop.

I learned that even though the tutor and I had intervened at various points, generally through conferencing, a number of students continued to be challenged by the process, though only one surrendered completely in frustration and did not finish the assignment sequence. Assigning a new genre (position paper) in a new form (memo) and a topic that required considerable building of new knowledge may have resulted in information-processing overload, even though a number of givens were presented. Bereiter and Scardamalia (1987) argue that instructors must "reduce the information-processing burden" (p. 255). Perhaps I need to scaffold even more – or design less ambitious assignments.

I adapted the I-Search paper to fit the research topic and sequence outlined in the first part of the chapter. However, an I-Search paper with reflective feedback can be employed in a variety of situations, following a number of research tasks. Through the reflective note-taking process and the I-Search paper, students inform the instructor and themselves about their strategies, problems, successes, and attitudes. I find that students are open and honest in their comments, and in their feedback they are quite accurate in their assessments of themselves, their strategies, and the class.

Notes

1. Student comments have been included as written; none have been edited.
2. It must be noted that this revision was encouraged by my feedback – and by his peer reviewers – though credit is not given.
3. Finally! A comment about instructor feedback!

References

Bawarshi, A. (2003). *Genre and the invention of the writer.* Logan, UT: Utah State University Press.

Bereiter, C., & Scardamalia, M. (1987). *The psychology of written composition.* Hillsdale, NJ: Lawrence Erlbaum.

Braine, G., & May, C. (1996). *Writing from sources: A guide for ESL students.* New York: McGraw-Hill.

Cotterall, S., & Cohen, R. (2003). Scaffolding for second language writers: Producing an academic essay. *ELT Journal, 57,* 158–166.

Donato, R. (1994). Collective scaffolding in second language learning. In J. P. Lantolf & G. Appel (Eds.), *Vygotskian approaches to second language research* (pp. 35–56). Norwood, NJ: Ablex Publishing.

Dudley-Evans, T. (2002). The teaching of the academic essay: Is a genre approach possible? In Ann M. Johns (Ed.), *Genre in the classroom: Multiple perspectives* (pp. 225–236). Mahwah, NJ: Lawrence Erlbaum.

Grabe, W., & Stoller, F. (2002). *Teaching and researching reading.* Harlow, UK: Longman-Pearson Education.

Harklau, L. (2003). *Generation 1.5 students and College Writing*. ERIC Clearinghouse on Language and Linguistics. ERIC Digest, ED 482491. Available at www.ericdigests.org/2004-4/writing.htm.

Harklau, L., Losey, K., and Siegal, M. (1999). *Generation 1.5 meets college composition: Issues in teaching writing to U.S-educated learners of ESL*. Mahwah, NJ: Lawrence Erlbaum.

Hyland, K. (2002). Genre-based pedagogies: A social response to process. *Journal of Second Language Writing, 12*, 17–29.

Hyland, K. (2004). *Genre and second language writing*. Ann Arbor: University of Michigan Press.

Johns, A. M. (1997). *Text, role, and context: Developing academic literacies*. New York: Cambridge University Press.

Johns, A. M. (2001). ESL students and WAC programs: Varied populations and diverse needs. In S. H. McLeod, E. Miraglia, M. Soven, & C. Thaiss (Eds.), *WAC for the new millennium: Strategies for continuing writing-across-the-curriculum programs* (pp. 141–164). Urbana, IL: National Council of Teachers of English.

Johns, A. M. (2002). Destabilizing and enriching novice students' genre theories. In A. M. Johns (Ed.), *Genre in the classroom: Multiple perspectives* (pp. 237–248). Mahwah, NJ: Lawrence Erlbaum.

Macrorie, K. (1980). *Searching writing*. Westport, CT: Heinemann-Boynton Cook.

Pennycook, A. (1996). Borrowing others' words: Text, ownership, memory, and plagiarism. *TESOL Quarterly, 30*, 201–230.

Raimes, A. (2005). *Keys for writers*, 4th ed. Boston: Houghton Mifflin Company.

Scarcella, R. All about words: Teaching vocabulary. http://e3.uci.edu/01s/34225/3000words.html. Web site of the University of California at Irvine.

Scarcella, R., & Zimmerman, C. B. (2005). *The academic word knowledge of California high school students*. Paper presented at the AAAL Conference, Portland, OR, May 2004.

Silva, T. (1990). Second language composition instruction: Developments, issues, and directions in ESL. In B. Kroll (Ed.), *Second language writing: Research insights for the classroom* (pp. 11–23). New York: Cambridge University Press.

Taylor, B. (1981). Teaching composition to low level ESL students. *TESOL Quarterly, 10*, 309–313.

PART III:
NEGOTIATING FEEDBACK:
INTERPERSONAL AND INTERACTIONAL
DIMENSIONS

10 Feedback and revision in second language writing: Contextual, teacher, and student variables

Lynn Goldstein

Teachers of second language writers often mention their concerns regarding the most effective means for providing feedback on text-level issues (content and rhetoric) to help students improve their texts in both the immediate sense and the long term. Over the past 20 years, beginning with Vivian Zamel's 1985 study examining the feedback practices of a small group of ESL teachers, a small body of research has developed addressing issues pertaining to teacher feedback and revision at the text level. In reviewing this body of literature, I have noted that "the research has largely been noncontextual and nonsocial, focused largely on texts and conducted within a linear model of teacher respond and student revise... however there are a good many factors that probably play an interactive role in how teachers comment, how students perceive and react to teacher commentary, and how students use such commentary when revising" (Goldstein, 2001, p. 77).

In Goldstein (2004), I argue for the need to take into account how contextual factors, as well as individual teacher and student factors, can influence teacher commentary and student revision. Contextual factors can include (1) sociopolitical issues that influence teacher status, the number of classes teachers need to teach, and the number of institutions at which teachers need to teach in order to make a living, resources available to students to ensure their success, and class size; (2) program and institutional attitudes toward second language writers; (3) program and curricular requirements; (4) program philosophies about the nature of effective feedback; and (5) entrance and exit requirements. Teacher factors may include attitudes toward particular students or the content of their texts. Student factors may include reactions to teacher feedback, outside commitments, and investment in the course content.

The relationship between teacher feedback and student revision

In light of these factors and their interaction, one major concern teachers and researchers need to address is the relationship between teacher

185

feedback (whether electronic, conference-based, or written) and student revision. At this point, we know the most about written feedback, a bit about conferencing, and virtually nothing about online feedback.

Electronic feedback

To date, the relationship between teacher feedback on text-level issues offered through electronic means, such as e-mail or the Comment function in Microsoft Word, and student revisions remains virtually unexplored. In a case study of three undergraduate students, Goldstein and Kohls (2002) report that individual teacher and student factors played a significant role in how the teacher gave feedback and the students revised. The fact that the students submitted their drafts electronically as e-mail attachments and the teacher gave feedback directly on these drafts, using the Comment function in Microsoft Word, seemed to play a relatively minor role. Ferris (2003) reports anecdotally that students may get greater amounts of feedback and more frequent feedback, but whether this feedback is better is not known. Clearly, we know almost nothing about how contextual, teacher, and student factors interact and influence both each other and teacher feedback, or student revision when this feedback is given electronically.

Conference feedback

Only a little more is known about the relationship between teacher feedback during conferences and student revision. Patthey-Chavez and Ferris (1997) found that teacher feedback in conferences did influence students' subsequent revisions. Goldstein and Conrad (1991), in their case study of three undergraduate students, found that the students differed greatly in how they interacted with the teacher in their conferences. They found differences in the degrees to which the students controlled or shared the discourse with the teacher, nominated topics, asked questions, and negotiated meaning when discussing possible revisions.

Goldstein and Conrad found a direct relationship between revision success and the negotiation of meaning when discussing the revisions. In almost all instances in which the student and teacher negotiated meaning, the revision was carried out successfully in the subsequent draft. In contrast, in almost all cases where a meaning was not negotiated, the resulting revisions were unsuccessful or revision was not attempted at all. Given how few studies have been carried out, little is known about the relationship between teacher and student discourse and teacher feedback in conferences and student revision. Virtually no research has looked at the interaction among context, student factors, and teacher factors and how such interactions influence conference feedback and revision.

Written feedback

A considerable number of studies have examined teacher written feedback and student revision. This research has shown that students sometimes find teacher commentary confusing (Arndt, 1993; Chapin & Terdal, 1990; Chi, 1999; Crawford, 1992; Dessner, 1991; Ferris, 1995, 1998; Goldstein & Kohls, 2002). Furthermore, students report that they may use teacher feedback without understanding the reasons behind it (Crawford, 1992; Hyland, 1998; 2000); that they sometimes think they have understood the feedback when they do not (Arndt, 1992; Goldstein & Kohls, 2002); and that even when students do understand a comment, they may not know how to use it in a revision (Chapin & Terdal, 1993; Cohen, 1991; Conrad & Goldstein, 1999; Goldstein & Kohls, 2002).

There is also evidence that the shape of written commentary, that is, its linguistic form, may play a role in student revision success. Conrad and Goldstein found that students had difficulty with comments that did not directly state that a revision was needed, and students either did not attempt revision or revised unsuccessfully in response to such comments. Other studies have shown that students may also have difficulty understanding the intent of comments that are hedged in some way (Conrad & Goldstein, 1999; Ferris, 1998; Hyland & Hyland, 2001).

However, Conrad and Goldstein (1999) and Ferris (2001) have found that the shape of teachers' commentary is not the only influence on how students revise in response to it. Indeed, the nature of what needs to be revised can play a more substantial role in students' revision success. Students were far less successful revising in response to more abstract difficulties, such as explaining their points of view, than they were to more concrete problems, such as adding necessary details. Furthermore, Conrad and Goldstein (1999) have found that the individual factors that each student brings to the process of writing and revision can influence how he or she uses teacher commentary. These factors include time constraints, beliefs about content, and views of teacher and student roles and responsibilities.

The influence of individual student factors on revisions has been demonstrated in other research as well. The factors include the following:

- The feeling that the teacher's feedback is not valid or is incorrect (Dessner, 1991; Goldstein & Kohls, 2002)
- A lack of content knowledge needed to undertake the revision (Anglada, 1995; Conrad & Goldstein, 1999)
- A lack of motivation (Pratt, 1999)
- A receptivity to or resistance to revision (Enginarlar, 1993; Radecki & Swales, 1988)

- A distrust of the teacher's content knowledge (Pratt, 1999)
- A mismatch between how the teacher responds and the students' expectations for response (Hyland, 1998, 2000)

There is much we do not know about teacher feedback and student revisions. No study has looked at all of the factors that can influence how teachers provide feedback and how students use this feedback and how these factors interact with each other. In addition, we know little about how these factors may influence students' motivations to revise with teacher feedback. In this paper I will look at two students in two entirely different contexts and examine instances where difficulties arose when these students attempted revisions using their teachers' commentary. These instances can be very instructive in considering how the commentary, along with other factors, influenced the students' motivations to revise and the success of their revisions.

The first case is a re-examination of Tranh, a student profiled in the research of Conrad and Goldstein (1999) and Goldstein and Conrad (1991). In this re-examination, I will look at the interaction of factors that come into play as the teacher gives both conference and written feedback and Tranh revises using the feedback. The second case focuses on a student from the research of Goldstein and Kohls (2002), Hisako. Here, I examine the interaction among contextual factors, teacher factors, and student factors and how these interactions influenced the teacher's feedback and the student's revision. The feedback was given electronically in an online writing course.

Tranh: An examination of a feedback experience

Tranh (all names of students and teachers are pseudonyms) was a junior, studying computer science at a large urban state university in California. He had been living in the United States for five years. Before coming to the United States, he had attended and graduated from high school in Vietnam, where he was born and raised. His native language was Chinese, but he spoke both Chinese and Vietnamese. He was enrolled in a full course load of 14 units, including the highest-level ESL writing course. A unit of work is equivalent to one hour of in-class time and roughly two hours of out-of-class assignments. Thus, the work load of 14 units is roughly 42 hours a week. In addition, Tranh was working 10 hours a week.

I was Tranh's teacher. At that time, in the mid-1980s, I had been teaching second language writing for nine years, and all of that teaching had taken place in academic writing programs at urban universities.

The course content was thematic and not tied to any particular university course content. Although we did some readings for the class, students were not required to do outside reading, and they were not required to use the class readings in their essays. In class, we focused on writing concerns – organization, development, audience and purpose, heuristics, and, on occasion, language – and on drafting and revision. Students wrote four papers, and on average each student, including Tranh, wrote three or four drafts of each paper.

Data collection and analysis

Copies of Tranh's drafts and my written feedback were collected over the course of the semester. I recorded all of the conferences on audiotape, and a research assistant transcribed them in their entirety. Rather than attempt to apply other researchers' systems for discourse analysis, my coresearcher, Susan Conrad, and I examined the transcripts to look for recurring patterns and variations among the three students in our study. We hoped that our review would suggest how the discourse was structured and identify the types and degree of interactional work each student did in the conferences. Through this process, we identified the number of topic nominations, turns, questions, and negotiations of meaning as our measures of interactional work. See Goldstein and Conrad (1991) for a full discussion of this process.

Tranh's conferences: Two instructive examples

In Goldstein and Conrad (1991) we found that, of the three students, Tranh was the most active participant. There is a real sense from looking at the discourse that Tranh felt co-ownership of the conferences. Across his conferences, half of the topic nominations were Tranh's. In terms of the conversational work, half of the conference episodes were marked by shared discourse, as Tranh and I took equal turns discussing the topic at hand. (An episode is defined as a continuous stretch of conference discourse in which the participants focus on a particular topic of discussion.) The other half of the episodes was split, with Tranh and I each controlling the discourse in a quarter of the episodes. In sum, Tranh either shared or controlled the discourse in the conferences for three-quarters of the episodes.

One conference on his paper "Two-Career Families" is particularly instructive, because we are able to see a number of intersecting factors that influenced his subsequent revisions. Tranh had strong negative feelings toward two-career families with children and placed the burden for problems he saw within these families on the women. I had diametrically opposed views, but I was trying to hide my opinion from Tranh, as I did not want to appropriate his text. Thus, my goal in this conference was to point out to Tranh places in his text where he had overgeneralized or had not considered other viewpoints, without trying to get him to change his views.

"Two-Career Families": Conference one

In one place, Tranh wrote the following:

During her pregnancy, a perspective mother suffers morning sickness and other symptoms of pregnancy. According to medical research, bearing a baby slows a woman's movements and at times causes her unnecessary anxieties. She worries over little things and became emotional easily. All of these undoubtedly affect a pregnant women's performance in the office.

In the conference, I brought up the overgeneralization and Tranh defended his view:

L: You know, I have to question something that you wrote. Do you know this is, this opinion where you say that when women are pregnant they worry over little things and become emotional easily and undoubtedly all this affects a pregnant woman's performance in the office?
   (*Laughter.*)
L: I don't know about that.
T: You don't know about that. Okay.
L: I don't have any evidence either, so I am reacting out of emotion as well, but I don't know that you – whether you can make a blanket overgeneralization like that.
T: Um, my friend told me she got breakdown and she depressed all the time.
L: Uh huh.
T: That's when I figure it out.

Next, I shifted my focus from the content to the source of his evidence, overlapping with the end of his turn:

L: So . . . from a friend?
T: Yeah.

Tranh then shifted back to whether I believed the overall idea was true:

T: You, you don't think it's true. I believe that it's true. I think that.

I responded, and although I did state an opinion, in the end I presented this as a case of overgeneralization.

L: Well I know that women undergo hormonal changes which can affect their emotions in a way that they don't affect their job performance . . . you know, I understand your point and I think it's a valid point, but I don't think it's a valid point for all women. So you might want to work in somehow you know, that for some women . . .

Tranh in turn picked up on my very implicit evaluation of using his one friend as evidence.

T: Okay (*laughter*) Better do some research before I write something.

I didn't respond to Tran's suggestion that he do some research, and we moved on to another topic.

In fact, Tranh never did this research and instead removed this content completely from his next draft. I do not have the sense that he removed his claim because I had convinced him that his point of view was wrong, as I had validated his view by saying "I think it's a valid point" and had attributed the problem in his text only to overgeneralization. We can also see from the conference that Tranh realized that evidence based on one friend's experience was not sufficient or effective and also understood that doing research would be an appropriate revision strategy. In the draft he wrote after this conference, he removed all mentions of individual friends, although he had made many such mentions as evidence in the draft we were conferencing on.

So why did he remove this text instead of doing research as he suggested he might do in the conference? He told me at the beginning of the conference that he had written the draft we were conferencing on only that morning and that he had not done certain things that would have strengthened his paper because, "I don't have time to do all the things." In several of his conferences the issue of time comes up in relation to his full-time studies and his part-time job. In addition, I was not teaching students how to do research and how to use sources in their papers, and I did not require students to do research or source-responsible writing. My rationale for this was based partly on the institution's curriculum, which did not require it, and partly on a fear of further taxing already overburdened students. Given these factors, I believe that Tranh took the most expedient path available: He removed the argument from his paper, knowing that there was no risk because the course did not require him to do research.

The preceding incident provides an example of how Tranh negotiates meaning for the revision, Tranh and I share the discourse work, my feedback is text-specific and clear to Tranh, and Tranh arrives at the appropriate revision strategy of doing some research. Nonetheless, despite what we might term ideal conditions for successful revision, Tranh removed the text in his next draft. This example lets us see that it was not the conference discourse per se that influenced Tranh's subsequent draft but the interaction of contextual factors outside the conference. I did not insist on research in the course or in students' texts and revisions, and Tranh did not have the time to do it.

"Two-Career Families": Episode two

In the next example from this conference, I continue to characterize my divergent views as places where Tranh needed to avoid overgeneralizing. In this episode, I began as follows:

L: Okay, so here you are telling me is that now that I'm 32 and still hadn't – have postponed having children, that wasn't a good idea.
T: Um, I don't know. I feel that people postpone and then they keep postponing and, and – until one day it's too late or it's too hard for them that they be maybe so.
L: Um, I have a friend who's 40 and she has a four-year-old and a six-month-old.
T: Oh (*laughter*). You know to me I think that over 30 is too late, yeah.
　　　　　　　　　　　　　　　　　　　　　　　　　　　　[
　　　　　　　　　　　　　　　　　　　　　　　　　　　too old
L: Most of my friends who have had children had their children in their early thirties. And when I have my first child I'll be somewhere around 33, 34.
T: Okay (*laughter*)
L: And the reason...
T: I'll think about that too and see.

Here with Tranh's last turn, we see that he was not convinced. I go on to concede that there are some negative aspects, such as a rise in cases of Down syndrome as women get older but also point out that there are positive aspects, such as having more patience. At this point, Tranh raised a cultural issue:

T: I don't know. I I feel, you know, that in the Chinese, um, Chinese culture it is is a big problem for people
L: Uhmm...
T: If a women gets old and have a baby... it is always good to have it when
L: Mhm.
T: One is young. So, um, I would think about that.

Instead of picking up on what Tranh saw as cultural difference and perhaps cultural conflict between us, I reiterated some of the pluses and minuses of women having children when they are older. Tranh actually brought the cultural differences to the forefront in his response:

T: Yes, I read the – what Newsweek and I know that many, some example say that women over 35, so maybe there is different culture and different people may have different ways, may have different ideal, but I write here and I feel that, um, you know, I heard people say, um, in our country or in the community is... I, I write down there.

I ignored the issue of how his culture influenced how he saw this issue. I did say I thought his point was valid but I then brought in what research might say, and Tranh reacted:

T: I really don't want to bring out this big piece about medical research. I just, um, I think that there is something is my, um, feeling about that.

My final comment in this episode was an implicit attempt to get him to avoid overgeneralizing:

L: There are, there are negative effects, there definitely are, and I agree with you, um, but there aren't negative effects for everybody. It's only a small proportion of the people, so people in a sense need to make informed decisions.

In Tranh's subsequent revision he kept the line "it is clear today that the older a woman, the harder she conceives a baby." To this he now added, "Even though the reports show only a very low percentages of women over 35 failed to be pregnant or had birth defects, yet the risk is there if women challenge the scientific find out." In his revision, Tranh attempted to avoid overgeneralizing and at the same time phrased his text in a way that allowed him to hold on to his belief about older women getting pregnant or having babies. Again, he avoided doing any research.

A number of factors interacted to influence his revision in the second example. As with the first example, we have conference discourse that is shared, and we have negotiation of meaning. Nonetheless, Tranh's revision is not really effective. This is due in part to the actual content of my feedback and in part to factors outside it. First, Tranh had a strong cultural belief that he wanted to hold on to and incorporate in his writing. I missed his explicit reference to this belief as culturally important and instead treated the difficulty as one of overgeneralization, a strategy that I chose to avoid confronting him with my strong negative reaction to his content, out of fear that this might result in appropriation. Thus, I failed to address the content of Tranh's interaction with me regarding Chinese culture, and I failed to engage him in meaningful dialogue about our differences. As a result, I missed the opportunity to suggest that he might want to examine the differences in cultural beliefs and acknowledge them in his paper so that his audience, who might not share the same culture, could understand the differences from his perspective. In turn, although Tranh's beliefs on this issue were clearly quite strong, he chose not to do any research to support or refute these beliefs, a choice to which the course curriculum and issues of time most likely also contributed.

Tranh's use of written feedback

As we turn to Tranh's use of written feedback, we will see that a number of factors interacted to influence his revisions. Some of these factors are the same as for conference feedback, for example, not asking for source responsible writing and issues of time. Added to this is Tranh's lack of important content knowledge; places where comments, although text-specific, are not clear; as well as his difficulty, one shared by all the students in Conrad and Goldstein, with providing analyses and explanations.

Tranh chose to write about the roots of discrimination for the first essay of the semester. The feedback that he received from me on his second draft was written on a separate sheet (we conferenced on his first and third drafts) and was text-specific. It focused on substantive revision concerns of support and the development of logical arguments, the issues most in need of revision, rather than addressing everything that could possibly have been revised.

On page five, in your discussion of greed, you need to work on your examples. In Ireland – who discriminates against whom? Why? Also how does your example about Blacks in South Africa show that greed causes this discrimination. I think you are right, but you haven't stated this explicitly.

Finally, on page seven, you say ancient feuds can cause discrimination. Can you go into this in more depth? You say discrimination results in war but you don't show/discuss how ancient feuds result in discrimination.

As before, Tranh did not use research as a strategy for gaining content knowledge that he lacked. Again, instead of revising the discussion about Ireland, Tranh removed it. Although he did attempt to revise the section about ancient feuds between Israelis and Palestinians, the revisions were not effective. He still had not shown the connection between ancient feuds and any current discrimination, and he still had not shown that anyone was being discriminated against. When we talked about these revisions, Tranh explained that he knew nothing about Israel, the current situation in the Middle East, or anything about any ancient feuds. Furthermore, he stated that instead of doing any research, he wanted to remove the content from his paper since he didn't know enough to be able to elaborate.

Tranh's revisions of his discussion about South Africa were also completely unsuccessful and seem to have been influenced by the clarity of my feedback and his developmental readiness to enact the type of revision called for. He added details showing how much better the living conditions were for whites in South Africa, but he did not show that conditions were bad for blacks because they were discriminated against, nor that the greed of the whites caused the inequality between the living conditions of blacks and whites. He may have revised in this manner because the feedback itself was not entirely clear. My question "How does your example about blacks in South Africa show that greed causes discrimination?" was intended as a directive that could have been better phrased as "You need to explain and illustrate how greed causes this discrimination." Analyses of other "how" or "how and why" questions show that, in general, Tranh, as well as the other students, had difficulty using them to revise successfully (see Conrad, 1999). In addition, Tranh, along with his classmates, was having consistent difficulties with writing the analyses and explanations needed to support the arguments he wanted to make. Regardless of how my comments were phrased, most of my requests in Tranh's papers for analyses and explanations were followed by unsuccessful revisions, suggesting that he did not yet know how to do this effectively.

In sum, Tranh's revisions following my written commentary, as we saw for conference commentary, did not represent a simple and direct response. Instead, we see how multiple factors, in addition to the clarity of the commentary, came together and influenced his revisions: his lack of content knowledge, motivation, and time to gain such knowledge through research, compounded by the absence of a course requirement or instruction to do so and his not yet knowing how to provide the depth of analysis and explanation his discussions required.

Hisako

I will turn now to an examination of Hisako. Here we look at a context completely different from Tranh's, with both similar and very different factors acting to influence the teacher's electronic commentary and Hisako's revisions in response to it.

At the time of data collection in fall 2000, Hisako, a native speaker of Japanese in her early twenties, was an international graduate student at a small private graduate school in California, studying for an MA in international policy. Hisako was enrolled in a full load of graduate courses in her major, as well as English Studies (ES) 325, the first course in a series of graduate-level courses for writing for academic purposes. The online section in which Hisako was enrolled focused on policy studies writing and had three students, including Hisako. The teacher, Anne, was a native speaker of English and had an MA in TESOL. She had been teaching in the English Studies program for approximately two years but had never taught ES 325 before. She was a relatively inexperienced teacher of academic writing.

The lessons and assignments were designed to build on each other as students learned to read academic sources in policy studies and to use these sources in their policy writing. Each student decided on a policy issue, read 10 articles on the issue, wrote an annotated bibliography of these sources and a reaction paper to one of the sources, wrote the introduction to a literature review about the issue they had selected, then wrote the literature review.

Hisako and her two classmates used Microsoft® Word and wrote multiple drafts of each component, submitting their drafts to Anne as attachments to e-mail messages. Anne used the Comment function in

Microsoft® Word to give feedback on the drafts, sending both the drafts and the feedback back to the students as e-mail attachments.

Data collection and analysis

Several sources of data were collected and used in the analyses. I copied all of Hisako's drafts and Anne's feedback and all of the electronic correspondence between Anne and Hisako. Anne kept a journal throughout the course, commenting on the successes and difficulties she saw in the course and in students' writing and revisions. I read this journal and interviewed Anne with follow-up questions. Anne also annotated all of her comments on Hisako's drafts, explaining her motivations behind each comment. Hisako met with me regularly to discuss each draft after she had completed her revisions. In our meetings, she detailed for me her reactions to Anne's feedback, including what she had done in response to each comment and why. Richard, an experienced teacher of ES 325 and my coresearcher and the cocreator of the online version of ES 325, and I coded each of Anne's comments to show whether or not Hisako had revised in response to the comment and, if so, whether each revision was successful, partially successful, or unsuccessful. Each of Anne's comments was also coded for the type of text problem it addressed, such as development or organization. Anne's journal, interviews, and annotations of her feedback were used to understand her motivations for the comments. My sessions with Hisako were used to understand why she had revised or not in response to particular comments and the factors that had influenced the success of these revisions.

Electronic commentary and revisions: Patterns of response and reaction

As seen in Table 10.1, Hisako's revisions in three out of the four major assignments show a pattern of removing problematic elements in her texts or not revising in response to Anne's commentary. For the annotated bibliography, the first paper of the semester, Hisako's lack of revision in response to Anne's comments ranged from 14.8 percent for draft one, 40.6 percent for draft three, and 75 percent for draft four to 100 percent for draft two. Hisako removed the text she was asked to revise in response to 12.8 percent of Anne's comments on draft one. Hisako removed the text in response to almost half of Anne's comments (47.2%) on draft one of the introduction to the literature review; made no revision in response to more than three-quarters of Anne's feedback (77.1%) on draft one of the literature review; and she did not revise in response to almost one-third of Anne's comments (30%) on draft two.

Table 10.1. *Instances of no revision or removal of text in response to written comments*

DRAFT	Paper One: AB		Paper Two: RP		Paper Three: ILR		Paper Four: LR	
	NAT	TR	NAT	TR	NAT	TR	NAT	TR
1	14.8% (7/47)	12.8% (6/47)	0	0	0	47.2% (17/36)	77.1% (27/35)	0
2	100% (27/27)	0	8.3% (1/12)	0	6.2% (1/16)	0	30% (9/30)	0
3	40.6% (13/32)	0						
4	75% (12/16)	0						

Key

NAT = % of comments after which revisions were not attempted
TR = % of comments after which text was removed

AB = Annotated bibliography
RP = Reaction paper
ILR = Intro to literature review
LR = Literature review

Table 10.1 shows the percentages of comments to which no revision was attempted and the occurrences in which text was removed from the draft in response to comments.

We can see from examining Table 10.2 that Hisako also had difficulty with revisions she did choose to make in response to Anne's commentary. Almost half of Hisako's subsequent revisions in response to comments on the first draft of her annotated bibliography were either only partially successful (12.7%) or unsuccessful (29.7%), and a quarter of her revisions in response to comments on the fourth draft were unsuccessful. A substantial percentage of her revisions in response to comments on the first draft of her reaction paper (38.1%) and on the third draft of her introduction to her literature review (81.2%) were also unsuccessful.

Analyses of Anne's feedback show that slightly more than half (52.4%) of her feedback to Hisako focused on sentence-level issues, whereas a third of her comments focused on text-level issues of development and organization. A small number of comments (2.3%) focused on issues of plagiarism, paraphrasing, and quoting. The focus on sentence-level issues was offset by many instances in which text-level and content issues in need of revision were not commented on. In fact, in her annotations of the comments to Hisako, Anne noted that her main goal had been to focus on content but that she saw that she had tended to focus on minor issues instead.

Table 10.2. *Percentage of successful or partially successful revisions in response to comments made on drafts*

DRAFT	Paper One AB PS	US	Paper Two RP PS	US	Paper Three ILR PS	US	Paper Four LR PS	US
1	12.7% (6/47)	29.7% (14/47)	4.7% (1/21)	38.1% (8/21)	0	5.5% (2/36)	0	5.7% (2/35)
2	0*	0*	8.3% (1/12)	8.3% (1/12)	0	81.2% (13/16)	0	0
3	9.3% (3/32)	3.1% (1/32)						
4	0	25%** (4/16)						

Key

PS = % of subsequent revisions that were partially successful
US = % of subsequent revisions that were completely unsuccessful

AB = Annotated bibliography

RP = Reaction paper

ILR = Intro to literature review
LR = Literature review

* Hisako did not revise at all in response to comments on draft two.
** Hisako did not successfully revise at all in response to comments on draft four.

Another salient feature of Anne's feedback to Hisako is the degree to which she repeated verbatim the comments she had given Hisako on the previous draft, something she never did with the other two students in the online course – doing so even in places where Hisako had revised in response to Anne's comments on the previous draft. All of the comments (34 of 34) on draft two of Hisako's annotated bibliography were identical to the comments on draft one; all but three of the 35 comments on draft three of the introduction to the literature review were identical to Anne's comments on draft two; and 20 percent of the comments (6 of 30) on draft three of the literature review were identical to the comments on draft two.

Anne and Hisako: Pieces of the puzzle

In response to Anne's commentary, why did Hisako either remove text or not revise with such frequency? Anne's policy was to grade only the final draft of each paper. All other drafts, regardless of quality or effort, were not graded and could not affect the students' course grade. Thus, in one interview, where we were discussing her work on the annotated bibliography, Hisako shared with me that "First I will finish my IPS (international policy) things. If it's the final draft, I'll focus on the ES course. Otherwise I'll do my best, but next to the main course." Overall, in my discussions with Hisako, she told me she had chosen to concentrate on her work for her policy classes, where her grades would be more greatly affected by her written work and where she was more invested. In contrast, she said she reserved her efforts on her ES 325 papers for the final draft because she knew that she would not be graded until that draft. She also said that in each draft, she chose to revise only those aspects that she felt she could do in time.

The elements she removed or did not revise fell largely into two categories: places where she would have to go back into her reading to find and bring into her text needed details and information and places involving citation formatting, something she told me she did not know how to revise in response to Anne's comments. In the first instance, the revisions would have entailed more work and in the latter instance would have involved getting help from Anne. We have already seen why Hisako did not go back into her reading, as this would be time consuming, and that she concentrated her efforts and time on her policy work.

As for the citations, Hisako told me that she did not know how to revise them and that she had not told Anne, despite the fact that Anne had online office hours (the course had built-in chat capabilities). Hisako stated in one of our interviews that "I couldn't find enough information about the citation online. But, yeah – unfortunately, I couldn't ask her how to find the information." I asked Hisako several times during this session if she had asked Anne about what she didn't understand, and in each instance she said no. When pressed she said, "I didn't have time to ask her." In this session, I also asked Hisako if there were any comments on her annotated bibliography that she did not understand, and she indicated "about the citation comments." When I asked Hisako what she planned to do to better understand how to work with citations, she replied, "I'll find out on the Web." In response to my suggestion that "You can ask Anne too, you know," Hisako replied "Yeah," but she never actually did. It appears that Hisako had decided that she would not ask Anne questions about the feedback or the writing problems she was experiencing because she did not have the time to do so.

The electronic communication between Anne and Hisako also shows that Anne did not directly offer such help nor ask Hisako why she was not revising in response to her feedback. Nor did she ask Hisako if she was having any difficulties in the places where revisions were not successful. This may also have affected Hisako's reluctance to approach Anne directly. I had the sense that Hisako did not feel that asking questions online would give her the help she needed and that she was hesitant to see Anne in her office because the course was online. In our final interview, Hisako commented, "I should have met her more during her office hour before this, before I realized I should meet her. Sometimes I need to talk. Mmm, to – that I couldn't understand her comments exactly."

In discussing Hisako's work with me, Anne told me that she had come to the conclusion that Hisako was "lazy," because Hisako often did not revise in response to her commentary. In reference to citations, the area in which Hisako indicated to me she was having the greatest difficulty, Anne's journals and annotations of her feedback show that she interpreted Hisako's lack of questions as an indication that she understood her feedback and knew how to use it appropriately. As Anne conveyed in one of our interviews, "Hisako didn't hardly incorporate any of my feedback, um, and it's not that I think she misunderstood it. I think that my feedback to her was task-specific, related to providing citations to some of her – full citations – and that would have meant that she would have had to go back and actually find the source and include the citation, and I think that was a lot of work for her." She also noted in her annotations of her comments on Hisako's literature review that ". . . most of my comments were related to citations or lack of. She was aware that citations were an integral part of the assignment. I think she just lacked time to complete this." Anne assumed that Hisako had understood how to revise using her comments about citations but had not done so because of the time involved. We also see that Anne had no way of knowing that Hisako was having difficulties, because Hisako had never asked her any questions about citations. In fact, when I asked Anne if she had any sense that the students didn't understand any of her comments, she replied, "I have not had one question about specific clarification of my feedback."

As a result, believing her feedback to have been understood and believing that Hisako knew how to do citations and seeing that Hisako had not revised in response to her comments about citations, Anne repeated the comments on the next draft. Anne's annotations of her repeated comments show her strategic use of this repetition. Next to several repeated comments on citations, she explained, "She didn't read my previous comment on the first draft." In another instance, she explained, ". . . sources are a problem even after third draft," and in another place where her comment to Hisako read "My comment remains the same," she explained, "I think I was getting frustrated."

We might also wonder why Anne focused so heavily on sentence-level issues in the face of Hisako's difficulties with text-level issues and in the face of Hisako's having strong control over written English at the sentence level. Although Anne mentioned when she annotated her commentary that she noticed the emphasis, she did not explain her reasons for doing so but merely stated in her annotations that "my main goal of feedback was content even though I tended to focus on minor issues." As an ESL teacher, Anne may have commented on areas where she felt she understood the content, that is, language, and thus she frequently commented on sentence-level issues. In addition, because this was the first time Anne had taught the policy writing course, and she had not been involved in the creation of the online course content and Web site, she may have felt she did not know the content of policy studies or the genres of policy writing well enough to comment effectively on those areas.

In sum, the pattern of commentary and revisions we see with Hisako and Anne was influenced by Hisako's time constraints and Anne's grading policies, by Anne's unfamiliarity with policy content and policy writing, and by how Anne and Hisako each constructed the other, based on Anne's interpretations of Hisako's revision behaviors and Hisako's interpretations of Anne's commenting behaviors. Hisako constructed Anne as (1) someone to whom she would not ask questions when she was having difficulty or when she did not understand her feedback, and (2) as someone who would not penalize her for failing to revise in response to feedback, since doing so did not affect her grades and Anne never commented on her lack of revision. Anne constructed Hisako as (1) competent, since she did not ask questions or indicate difficulty, and thus seemed capable of understanding and using what she believed to be clear feedback, and (2) "lazy" for not revising in response to her commentary. Anne and Hisako were effectively working at cross-purposes, neither communicating with each other nor understanding what was motivating the other's behaviors.

Lessons learned

The concept of motivation seems particularly important in understanding how students might use their teachers' commentary. For Tranh, some aspects of my pedagogy (that is, what we wrote about, the fact that we had no real audiences and purposes, and the fact that we did not use readings in the writing) did little to tap into any intrinsic motivation or provide extrinsic motivation. Without such motivations, and in the face of time pressures, Tranh did not go the extra mile to find and read the content needed for his papers. Nonetheless, it is clear to me that he was intrinsically motivated to be a good student and that he worked diligently with my commentary in the effort to be a good student. I also think the fact that I was engaging with him about the content of his writing as a writer, not only as a second language student, was motivating.

Unlike the case with Tranh, the genres of writing that Hisako was working on were directly related to the genres she was being asked to work in for her policy courses, and she was reading and writing about policy issues and topics of her own interest and choice. I would expect this to be both intrinsically and extrinsically motivating, but I believe that it is difficult to tap into these motivations if the student is being overwhelmed. Hisako was clearly up against a situation in which the graduate-level reading and writing demands of her policy MA courses overwhelmed her. Overloading students with degree courses for which they are underprepared while having them enroll simultaneously in a writing course designed to prepare them for the writing demands of the degree courses makes little sense. Being in this situation often has negative effects on students' success in all of their courses, because they are neither ready to handle the reading and writing demands of their degree work nor able to invest themselves in the writing courses that will help them develop the reading and writing proficiencies they need. Here, something needs to change fundamentally in the way universities accept students before they are ready to carry that amount of demanding work.

Also, Anne's commentary may also not have succeeded in motivating Hisako to revise. It is difficult for students to be motivated to work with commentary that focuses heavily at the sentence level; does not engage with the ideas of the writing or with issues of audience, purpose, and genre; and is repeated verbatim from one draft to the next. Finally, the lack of grades on drafts may also have served to lessen Hisako's extrinsic motivation for revision, though I want to be careful not to suggest that grades should be used in a punitive sense to provide extrinsic motivation.

There are some direct lessons that Tranh and Hisako can teach us in terms of pedagogy. (See Goldstein, 2004, and Goldstein, 2005, for detailed discussions of pedagogy.) From Tranh we learn the importance of incorporating source-responsible writing, that is, writing that requires students to use sources from their reading, into our courses and we learn how a teacher's fear of appropriation may result in beneficial discussions not taking place where beliefs differ. We learn that difficulties in revising in response to teacher commentary may sometimes be developmental and that students may thus need to learn certain rhetorical skills, such as providing explanations. We also learn that teachers need to listen well in conferences, so as not to miss, as I did with Tranh's cultural beliefs, what is really motivating a student's writing.

From Hisako we learn that our grading practices can influence how students use our commentary. We learn not to assume that laziness or poor time management underlie student difficulties or that students know how to do something because they have been exposed to it or because they have not indicated any difficulty by asking questions. From Hisako we also learn how a teacher and a student's misperceptions can influence their construction of each other, which in turn can influence commentary and revision behaviors. We learn the need to provide opportunities for open and honest communication.

From both Hisako and Tranh, we learn how difficult it is for matriculated students to juggle content courses along with writing courses and understand the need to consider how this may affect our pedagogy and our students' work. We also learn that sometimes our comments may not be clear to students and that we need to build into our courses the means for students to communicate with us about our comments and their needs; in that way, we can see where we are not clear and we can see where students lack the resources or knowledge they need to enact revisions.

We would all agree that the quality of feedback matters and that students will most benefit from feedback that is text-specific, relevant, and clear; does not appropriate the text or the writer's responsibilities; and allows students to determine a way to revise in response to the feedback. Nonetheless, if researchers and teachers concentrate their examinations on the shape of feedback alone, we will miss the incredible complexity of factors that interact with each other as students write, teachers comment, and students revise with this commentary. The examples of Tranh and myself and Hisako and Anne illustrate that no matter whether feedback is given electronically, through written comments, or through conferences, it is the unique constellation and interaction of variables – contextual, teacher and student – that must be looked at to truly understand what happens in the commentary and revision process and to understand what may or may not motivate students when they revise in reaction to this commentary. Clearly, this makes our work as teachers and researchers much more complex.

Regardless, this brief look at two cases shows why it is necessary for us as researchers to do case studies to develop a sound understanding of the feedback and revision process and why as teachers we need to look at each student and his or her context individually if we are to give optimal feedback to all students.

References

Anglada, L. (1995). *On-line writing center responses and advanced ESL students' writing: An analysis of comments, students' attitudes and textual revisions*. Ph.D. dissertation, Texas Tech University.

Arndt, V. (1992). Response to writing: Using feedback to inform the writing process. In M. Brock and L. Walters (Eds.), *Teaching composition around the Pacific Rim: Politics and pedagogy* (pp. 90–116). Cleveland, Philadelphia, and Adelaide: Multilingual Matters.

Chapin, R., & Terdal, M. (1990). *Responding to our response: Students' strategies for responding to teacher written comments*. ERIC Document Reproduction Service, ED328 098.

Chi, F. (1999). *The writer, the teacher, and the text: Examples from Taiwanese EFL college students.* ERIC Document Reproduction Service, ED442 272.

Cohen, A. (1991). Feedback on writing: The use of verbal report. *Studies in Second Language Acquisition, 13,* 133–159.

Conrad, S., and Goldstein, L. (1999). ESL student revision after teacher written comments: Texts, contexts and individuals. *Journal of Second Language Learning, 8,* 147–180.

Crawford, J. (1992). Student response to feedback strategies in an English for academic purposes program. *ARAL, 15,* 45–62.

Dessner, L. (1991). *English as a second language college writers' revision responses to teacher-written comments.* Ph.D. dissertation, University of Pennsylvania.

Enginarlar, H. (1993). Student response to teacher feedback in EFL writing. *System, 21,* 193–204.

Ferris, D. R., (1995). Student reactions to teacher response in multiple-draft composition classrooms. *TESOL Quarterly, 29,* 33–53.

Ferris, D. R., (1997). The influence of teacher commentary on student revision. *TESOL Quarterly, 31,* 315–339.

Ferris, D. (1998). *How does teacher feedback affect student revision? A pilot comparison between ESL and NES writing teachers and their students.* Paper presented at the 32nd Annual TESOL Convention, Seattle, WA.

Ferris, D. (2001). Teaching writing for academic purposes. In J. Flowerdew & M. Peacock (Eds.), *Research perspectives on English for academic purposes,* (pp. 298–314). Cambridge: Cambridge University Press.

Ferris, D. (2003). *Response to student writing: Implications for second language students.* Mahwah, NJ: Lawrence Erlbaum.

Goldstein, L. (2001). For Kyla: What does the research say about responding to ESL writers? In T. Silva and P. Matsuda (Eds.), *On second language writing* (pp. 73–90). Mahwah, NJ: Lawrence Erlbaum.

Goldstein, L. (2004). Questions and answers about teacher written commentary and student revision: Teachers and students working together. *Journal of Second Language Writing, 13,* 63–80.

Goldstein, L. (2005). *Teacher written commentary in second language writing classrooms.* Ann Arbor, MI: The University of Michigan Press.

Goldstein, L., and Conrad, S. (1990). Input and the negotiation of meaning in ESL writing conferences. *TESOL Quarterly, 24,* 443–460.

Goldstein, L., and Kohls, R. (2002). *Writing, commenting and revising: The relationship between teacher feedback and student revision online.* Paper presented at the American Association of Applied Linguistics Conference, Salt Lake City, UT.

Hyland, F. (1998). The impact of teacher written feedback on individual writers. *Journal of Second Language Writing, 7,* 255–286.

Hyland, F. (2000). ESL writers and feedback: Giving more autonomy to students. *Language Teaching Research, 4,* 33–54.

Hyland, F., & Hyland, K. (2001). Sugaring the pill: Praise and criticism in written feedback. *Journal of Second Language Writing, 10,* 185–212.

Patthey-Chavez, G. G., & Ferris, D. (1997). Writing conferences and the weaving of multi-voiced texts in college composition. *Research in the Teaching of English, 31,* 51–90.

Pratt, E. (1999). *A qualitative study of peer and teacher response in an ESL writing classroom in Puerto Rico*. Ph.D. dissertation, Indiana University of Pennsylvania.

Radecki, P., & Swales, J. (1988). ESL student reaction to written comments on their work. *System, 16*, 355–365.

Zamel, V. (1985). Responding to student writing. *TESOL Quarterly, 19*, 79–102.

11 Interpersonal aspects of response: Constructing and interpreting teacher written feedback

Ken Hyland
Fiona Hyland

As a pedagogical genre, teacher written feedback is designed to carry a heavy informational load, offering commentary on the form and content of a text to encourage students to develop their writing and consolidate their learning. The information offers the assistance of an expert, guiding the learner through the "zone of proximal development" (Vygotsky, 1978) and providing opportunities for students to see how others respond to their work and to learn from these responses. Feedback plays a pedagogical role by pointing forward to other texts students will write, assisting students to work out the text's potential and to comprehend the writing context, and providing a sense of audience and an understanding of the expectations of the communities they are writing for. The substantial comments that many teachers write on student papers thus do more than simply justify a grade. They provide a reader reaction and offer targeted instruction.

Often, however, written feedback has been seen as *purely* informational, a means of channeling reactions and advice to facilitate improvements. Response is therefore discussed as if it were an objective, impersonal, and purely didactic discourse – simply an interaction between a teacher and a text. But, although the information in feedback is a key factor in learning to write, it is effective only if it engages with the writer and gives him or her a sense that it is a response to a *person* rather than to a script.

In this chapter, we look at the role of the interpersonal in constructing feedback, focusing on the part it plays in negotiating a relationship with students. Drawing on a study of six EFL learners in a university pre-sessional course, we elaborate why the interpersonal is important in teacher written feedback; how it is realized in comments through mitigation and the expression of praise, criticism, or suggestion; the part played by teachers' construction of an interpersonal and pedagogic context in this process; and how students actively interpret, comprehend, and respond to these comments.

Study purpose and design

Why is the interpersonal important in feedback?

Allwright (1989) points out that classroom interaction data often reveal that teachers and learners are trying to solve a recurring discoursal dilemma: the need to maintain social harmony. Establishing and preserving genuine opportunities for learning involves minimizing or avoiding conflicts and incompatibilities, and the culture of most classrooms assumes that there will be trust, cooperation, and a broad meshing of teacher-learner agendas. However, whereas interpersonal considerations have been discussed in peer and oral feedback studies, research on teacher written response has largely ignored how feedback is framed to achieve such harmony. The ways teachers choose to express their feedback can affect both students' reactions to it and the extent to which they use it in their revisions, and may have a significant impact on writing development. The effects are likely to be particularly telling for L2 students, whose linguistic proficiencies and cultural expectations may affect either their acceptance or processing of feedback.

Like all texts, teacher feedback is a concrete expression of recognized social purposes, which means that although it is shaped by the teacher's personal goals, it is also mediated by the institutions and cultures in which it occurs. Every feedback act carries assumptions about participant relationships and how teachers think these should be structured and negotiated. Our experiences and perceptions as teachers thus influence not only what we choose to focus on but also how we structure our responses, the relationship we seek to establish with students, and the extent to which we personally involve ourselves in our comments. In giving feedback we simultaneously offer a representation of ourselves as teachers and as individuals, revealing our beliefs about language, learning, writing, and personal relationships. We can be impersonal, critical, and autocratic, or informed, sympathetic, and helpful, and controlling this representation of self can be crucial to maintaining interaction with students and providing feedback that will be taken seriously.

The main point we want to make in this paper is that teachers face choices when responding to student written work, selecting from available options that carry very different pragmatic force. We will argue that these decisions are often based on a desire to negotiate interactions that recognize both the learner's struggle to make meaning in a foreign language and the fragile intimacy of the teacher-student relationship. Teachers thus make assessments of their teaching context and their students as much as the texts they comment on, and these assessments have the potential to influence how they express their feedback and how students respond to it.

Study participants and data

Participants in the study were ESL students from various language backgrounds in two classes of a 14-week full-time pre-sessional English proficiency course at a New Zealand university. One class was preparing students for undergraduate admission (class A) and contained 15 mixed nationality students of low- to mid-intermediate ability, and the other class comprised 16 students of high-intermediate to advanced proficiency, mostly from Thailand and China and preparing for postgraduate studies (class B). Six case studies were selected for detailed focus. These were Maho, a 19-year-old woman from Japan; Keith, a 26-year-old man from Taiwan; Seng Hee, a 20-year-old Korean woman in class A; Liang, from Taiwan, and Samorn, from Thailand, both women in their thirties; and Zhang, a 27-year-old man from China in class B.

The teachers of the two classes were experienced ESL writing instructors who had taught the course several times before. They were both well aware that the type of comments they gave acted both to contribute directly to learning and to create the interpersonal conditions in which learning might occur.

Writing was an important aspect of this course, with about two hours each week given over to teaching academic writing and another two hours devoted to writing workshops. Feedback was collected for all the students in two classes, and all the feedback on all the case studies' writing assignments was analysed. This amounted to 10 pieces of work for class A and seven pieces of writing for class B. Three pieces of writing in both classes involved a feedback/revision cycle, consisting of the writing of a draft followed by written feedback, and then preparation of a revised version in response to the feedback.

We examined teachers' end comments on these texts, including both comments written at the conclusion of the essay and those on a separate feedback sheet, since these represent longer, more substantive, and more discursive remarks on the student's writing than margin notes. Altogether a total of 495 feedback points were examined, amounting to 4,700 words from 51 student essays. The classes and workshops were also observed regularly, and interviews with the teachers and students were conducted. For each case study participant, teachers also conducted think aloud protocols as they gave written feedback to the draft of one piece of writing. Before they did this, a training session was held in the presence of one of the researchers, but the actual think aloud protocols were carried out naturalistically and recorded by the teachers while doing their marking at home. A retrospective interview was then carried out with the students within a day of their revising draft. Respondent validation, or "member checking" (Lincoln & Guba, 1985), was achieved by seeking participants' input and their evaluation of the authenticity of the data.

All class observation notes were commented on by the two class teachers to help validate the interpretations and minimize misrepresentations.

Realizing the interpersonal in feedback

As teachers we are usually conscious of the potential feedback has for helping to create a supportive teaching environment and aware of the need for care when constructing our comments. We know that writing is very personal and that students' motivation and self-confidence as writers may be damaged if they receive too much criticism (e.g., Connors & Lunsford, 1993). We may also believe that praising what a student does well is important, particularly for less able writers, and use praise to reinforce good writing and foster students' self-esteem. We may also feel that some of our suggestions for improvement carry an implied criticism and choose to take the sting from these by toning down the force of our comments. The ways we convey our praise or criticisms, and how we phrase our suggestions, are central to effective feedback; they represent key interpersonal resources for negotiating judgments and evaluations of student writing (Hyland & Hyland, 2001).

Essentially, teachers have to weigh their choices of comments to accomplish informational, pedagogic, and interpersonal goals simultaneously. It is possible that negative feedback has a detrimental effect on writer confidence (Gee, 1972; Taylor & Hoedt, 1966), whereas premature and gratuitous praise can confuse students and discourage revisions (Hyland & Hyland, 2001). In short, interpersonal aspects of response have the potential to construct the kinds of relationships that can either facilitate or undermine a student's writing development. In interviews, both teachers in our study showed that they were very aware of these interpersonal effects of feedback, and this awareness had an effect on their comments. Joan (teacher A) said that she generally tried to find something positive to say in her feedback and to look for the most important and most generalizable problems to comment on. Nadia (teacher B) reported that she felt that it was necessary to show both the positive and negative parts of the writing. In the data, we found that 44 percent of the nearly 500 feedback points related to praise and 31 percent were critical. Only a quarter were suggestions, offering explicit recommendations for improvement (Table 11.1). Both teachers were acutely aware of the potential of their comments to create a positive or negative learning context (see also Bates et al., 1993). They therefore used praise frequently as an important means of engaging with writers and building their confidence in their composing and revision choices. The greater number of comments by Joan, however, reflects her stance as an "expert guide" and her preference for dealing with discrete points on a

Table 11.1. *Teachers' use of feedback acts (Hyland & Hyland, 2001)*

	Praise	Criticism	Suggestion	Overall
Joan	160 (42%)	114 (30%)	109 (28%)	383
Nadia	58 (52%)	39 (35%)	15 (13%)	112
Totals	218 (44%)	153 (31%)	124 (25%)	495

feedback sheet rather than responding, as Nadia did, with global end comments on the student papers. Interviews revealed that Nadia felt happier offering critical comments on drafts when there was potential to improve them, and that Joan was uncomfortable making critical comments without appending a positive comment. Interestingly, although criticism and suggestion were fairly evenly distributed between drafts and final versions, nearly three-quarters of all praise was reserved for final drafts, where it was designed to motivate the students in their next writing.

The expression of feedback shows that teachers consider the possible interpersonal impact of positive and negative feedback. Joan, for instance, did not want to overwhelm her students by addressing all their problems and described why she was reluctant to be directly critical.

I had a Korean student who was kind of a fossilisation problem I guess. . . .
On the very first test I think I made some criticisms . . . and she wrote in her journal that she found this very devastating and "please try and encourage me" and so after that I modified my feedback to try and be more positive. . . . I mean it's hard sometimes to get a balance between being a realist and being positive. But once she told me that I made a conscious effort.

Nadia also discussed the potentially demotivating impact of negative feedback and related it to her own feelings as a creative writer and her conception of the students' feelings as ESL writers:

I'm really insecure about my writing and I think that if people gave me negative feedback all the time, without very much positive feedback, I would probably never write again. I would feel more and more insecure. So I know what positive feedback does for me and I know what negative feedback does as well and so I know that I want a bit of both. . . . But I think the positive is incredibly important. Especially for such insecure students, you know. I mean these are ESL students who are writing in a second language and they are terribly insecure. They are terrified all along the way. So if you can show them that there are some things which they do which are great . . . I think you are going a long way.

In addition to using praise as an interpersonal strategy, we found also that teachers extensively mitigated their comments to reduce their critical force. It has been suggested that unmitigated imperatives assert authority and sustain the boundaries between expert and novice (Lea & Street, 2000). The evaluative nature of teacher feedback, the fact that it judges

Paired comments Combining criticism with either praise or a suggestion (43.8%)

Vocabulary is good but grammar is not accurate and often makes your ideas difficult to understand.
Good movement from general to specific, but you need to make a clearer promise to the reader.

Hedged comments Modal verbs, imprecise quantifiers, usuality devices (37.9%)

Some of the material seemed a little long-winded and I wonder if it could have been compressed a little.
There is possibly too much information here.

Personal attribution Teacher responds as ordinary reader rather than expert (11.8%)

I'm sorry, but when reading this essay I couldn't see any evidence of this really. Perhaps you should have given me your outline to look at with the essay.
I find it hard to know what the main point of each paragraph is.

Interrogative form Express element of doubt or uncertainty in the comment (6.5%)

The first two paragraphs – do they need joining?
Did you check your spelling carefully? Why not make a spelling checklist of words you often get wrong and use this before handing in your final?

Figure 11.1. Mitigation strategies in end comments as a percentage of all mitigation strategies

and pronounces on student work, means that it always carries the risk of disharmony. Although criticism can undermine a writer's developing confidence, praise also carries risks because it implies a clear imbalance of authority between the teacher and student as evaluator and evaluated. Commentary is thus not limited to broad functions of praise, criticism, and suggestion, but involves delicate social interactions that can enhance or undermine the effectiveness of the comment and the value of the teaching itself. For that reason, baldly negative comments such as "Poor spelling" or "Incomprehensible" were rare in our data. In fact 76 percent of all criticism and 64 percent of suggestions were mitigated in some way, and praise was widely used to tone down the negative effect of comments. Figure 11.1 summarizes the main mitigation strategies employed by these two teachers (Hyland & Hyland, 2001; Hyland, 2003) and the percentage of their use in relation to all mitigation strategies.

The use of such mitigation strategies may not only build a positive teaching relationship but may also help to moderate the teacher's dominant role and tone down what might be seen as over-directive interventions in students' writing. Such strategies help assuage teachers' anxieties about *appropriating* student writing and how students might respond to comments that are too directive and prescriptive.

Contextual factors and the construction of feedback

Context is a combination of factors related to the institution and the writing program and to the factors that teachers and students bring to the interaction. Central to understanding interpersonal aspects of teacher response is the fact that feedback occurs in a classroom context and through the teacher's construction of the individual student and his or her personality and learning needs. Few studies have addressed interactional aspects of written feedback, however, despite Knoblauch and Brannon's (1981) plea over two decades ago that response should be considered in relation to "the larger conversation between teacher and student" (p. 1). In fact, a major criticism of feedback studies is that analyses too often treat comments as contextually disembodied, thereby eliminating a key dimension needed to understand teachers' responses and making their comments appear problematic and idiosyncratic (Reid, 1994).

It is important to see teachers' actions in relation to their assessment of the context, which is partly influenced by their personal belief systems and reflected in the ways they judge writing and define their role (Anson, 1989). But these beliefs are not entirely personal; they are firmly anchored in the social and institutional context in which the teacher works. Often, teachers are not simply appraising writing but are also hoping to use the opportunity for teaching and reinforcing writing behaviors. In fact, they may be fulfilling several different and possibly conflicting roles as they give feedback: teacher, proofreader, facilitator, gatekeeper, evaluator, and reader, all at the same time (Leki, 1990; Reid, 1994). They are also considering their personal knowledge of the writer, the task, and the wider learning context in constructing the feedback context.

Hillocks (1986) has suggested that effective feedback is strongly tied to instruction. In much of our data, we observed a close relationship between written and oral feedback and particular teaching points raised in the writing workshops. In week 5, for example, the students in class A were given a worksheet on introductions.

An introduction ... gives the reader a good idea of the direction of your essay so that they know what to expect. This is sometimes called a "promise to the reader."

At the beginning of the next workshop, before the teacher entered, the students were already discussing the comments on their drafts.

Van is talking about the comment on his draft "no promise to the reader." He is not sure what it means and is canvassing different people on his table as to what it could mean. (From observation notes)

During this workshop there were five student-teacher interactions where students discussed comments, relating to a "promise to the reader" and two further peer interactions on the same topic. The indications were that Joan was consciously linking the class teaching and the written feedback, and this was supported by an extract from the protocol of Joan's response to Maho's essay.

I think I'll make a positive comment about that sentence about culture and festivals – Um the promise to the reader – cos we've dealt with that today. (Joan/Maho)

Thus the points made through explicit teaching were picked up and reinforced by the written feedback and then recycled in both peer and student-teacher oral interactions.

To summarize, we strongly argue that teacher comments are always related to specific pedagogic and interpersonal goals that both help to construct and are influenced by the teaching context. Commentary is always situated in an ongoing dialogue between teachers and students, and we respond not just to texts but also to our knowledge of our learners' personalities and our experience of the entire classroom situation. In other words, we actively construct a context that relates feedback to specific *learners*. Thus, any study of teacher written feedback must take into account the connections between teachers, students, texts, and writing purposes, and so consider written comments as "multidimensional social acts in their own right" (Sperling, 1994, p. 202). Here we briefly illustrate how the two teachers in our study drew on their conceptualizations of individual students and the pedagogic context in designing their commentary.

Conceptualizing the student and her or his needs

Goldstein (2004) has recently argued that the basis of helpful feedback is understanding what students are hoping to accomplish with a text – their intentions, audiences, and points of view – so that we can read and respond appropriately and avoid appropriation. The teachers in this study almost always tailored their responses to student essays by drawing on their knowledge of the student, their problems, and their wants. To assist them, the teachers made considerable use of the information provided in the cover sheets that students were required to submit with each piece of writing. From the sheets, teachers could learn what pleased the students most about the writing, what they found most difficult, and what they wanted feedback on. As these extracts from the teacher think-aloud protocols show, both teachers usually began their response by using this information to conceptualize the student. In the following paragraphs, italic type indicates what the teacher is reading aloud from the student's sheet, and bold type represents the teacher's written comment:

I'm going to do Liang's first – and looking at her cover writing cover sheet. Here we go – *Aspects of this essay that I'm pleased with – when I finished the first draft and gave someone to revise that – when I finished the final draft tried to improve while writing it – grammar mistakes and vocabulary, organisation -is it easy to understand the whole essay?* So she worried about grammar, vocabulary, organisation, which is what I'm going to concentrate on – *it is difficult for me to have more ideas about this topic, to make a conclusion.* So we'll need to look at the conclusion. Yes. (Nadia/Liang)

I think he thinks about the language, i.e. the grammar, more than he does about the content and organisation – I think that comes out quite clearly with the writing cover sheet where he talks about *"please correct all the grammatical mistakes – and give me some suggestions on how to improve my writing"* – doesn't really set store very much by organisation and I think that's what he needs to concentrate on – um – yeah has to be reworked – has some problems with sentence fragments – which I'm going to talk to him about. (Nadia/Zhang)

Now Keith's – this one's going to be a bit more tricky to mark because he's negotiated – he's done it as a business report, not an academic essay – so I'll have to try and assess it in a different way. OK, so he wants feedback on grammar basically – oh well I'll just have to take his word for it that this is the kind of thing he has to write. (Joan/Keith)

She's pleased with the introduction and conclusion – *more information* that's rather – what does that mean? – oh, ah – she's aware of the topic being wide -good questions for feedback – can I understand her ideas? (Joan/Seng Hee)

It is obvious here that the teachers are not simply marking a text; they are using the information they have about the student to contextualize the writing being done, the strengths and weaknesses of the individual student, and his or her explicit requests for particular kinds of help. In addition, the protocols also showed that the teachers considered the personality and possible response of the student to specific feedback points, both before and while giving feedback.

I've been looking forward to marking Maho's – to reading Maho's draft because I had an interesting wee talk with her in the writing workshop and she has an interesting approach – she's an interesting person. (Joan/Maho)

The wastes would be removed from their sources, where they would be harmful – right I don't understand that – **I don't understand this sentence** – alright that fits in with the kind of feedback that she wants too – whether I don't understand. (Joan /Seng Hee)

I feel that I'm giving quite detailed feedback here, but she is a quite serious student so I feel that it is worthwhile. (Joan/Maho)

The essay itself – what did I do? I looked through the whole thing first, recognized that this woman had put in a lot of effort into organisation and structure. (Nadia/Liang)

Research confirms that students value feedback and believe it helps them, and it is possible that students who do not get what they believe they need may lose motivation (Ferris, 2003). Our data suggest that teachers often recognize students' needs and do their utmost to accommodate them. Teachers do not give feedback in a vacuum but create a context for their remarks, making use of what they know of the writer to create an inter-personal link and target feedback to the student's personality and needs. In using mechanisms such as cover sheets (Leki, 1990), questionnaires, or autobiographies detailing students' past experiences as writers and of recipients' feedback (Goldstein, 2004) to uncover student feedback pref-erences, we open up a process of communication between teachers and students that can enhance the effectiveness of the teacher's commentary and the students' revisions.

Pedagogic context

In addition to constructing the student, the teachers showed an aware-ness of the pedagogic context in their responses to the students as they constantly referred to previous learning experiences of the class and to individual conversations with students as they wrote their comments:

Oh has she put references? – good – she's got that from the last assignment. (Joan/Seng Hee)

He's definitely using his own words – and he's using new words from our last class theme as well. (Joan/Keith)

She's pleased with the outline. Wants to improve coherence and ideas. What we dealt with in class – that's good. (Nadia/ Samorn)

The teachers also looked ahead, highlighting the close link between feed-back and teaching, both as a reinforcement of what had been done in the classroom and as a way of indicating future directions to students. Thus, the feedback was not treated simply in reference to student texts but as an interactive part of the whole context of learning, one that would help to create a productive interpersonal relationship between the teacher and individual students:

She recognised that she had a fragments problem um and identified her problems with articles and that's what I know I need to follow up on with her and perhaps just make sure that she gets on to that one. (Nadia/Liang)

You need to say where you got the information from in an academic essay. References – I'll just say we'll be doing them next week – **we'll look at this next week.** (Joan/Seng Hee)

Table 11.2. *Focus of teacher feedback acts (%)*

	Ideas	Form	Academic	Process	General	Totals
Number	283	139	122	20	24	588
Praise	63.8	13.8	13.3	2.3	6.8	100
Criticism	43.8	23.5	30.1	2.6	0.0	100
Suggestion	36.3	23.4	36.3	4.0	0.0	100
Overall	48.1	23.6	20.8	3.4	4.1	100

These extracts show quite clearly that the two teachers had pedagogic goals that were best served by considering interpersonal issues and mitigating their feedback. In considering the writer as much as the text, the teachers sought to make their responses more effective and continue the student-teacher dialogue, which is central to successful teaching and learning.

Focus factors and the construction of feedback

Another area in which interpersonal issues may affect the construction of feedback is teachers' choices of what to focus on in student writing. Many teachers are aware of the form/meaning dichotomy originally proposed by L1 researchers and the admonishments that teachers should avoid over-attending to form and respond more to meaning (Zamel, 1985). In practice, of course, this has never been a productive distinction, beacuse language is a *resource* for making meanings, not something we turn to when we have worked out what we are going to say (Ferris, 2003; Hyland, 2003). But whereas it is hard to separate form and function when giving feedback, the dichotomy forms a conscious part of the way many L2 writing teachers respond to student texts and can potentially influence the interpersonal strategies they adopt when giving feedback.

Our analysis identified five main areas of feedback focus: the students' ideas, their control of form, their ability to employ appropriate academic writing and research conventions, their approach to the processes of writing, and global issues related to the entire essay. Table 11.2 shows that the teacher end comments overwhelmingly addressed the ideational content of the writing and that the teachers focused most of their praise (64%) and much of their criticism (44%) on ideas. Suggestions focused evenly on ideas and academic concerns, with slightly less focus on language issues.

We also hypothesized that teachers might tread more softly and be less prescriptive when they were responding to meaning, particularly as both Joan and Nadia were sensitive to appropriation issues and took

Table 11.3. *Mitigation of suggestions and criticisms by main area of feedback focus*

	Ideas	Form	Academic	Process	General	Totals
Suggestions	79.2	29.6	37.1	68.0	0.0	71.0
Criticisms	88.4	31.2	45.2	80.0	0.0	84.3
Unmitigated	16.2	69.6	59.7	26.0	0.0	22.4
Totals	100	100	100	100	100	100

seriously the need to avoid taking control of student texts – shifting the student's purposes to their own with over-prescriptive and over-directive feedback on their ideas (Brannon & Knoblauch, 1982). We therefore looked at the distribution of mitigation across the five categories to see if interpersonal issues affected the ways the teachers constructed their criticisms and suggestions in different focus areas. Table 11.3 confirms our hypothesis and shows that these teachers overwhelmingly softened the expression of their remarks, mitigating 88 percent of all criticisms and 79 percent of suggestions on ideas.

Students are often committed to the ideas they produce and invest something of themselves in them. The content of their writing represents their views as *thinking individuals* rather than as *second language students*. Unhedged criticisms can therefore carry a possible threat to the "face" or public self-image of students, weakening their confidence in what they believe and damaging the relationship of trust with the teacher. Teachers may therefore mitigate the force of their comments to avoid causing resentment and hostility and to preserve the relationship. This desire to reduce the potentially devastating effects of negative commentary on students' ideas was clearly illustrated in our teacher protocols. These data contain many examples of the teachers being very direct and to the point when thinking aloud but then toning these thoughts down in their written comments:

Spoken comment: OK. Theory's good but absolutely no examples given.
Written comment: You have dealt with the points in a logical manner and your introduction and conclusion are well developed. However, I would have liked you to give some examples of countries which have one or the other system as the material is rather difficult to grasp /understand without concrete/real life examples. (Nadia/Liang)

Spoken comment: Hum, definitely needs to use subheadings – the first bit is about tours and the second is about duration, accommodation, mm – I might suggest that.
Written comment: It might be a good idea to use sub-headings here, e.g., activities, length of stay, accommodation. (Joan/Keith)

The protocols also contain numerous cases of the teachers consciously selecting the mitigating strategy they will use, carefully picking over expressive options before selecting forms that convey an appropriate degree of softening. In these examples, for instance, Joan chooses to weaken her statements using interrogatives, hedges, and personal attribution, and Nadia uses the hedges; *a bit* and *rather* to weaken the force of her criticisms.

Conclusion is a bit vague – it is vague – need to question that – suggest – err – mmm – I'm not sure that is the conclusion so – I'm not sure that is the conclusion so – did she say anything about another sheet? – no, no mention of conclusion – **Is this the conclusion? It is** too – no – I've written **a bit – too general.** (Joan/Maho)

In addition many other non governmental groups are strongly against pollution – Ah that has to be a separate paragraph – **is this a separate paragraph?** – and then in brackets – **I think it should be.** (Joan/Seng Hei)

The main idea is clear – but the organisation of sentences in the introduction – and conclusion – is confusing? – no- is chaotic? – Ha ha – *but the organisation of sentences in the introduction and conclusion* – is jumbled? – Um – Could be improved? – Err **– could be improved –** Sometimes students don't understand that as a criticism, but he should. (Joan/Keith)

In a free market economy there are more productive efficiency than in a planned economy and consumers are happier for they can choose and get the goods they want and are willing to buy most by themselves. Ha ha she clearly knows which one she wants, but a very sudden end – Ok **– the conclusion is a bit abrupt – you need to re-state some of the main points – the essay is rather –** it's way too much **– middle heavy.** (Nadia/Samorn)

We can also see in Table 11.3 that the teachers were far more direct when responding to form, with some 70 percent of these comments unmitigated. It is possible that the teachers felt more comfortable in adopting an authoritative stance in a domain where their expertise was likely to be more assured and less threatening to students. L2 students often expect directive comments on their grammar and lexical choices and often feel this is the teacher's primary responsibility when giving feedback. The greater assurance that teachers seemed to have in acting as experts in their comments on form also comes through clearly in the protocols:

Hmm it's a good essay. Right what have we got? She has to practise her articles. I'll put **Work needed on articles.** (Nadia/Liang)

In conclusion ... to solve its problems – ha I like that one – *of overpopulation pollution and national welfare* – oh my god that's a confusing sentence – let's try again – yes it's not a proper – it's not a complete sentence – oh dear – I'll ask her to identify the subject and the verb – **Very long sentence! Not clear! Which is the subject and which is the verb?** (Joan/Keith)

I wonder if he understands the comma punctuation – it's a such simple thing – it should be an easy correction – **don't leave a space before commas or full stops.** (Nadia/Zhang)

Another important focus of feedback in these presessional university courses, as in many EAP contexts, is that of academic issues. In this area, teachers may see their primary role as expert and gatekeeper, helping students to understand the appropriate conventions to gain entry to the academic discourse community. Teachers may therefore be willing to offer more directive feedback on such elements as these issues, choosing not to mitigate their comments on such elements as referencing conventions or questions of appropriate formality, for instance. Generally, this is the case, but in one area of academic issues we found that teachers extensively mitigated their comments: plagiarism.

This issue is very sensitive for feedback and one teachers are often unwilling to address directly. Teachers may also be aware of the literature that suggests that plagiarism is, at least partly, a Western cultural concept and that many nonnative writers are unfamiliar with the individualistic authorial role implied in English academic writing conventions (e.g., Pennycook, 1996). This understanding places ESL teachers in a dilemma, because they often feel it is important to address these concerns when giving feedback but are reluctant to do so directly. Joan, for example, expressed her unwillingness to accuse Seng Hee directly of a possible instance of plagiarism in one of her protocols.

...thereby enabling the people to live healthfully and pleasantly – it doesn't sound like her words – I hate accusing people of plagiarism, but when you think it is what do you do? – *the government implemented regulations of each items in terms of category, size, capacity and kind* – items – *the law also established quality standards for air, fresh and marine water, noise, discharge of chemicals and motor vehicle emissions* – I'd better ask her where did she get this information from – **Where did you get this information? Have you used quotations?**– a subtle way of saying it – of course. (Joan /Seng Hee)

Joan's decision to be subtle here attempted to obscure a potentially volatile issue, but the comment was too indirect for the student to recognize, and the offending section remained in her final draft.

Joan felt uncomfortable with this issue in another case and debated how to tell Maho that she thought she had plagiarized:

uh so bother – do I accuse her of plagiarism? – I can ask her where she got this information from anyway – **Where did you get this information?** – we'll deal with referencing next week. (Joan/Maho)

Once again she used the formula *Where did you get this information from?* in her feedback to tone down the comment rather than confronting the issue directly. Nadia, when confronted with the plagiarism of an entire essay, was also unwilling to be direct. She responded with a personalized and hedged criticism, followed by a second criticism, also hedged.

I am afraid that this may not be your own work. You may have got some/ considerable help with it.

As before, this comment failed to open a dialogue with the student on the topic.

Student interpretation and response

A final interpersonal dimension concerns the ways that students respond to comments. In discussing a sociocultural perspective on second-language acquisition (SLA), Lantolf and Pavlenko (2001, p. 145) argue that learners are "more than processing devices that convert linguistic input into well-formed (or not so well-formed) outputs." They are individuals with human agency who "actively engage in constructing the terms and conditions of their own learning." In other words, learners are historically and sociologically situated active agents who respond to what they see as valuable and useful and to people they regard as engaging and credible. They learn through purposive interaction with teachers and their learning environment to develop knowledge and strategies and to engage with others in communities of practice.

The factor of student agency and decision making has not always been fully explored in the research on feedback, and we have space only to mention it briefly here. It is worth observing that agency is not an individual phenomenon, and decisions about what to act on and how to act on it are always co-constructed in interaction with other agents, particularly the teacher's feedback itself. SLA research tells us that learners are interpretative, accommodating, and strategic and that their response to meaningful input and attempts to express meaning drive learning (Breen, 2001). Teachers position students in particular ways by their feedback, and students respond selectively as they try to make sense of their learning. Therefore, it is not surprising that research shows that comments that are vague, cryptic, authoritarian, generic, or a combination of these fail to engage this kind of selective response and neither inform students nor motivate revisions (e.g., Ferris, 1995; Straub, 1997).

The students in our study were very clear about what they wanted from the teacher in terms of feedback and were sensitive to the interpersonal dimensions of how it was expressed. Several students said they found positive remarks to be motivating and attached considerable importance to them.

> If teacher give me positive comments it means I succeed – just only two sentence but I succeeded with these sentences, so I feel satisfied with this. These comments will give us some enjoyment. It's more enjoyable to write if someone enjoys my writing. It makes me feel better. (Maho)

> I always look for what she says is good in the essay first, this gives me the support. Then I can look for the corrections I must do. (Samorn)

But students also expect to receive constructive criticism rather than simple platitudes (Ferris, 1995). Even Maho said that despite appreciating positive comments, what she felt she needed most from teacher feedback was "some help not admiration." Students are adept at recognizing formulaic positive comments that serve no function beyond removing the sting from criticisms and do not generally welcome empty remarks. A student in Nadia's class, Zhang, for example, believed positive remarks were "useless" unless they were backed up by "serious" comments that he could act on, and another student, Mei Ling, discounted positive comments because "I want to know my weaknesses most." For her, positive comments were insincere and therefore worthless.

> Sometimes maybe the teacher doesn't mean it, but they just try to encourage you. [...] Because there is always "but" after the positive ... may be that strength is not the main point. ... I want the teacher to always tells me the weaknesses of my writings and then I know how to improve. (Mei Ling)

Teachers' use of mitigation strategies to help maintain or develop good relationships with their students seems to be appreciated. Although positive comments need to be used with care, failing to mitigate criticism can have a serious impact on students' attitudes toward writing and their reception of feedback.

> I am very interested in teacher's comments every time. I like to read it and when I read it and if it says "it's good but your problem is grammatical problem", then I will turn back to see how many mistakes I have. But if the comment is very bad and maybe not good enough, maybe I'll stop for a while and keep it and take it out and look at again later.

> If feedback is not so good, I mean that teacher criticise many mistake I have, then I feel – "Oh I don't like writing." (Samorn)

There are, however, dangers in indirectness, and we have pointed to the potential for miscommunication in mitigated feedback elsewhere (Hyland & Hyland, 2001). Each case study provided several examples where students failed to understand, or only partly understood, mitigated comments, and this practice clearly carries potential dangers and requires careful consideration. Although teachers need to develop rapport with students and guard against being overly directive, indirectness carries its own problems, especially for learners of low English proficiency, since they may fail to understand implied messages. Although mitigation helps make critical comments more palatable, it has the potential to cloud issues and create confusion. For instance, when we asked one of our case study writers, Zhang, why he had failed to respond to a teacher suggestion on his draft, he made it clear that he had not refused to respond to this comment on purpose, saying, "I didn't mean to ignore it, but I did not understand it. I think the teacher is always right."

Conclusions and implications

Our purpose in this chapter has been to take a preliminary look at an under-researched aspect of teacher written feedback: the ways that interpersonal considerations influence the construction and interpretation of response. We have attempted to show in the extracts that feedback not only communicates beliefs about writing, language, or content but also expresses and negotiates human relationships. Teachers often take great care in phrasing their end comments on ESL learners' essays, using praise, criticism, and suggestions to structure their response and mitigating directness in various ways. We also found that the teachers tended to be more reticent about criticizing students' ideas than about commenting on form and that issues of plagiarism were rarely addressed directly.

Analysis of our data leads us to believe that teachers' comments and students' appreciation of them are underpinned by attempts to foster and maintain social harmony and encourage a cooperative pedagogical environment that can promote learning. Evidence from the protocols, interviews, and teacher commentary shows that the two teachers were very aware that their responses had the potential to construct the kinds of relationships that could either facilitate or undermine writing development. They recognized that offering praise and criticism expresses and confirms the teacher's right to evaluate a student's work, and as a result they sought to blur the impact of this dominance. In other words, their feedback practices were guided by interpersonal strategies to enhance the teacher-student relationship, minimize the threat of judgment, and mitigate the full force of their criticisms and suggestions.

Our research has a number of clear implications for teachers and researchers. As our discussion has shown, students vary considerably in what they want from their teachers in the form of feedback. Some students value positive comments, whereas others discount them as mere dressing. Students often have their own concerns and agendas, and it is important that teachers seek to discover these and, to the extent possible, address them in their feedback. We need to tailor our comments to specific students and their needs and personalities, as well as to the teaching context.

Teachers are largely aware of the importance of feedback in providing helpful advice on writing and in negotiating an interpersonal relationship that will facilitate its development. However, they need to keep the individual student in mind at all times when responding to writing. The ways that we frame our comments tell students a lot about us, what kinds of teachers we are, and what we believe about writing and learning. Our comments can transform students' attitudes to writing and lead to improvements, but our words can also confuse and dishearten them. We need, then, to be sure that we monitor our feedback so that it is consistent, clear, helpful, and constructive.

While further research into the ways teachers and students co-construct each other in the feedback relationship is needed to explore these findings, we believe that interpersonal considerations are central to the ways we express comments and are crucial to good feedback practices.

References

Allwright, R. (1989). *Interaction in the language classroom: Social problems and pedagogic possibilities.* Paper presented at les États Généraux des Langues, Paris. April, 1989.

Anson, C. (1989). Response styles and ways of knowing. In C. Anson (Ed.), *Writing and response: Theory, practice, and research* (pp. 332–65). Urbana, IL: NCTE.

Bates, L., Lane, J., & Lange, E. (1993). *Writing clearly: Responding to ESL composition.* Boston: Heinle and Heinle.

Brannon, L., & Knoblauch, C. H. (1982). On students' rights to their own texts: A model of teacher response. *College Composition and Communication, 33,* 157–166.

Breen, M. (2001). Navigating the discourse: On what is learned in the language classroom. In C. Candlin, & N. Mercer (Eds.), *English language teaching in its social context* (pp. 122–144). London: Routledge.

Connors, R. J., & Lunsford, A. (1993). Teachers' rhetorical comments on student papers. *College Composition and Communication, 44,* 200–223.

Ferris, D. R. (1995). Student reactions to teacher response in multiple-draft composition classrooms. *TESOL Quarterly, 29*(1), 33–53.

Ferris, D. (2003). *Response to student writing: Implications for second language students.* Mahwah, NJ: Lawerence Erlbaum.

Gee, T. C. (1972). Students' responses to teacher comments. *Research in the Teaching of English, 6,* 212–221.

Goldstein, L. (2004). Questions and answers about teacher written commentary and student revision: Teachers and students working together. *Journal of Second Language Writing, 13 (31),* 63–80.

Hillocks, J. R. (1986). *Research on written composition. New directions for teaching.* Urbana, IL: ERIC Clearinghouse on Reading and Communication Skills, ED265 552.

Hyland, F., & Hyland, K. (2001). Sugaring the pill: Praise and criticism in written feedback. *Journal of Second Language Writing, 10 (3)*, 185–212.

Hyland, K. (2003) *Second language writing.* New York: Cambridge University Press.

Knoblauch, C. H., & Brannon, L. (1981). Teacher commentary on student writing: The state of the art. *Freshman English News, 18* (2), 1–4.

Lantolf, J., & Pavlenko, A. (2001). (S)econd (L)anguage (A)ctivity theory: Understanding second language learners as people. In M. Breen (Ed.), *Learner contributions to language learning* (pp. 172–182). London: Longman.

Lea, M., & Street, B. (2000). Student writing and staff feedback in higher education: An academic illiteracies approach. In M. Lea & B. Stierer (Eds.) *Student writing in higher education* (pp. 32–46). Buckingham, UK: Open University Press.

Leki, I. (1990). Coaching from the margins: Issues in written response. In B. Kroll (Ed.), *Second language writing: Research insights for the classroom* (pp. 57–68). Cambridge: Cambridge University Press.

Lincoln, Y. S., & Guba, E. G. (1985). *Naturalistic inquiry.* Beverly Hills, CA: Sage.

Pennycook, A. (1996). Borrowing others' words: Text, ownership, memory and plagiarism. *TESOL Quarterly, 30*(2), 201–230.

Reid, J. (1994). Responding to ESL students' texts: The myths of appropriation. *TESOL Quarterly, 28*(2), 273–294.

Sperling, M. (1994). Constructing the perspective of teacher-as-reader: A framework for studying response to writing. *Research in the Teaching of English, 28*, 175–203.

Straub, R. (1997). Students' reactions to teacher comments: An exploratory study. *Research in the Teaching of English, 31*, 91–119.

Taylor, W. F., and Hoedt, K. C. (1966). The effect of praise upon quantity and quality of creative writing. *Journal of Educational Research, 60*, 80–83.

Vygotsky, L. (1978). *Mind in society: The development of higher psychological processes.* M. Cole, V. John-Steiner, S. Scribner, & E. Souberman (Eds.). Cambridge, MA: Harvard University Press.

Zamel, V. (1985). Responding to student writing. *TESOL Quarterly, 19* (1), 79–101.

12 Formative interaction in electronic written exchanges: Fostering feedback dialogue

Ann Hewings
Caroline Coffin

In this chapter, formative feedback is examined within asynchronous exchanges between native and nonnative English-speaking (NS and NNS) master's degree students, using computer conferencing software. The styles of peer and tutor interaction in three separate tutorial groups are observed to promote different levels of discussion and reflection on content and academic writing. We analyze how the task sets and the tutors' input influence the development of these interactions and the degree of critical reflection exhibited by students in their feedback to each other. From these case studies, we argue that asynchronous computer-mediated communication (CMC) has the potential to help students learn the disciplinary norms of a new area of study in terms of content knowledge, expression, and epistemology. The realization of this potential is influenced by the role the tutor adopts and the tasks that are set. It is these aspects that we examine in detail through an analysis of feedback.

Much of the literature on learning highlights the importance of talk or dialogue, particularly as a way of scaffolding learning (Bruner, 1986). Here, we foreground the potential for written CMC to scaffold understanding of not only disciplinary knowledge but also disciplinary writing demands. The relative durability of CMC, in contrast to ephemeral face-to-face discussions, allows opportunities for students to reflect on contributions already posted to a conference and to consider and revise their own contributions before posting them to a group. In addition, with prompting from the tutor, students can be encouraged to evaluate their own and others' writing in terms of disciplinary expectations and to feed back that evaluation. At a master's level, such metacognitive reflection on learning and writing processes can make students aware of what is acceptable in terms of knowledge claims and evidence and how both may be expressed within a subject area.

We begin by reviewing briefly some of the literature on learning as a dialogic process and then relate it to our knowledge about educational interaction using CMC. The central part of the chapter is an analysis of tutor and peer feedback with an emphasis on how the interventions of the tutors influence the level of critical engagement and reflection on both writing and the discipline. We draw out areas of significance for those using CMC in their own teaching.

Dialogue and computer-facilitated learning: Study viewpoints

Our starting point for examining CMC is that interaction per se provides the possibility that some form of learning will take place. Support for this view comes from both educational theorists and linguists. Vygotsky (1962) assigns a privileged role to speech in the development of thinking, and Halliday (1994) emphasizes language more generally. Gee (1990, 1994), in taking a sociocultural / sociohistorical perspective, foregrounds the importance of interaction in his concept of "discourses." We therefore take as a foundation that dialogue, whether face-to-face or computer-enabled, can facilitate, or scaffold, the process of learning. There are, however, fundamental differences associated with the electronic medium. Clearly, in asynchronous CMC there is a lack of visual and aural clues about participants and their views, a time delay in receiving responses and feedback, and a need for at least moderately effective writing skills. On the other hand, it has been argued that the asynchronicity provides time and space for participants to reflect on their ideas and those of others (Lea, 2001; Light et al., 1997; Wilson & Whitelock, 1998). It can create a safe site for students to try out ideas, to co-operatively brainstorm problems, and to rehearse the articulation of their thoughts (Belcher, 2001, p. 145). It can enable those who are hesitant in face-to-face situations, particularly those NNSs socialized to be quiet in class, to join in (Warschauer, 2002). A number of studies have also pointed out the influence of CMC on argumentation processes, with several researchers claiming that by providing the text of messages in a form that can be reviewed and manipulated, asynchronous electronic conferencing aids the articulation, critique, and defense of ideas (Harasim, 1989; Henri, 1995; Lea, 2001).

Not all the research has been clear-cut in pointing to the educational benefits of interaction using computers. On argumentation, Marttunen and Laurinen (2001) found that during e-mail discussions students learned to identify or choose relevant grounds for an argument, but that face-to-face discussions improved their skills in putting forward counter-arguments. The ability to encourage NNSs or more hesitant speakers to participate has been questioned by Goodfellow (2004). For some students, it is not the language but the style of interaction that can cause problems (Hara & Kling, 1999; Lea et al., 1992). Participants may deliberately or unwittingly subvert conference discussions; what to some may be a legitimate challenge that can aid learning (Tolmie & Boyle, 2000) may seem to others a threat to face.

The lack of agreement on the educational benefits of CMC may be due, in part, to its relative newness. Unlike the classroom or other face-to-face situations to which we all bring years of socialization, CMC is a relative newcomer in education and is still rapidly evolving; thus, it represents a process that students and tutors alike are learning to handle. In this study, we show how feedback within CMC can promote reflection on both disciplinary content and its associated literacies and at the same time foster an inclusive and supportive learning community. We argue that the interpersonal dimension, and particularly the role of the tutor, is significant in influencing the dynamics of the conference and thus the opportunity for reflection to come about (see Light et al., 2000).

Our concern for written interaction moves us away from a focus on writing as a skills issue for NNSs. Rather, at this level, we see academic writing or literacy, both CMC and traditional essays, less as a matter of correct grammar and relevant content knowledge, and more as a means of helping students to understand and enter into the ways of knowing sanctioned by the academy and by their discipline (Becher, 1994; Hewings, 2004; Hyland, 2000; MacDonald, 1994; Myers, 1990). Students need to grasp what constitutes knowledge and evidence and learn how to express this within disciplines. Difficulties in accomplishing these goals can affect both NS and NNS students. In recent years, there have been calls for academic and disciplinary expectations to be made more explicit particularly as more nontraditional students move through the higher education system (Coffin et al., 2003; Gee, 2000). Lillis (2001) has suggested that one way of doing this is to replace traditional feedback with "talkback." She likens this to exploratory talk (see also Mercer, 2000), which is aimed at "opening up discussion and . . . [moving] away from a tutor-directed talking space" (Lillis 2001, p. 10). This definition provides a useful way of characterizing what we might aim to achieve in conferencing interactions.

What we mean by "feedback"

We consider feedback broadly as that part of a dialogue that acknowledges, comments on, or extends the discussion of academic content or its expression. Like the typical initiation-response-feedback (IRF) sequence noted by Sinclair and Coulthard (1975) in classroom discourse, feedback in our CMC data is identified in part by its position in the interaction. However, although traditionally associated with evaluation, our conception of successful feedback is as a positive strategy, with the aim of expanding dialogue as a means to extend students' thinking. It is important in both interpersonal and experiential domains, creating a cooperative and supportive learning community, as well as focusing on content. Feedback often provides building blocks, points at which a student's understanding can be acknowledged and built upon to encourage deeper reflection. The written aspect of asynchronous conferencing creates time and space for this reflection. However, the degree to which these opportunities are taken up and acted on appears to be strongly influenced by the tasks students are set and by the type of feedback model provided by tutors.

There is some evidence that tutors and students have different views on the role of the tutor and importance of feedback in the CMC environment. Collaborative learning prioritizes peer interaction based on tasks designed by a tutor who has adopted a facilitator role (Thorpe, 2002). However, this teacher role does not satisfy some students, who want feedback not from peers but from their tutor (Jones et al., 2000, Lea, 2001). An alternate model is Salmon's (2003) view of conferencing as a series of stages where the tutor role evolves as the independence of the students increases. In the data presented in this paper we see a number of these views.

Research aims and context

The research reported here is part of a larger project[1] (see Painter et al., 2003, for a summary) designed to investigate the effect of different tutorial tasks on the way students in a globally available master's course in TESOL put forward discipline-based arguments in CMC and in subsequent traditional written assignments. The primary aim was to explore how particular types of feedback might support a deepening awareness of the academic conventions of argumentation needed in both CMC as well as in traditional essay writing. In particular, we wanted to encourage awareness and reflection on the disciplinary expectations of applied linguistics with regard to putting forward and supporting opinions. We observed that the effect of emphasizing argumentation in the conference discussions is a means of rehearsing the language expected in the traditional essay assignments that students need to write.

The participants in this study were all working or studying with the Open University, the U.K.'s biggest university with more than 150,000 mainly part-time students studying at a distance. The data come from one of three modules that form a globally presented master's level distance-learning program in applied linguistics. Teaching was conducted using a mix of print materials, videotapes, and audiocassettes. Tutorials took place using asynchronous electronic conferencing that allowed the posting of messages to the conference at any time, to be read and responded to at any time.

Each tutor group was generally between 10 and 18 students. The students were a mixture of U.K.-based and continental Europe-based NS and NNS English language teachers. Although their proficiency in English was excellent, there was variation in their understanding of the writing requirements of applied linguistics. The tutors assigned tasks to be completed using the computer conference, participated in the conference discussions to a greater or lesser degree, made themselves available to answer individual e-mail queries, and also marked and commented on assessed work. Six tutorials were conducted using the commercial First-Class software by Open Text. Messages were retained in the conference for the duration of the course.

Three tutors volunteered to allow us to collect the messages posted during two of their computer-mediated tutorials. All were tutoring the course for the second time and were experienced subject specialists. Only one tutor (for Group C) had had significant CMC teaching experience for the Open University before beginning work on this course. In this chapter, we are reporting on only the interaction that took place during the first tutorial for each of the three groups, A, B, and C, because the first tutorial was the only mandatory CMC element of the course. The tutorials took place over approximately two weeks, and students' interactions in the conference formed part of the first summative assessment, which also included an essay on second language acquisition. In addition to the tutorial conferences, we sent online questionnaires to all tutors and students involved in the course during the year.

The tutor for Group A was given no instructions beyond what all tutors for the course received. He provided the general instruction that students should introduce themselves to the group and describe from their own experiences a problem in language learning and a factor relevant to success. They should then respond to another student's posting, giving their own views.

In Group B, the tutor was asked to draw the attention of his students to the putting forward of logical arguments during the conference, and the way in which to do this was left to his judgment. We expected that this instruction would lead to greater involvement in the discussion by the tutor, and our interest was in how students might be supported by his discursive interventions. The tutor invited students to give an example from their experience of a "problem" and a "joy" in learning a language. These problems and joys were the focus of our analysis.

For Group C, four tasks were designed by us in collaboration with the tutor. These tasks were intended to provide scaffolding for the assignment through structured activities that would rehearse argumentation skills, among them the sourced provision of evidence and increased understanding of the requirements of academic argumentation. The tasks are described in the following section.

A framework for analysis

In order to isolate peer and tutor feedback, each tutorial conference was analyzed in terms of initiations, responses, and feedback. This approach allowed us to see whether and how feedback led to a continuation of the learning interaction. The assignment task that students were to undertake during the conference was categorized as the primary initiation. There followed initial responses from students. Feedback then came both from the tutor's comments on the students' responses and from the students' comments on each other's messages. Feedback postings were complex and often included text copied from earlier messages, comments on the messages, and follow-up questions. As such, they had the potential to extend the dialogue and exploration of the topics. Tutors and peers were able to encourage others, endorse their views with experiential information, probe aspects of what had been said, and challenge remarks that were not clear or did not apply universally. Because feedback was itself part of the ongoing dialogue, it often served also to initiate subsequent responses. These different purposes were captured through our qualitative analysis of the interactions. In the next section, we trace the development of CMC exchanges during the first tutorial, with emphasis on how tutor feedback influenced the interpersonal nature of peer interaction and reflection on disciplinary argumentation and academic writing. We focus in particular on those tutor roles and strategies that fostered richer dialogue, creating more opportunities for reflection and peer feedback, because these provide indications of how to promote "talkback."

Findings and discussion

Our findings led us to concentrate on how feedback provided the following benefits:

- Support for the interpersonal side of interactions in CMC
- Assistance in extending and expanding the learning dialogue
- Support for reflection on personal experience and academic content (moving from the personal to the abstract)

These last two points are particularly relevant to the development of argumentation skills, as we shall demonstrate.

The tutor groups reported on here were all focusing on the topic of second language learning, and all three tutors aimed to create a welcoming

Table 12.1. *Overall participation in the tutorial conference by the three groups*

	Group A	Group B	Group C
No. of student contributors	29[2]	15	18
Student messages	80 posts	87 posts	213 posts
Mean no. of student contributions	2.8 posts/student	5.8 posts/student	11.8 posts/student
Tutor messages	11 posts	39 posts	44 posts

and supportive community. Beyond these basic similarities, each tutor used contrasting strategies and tasks to stimulate discussion around the topic and took up different roles in relation to their students, thereby creating different types of interactional spaces for students to respond to each other.

Group A: Feedback in a symmetrical power structure

In Group A, the tutor focused on creating a symmetrical power structure. He initiated the tutorial activity and welcomed students and their ideas, but then took a backseat role. The floor was left open to the students to discuss matters and give peer feedback, an opportunity that was only minimally exploited. In terms of stimulating interaction, this strategy was not highly successful, with the average number of posts per student being much lower than for either of the other two groups (Table 12.1).

The tutor's first and only substantive post after initiating the task was his own response to the task. His feedback on students' messages was welcoming but not extensive, as illustrated in the example in Figure 12.1, a response to a posting about past problems with pronunciation by a London-based Brazilian student. The feedback had an interpersonal element – an acknowledgement of the posting through a welcome message – and also endorsed the student's experience through reference to an earlier posting by the tutor, PK.

The reference to a shared language-learning problem strengthened the interpersonal role of the exchange without reinforcing an asymmetrical relationship between the tutor and student and without setting up an expectation that the tutor would evaluate all postings. In discussion with this tutor we found that he viewed his role as creating a forum that was open and welcoming and in which the students, as autonomous adult learners, could interact. His aim was to encourage peer interaction, not to be the arbiter for all exchanges. This lack of a visible presence by the tutor led to little follow-up interaction among peers or between tutor and students after the initial responses and feedback. For this reason, we

Tutor PK:	Hi J Welcome to the conference.	Tutor feedback: Acknowledgment
	As my earlier message said, I've shared your pronunciation problems when learning another language. P	Endorsement of an aspect of the student's experience

Note: In the examples, the left-hand column indicates the initials of the person who posted the message. Where this is the tutor it is explicitly noted. The column contains the text of messages. Extracts from earlier messages are shown in bold. Typographical errors remain as in the originals. The right-hand column provides a brief analysis of the text.

Figure 12.1. Feedback example from Group A

Tutor SJ:	**Living here in the North East of England has been in some situations like learning a whole new language and culture for me. The accent used by some individuals has been very difficult for me to understand, not to mention the abundant use of idioms.**	Tutor feedback: Acknowledgment / contextualizing
	I can also attest to the difficulties of the "Wayay, hinny, I'm gang nyaem"[3] strong dialect utterances sometimes heard in the North East.	Endorsement + personal observation
	But what do you think is the motivation of the user, and what effect does it have on the non-dialect-using listener?	Open question (further initiation)

Figure 12.2. Feedback example from Group B

will concentrate on the feedback strategies used by tutors and students in Groups B and C.

Group B: Feedback through probing with open questions

In Group B the tutor, SJ, rarely used a feedback message to simply acknowledge a post or welcome a student. Rather, he established an open and friendly tenor through the jokey nature of some of his responses and, in addition, endeavored to deepen the discussion by asking questions that required the students to consider their experiences and views on language learning more carefully (Figure 12.2). This probing was addressed to the whole group and thus invited anyone to respond, not just the individual whose post had occasioned the questioning. In this way, SJ avoided any threats to face associated with the

NE: **I never thought it would be so difficult to communicate in my native language.**	Peer feedback: Acknowledgment / contextualizing
I agree, being a northerner and also finding "Geordie" terminology confusing or indecipherable at times I can empathize with any native speaker who seems totally bewildered when trying to communicate.	Agreement / positive evaluation, with personal observation to support position
When inner circle speakers struggle to interact successfully and if the suggestions of Smith and Rafiqzad are true (the native speakers in their study were always found to be among the least intelligible speakers).	Abstraction (using academic source material)
Are monolingual English speakers ultimately going to become isolated from speakers of other varieties of English if a standard form of language cannot be introduced?	Open question (further initiation)

Figure 12.3.   Second feedback example from Group B

questioning technique. The response style modeled by the tutor also facilitated interaction by copying just that part of a message that he was addressing on. Many messages were relatively short, which meant that students did not feel the need to present carefully considered and polished prose, but could enter and influence the debate as it moved along.

In early exchanges, SJ structured his messages in three parts, as shown in the example in Figure 12.2. It begins with a short extract from a student's earlier message (shown in bold) and continues with the tutor's relating it to a personal experience of his own that endorses the student's observation. He finishes with open questions to the whole group, which moves the discussion away from particular personal experiences to more generalizable considerations. That this is a deliberate strategy is shown by his questionnaire comment, "I can and do try to turn conference messages more towards debate."

In Group B, the tutor's use of open questions as the final part of the feedback led to students copying them as the context for their responses, thereby continuing and elaborating the discussion. Some students also used the questioning technique in their own peer feedback. The example in Figure 12.3 comes from a discussion thread on the difficulties of understanding different dialects of languages. This exchange led to peer evaluation of the experiences and ideas of others, and the opening of areas for further discussion through questions.

Peer feedback often included a positive evaluation, such as "I agree...," and when questions were raised they were generally open to the whole group rather than addressed to a particular student. This strategy appeared to diminish any potential loss of face that might be implied by the question to an individual and also followed the lead set by the tutor.

Within feedback, overt challenges to opinions were rare, though they did occur. The tutor adapted his three-part structure: quoting a student, then indicating a counter opinion, and in the final part opening the discussion by addressing a more general question to the conference as a whole. The example in Figure 12.4 shows how this style of challenge was taken up and adapted by students. A student (NE) wishing to challenge another student (HJG) adopted a similar style to that of the tutor – putting forward a counter point of view. The counter elicited a further feedback – support for the challenge by another student (SB). The challenged student responded by reflecting on her choice of language.

This type of peer interaction is illustrative of the challenging dialogue considered so useful by Tolmie and Boyle (2000), in which evidence is required to support statements or claims. In this extract it leads to a deeper level of reflection on how to put forward opinions in an academic context. Another comment by the same student at around the same time, "I must try to be more tentative with my replies in this short form of communication," indicates a concern with linguistic expression related to CMC. The way in which the opinion is supported using the modality marker *perhaps* shows both awareness and an adjustment to the rules of argumentation in this field. It is not generally acceptable to state something categorically without strong evidence, and markers of modality are therefore necessary to indicate the provisionality of an opinion or claim. This is certainly the case in traditional essay assignments, and it is shown to influence the CMC discussion here too.

Peer challenges of the type illustrated in Figure 12.4 were relatively rare in Group B, despite the modeling by the tutor, and rare in the conferences overall. We have argued elsewhere (Coffin & Hewings, 2005) that challenges are not a compulsory element of the argumentation in our data. Rather, most extended interaction on a particular topic tended to be additive – students made supportive comments about earlier postings and then added new thoughts and examples. The result was a cumulative buildup of evidence and experience around a topic without putting the interaction at risk through interpersonal clashes. This pattern held in both Group B's and C's discussions. In Group B, the feedback style adopted by the tutor led to a high level of interactivity, with reflection on concepts facilitated by the questioning technique and peer feedback. The conference, however, remained asymmetrical, as only 10 questions were asked by students, in

NE:	HJG wrote: ...so, more advanced learners will be hungry to see many different forms and enjoy the culture of other English speakers, too.	Peer feedback: Acknowledging / contextualizing
	Within Arabic the opposite appears to be true...The most advanced native learners of the language aspire to master Classical Arabic which is regarded as highly complex and very formal. (so there is little hope for us second language learners!) To quote an acquaintance, the language of The Holy Quran is so grammatically correct and beautifully written that it's origin must be inspired. Of course I don't want to bring the discussion into the realms of religion. I thought that maybe this could suggest not all learners wish to deviate from what is regarded as a standard variety of language.	Challenge (counter-example followed by generalization)
SB:	Greetings, N, I must agree, learning the "standard" dialect was more reassuring to me as well when studying Spanish. In my experience with Spanish, it is the form that will see you through most situations.	Peer feedback: Agreement / positive evaluation with personal observation to support position (implicit challenge of HJG's comment)
HJG:	I should be more tentative of course, not all learners will be hungry for different forms...perhaps the case of English today is different from Arabic though, if we think in terms of new varieties. Someone using English might be operating in a wide variety of contexts and experiencing English from many sources. [ellipsis in original]	Student response: Metacognitive reflection (considers problem of appropriate language; defends viewpoint using modalized expressions)

Figure 12.4. Interactive feedback example from Group B

contrast to 46 asked by the tutor. Of these 10 questions, only 5 received a direct response – possibly due to their rhetorical flavor. The tutor's questions, in contrast, almost always received a response and sometimes multiple responses. Students' postings did, however, receive peer feedback that used supportive strategies, such as validating the writer's experiences through recalling a similar experience, and positive feedback, such as "This is interesting." For a less asymmetrical conference, but one that was highly interactive, we can turn to Group C, where more overt efforts were made to focus attention on aspects of argumentation.

| Tutor PJB: | Hi, I've been very impressed with the number of detailed argued responses to the first activity, and I'm particularly pleased to see the way you've taken up certain issues to debate together. Your responses have certainly gone well beyond a simple listing of the factors which, based on personal experience, you believe affect language learning. | Tutor feedback: Positive evaluation + reason |

Figure 12.5. Tutor feedback: Positive evaluation of interaction

Group C: Activity-based feedback and response

Group C had the same basic task as groups A and B – discussing factors affecting language learning – but the task itself was broken down into activities. Activity 1 required the students to brainstorm factors affecting language learning, drawing on their own experiences. It also served as an icebreaker. Like the tutor in Group A, the tutor (PJB) in Group C tried to encourage peer dialogue by staying in the background while the students posted their experiences. He entered the conference only to respond to specific concerns, though he did give feedback to the group as a whole at the end of the first tutorial activity and before initiating the next activity. This feedback highlighted the way the interaction had taken place and the importance he attached to dialogue, as shown in Figure 12.5.

Activity 2 focused on the academic discourse skills of reasoning, debating and supporting claims with evidence. Students were instructed to comment – in effect, to give feedback – on the messages from Activity 1 and challenge or endorse at least one of the factors put forward, saying why they thought the factor was convincing or unconvincing. They were asked to draw first on their own experience, then on that of their peers, and finally through reference to specified readings for the course.

The students in this activity were careful to maintain positive relationships with each other, and most chose to endorse rather than to challenge. Some, however, used an endorsement or partial endorsement followed by a challenge on an item of detail. This pattern seemed designed to maintain the friendly and encouraging interpersonal tenor of the conference while at the same time enabling deeper reflection on the views of others. The activity also supported the dialogic interaction by requiring students to read and reread the views of their peers. The tutor in these activities shared his own experiences but did not take a stand on those of the students.

It was notable that the challenges offered in the peer feedback were rarely responded to. There are two possible explanations. First, as the

DS: The conferencing system becomes a bit like a rough sketch book, or scrap paper, with comments from other people about our own ideas. We can then reformulate our ideas taking into consideration reactions from others. On the other hand the purpose of writing about language learning becomes more formal in the [assignment]. We are able to draw on other people's experiences and ideas which have been proposed and dissected in the conference and reformulate them into a structured argument . . .We can also consolidate our ideas in a formal piece of writing.	Peer feedback: Acknowledging/ contextualizing (demonstrating metacognitive reflection on conferencing and writing in different genres)
I liked this analogy very much! I think you've hit the nail on the head.	Positive evaluation

Figure 12.6. Student's comparison of CMC and writing for assessment

challenging feedback came from their peers, students perhaps did not feel that they were obliged to respond. If this is the explanation, it might indicate that the symmetrical interpersonal role taken by the tutor was not facilitating deeper engagement with ideas. Second, the volume and length of messages generated may have meant that students were too overwhelmed just reading and responding to really engage in an ongoing dialogue about a particular point. Students commented negatively on the amount of time required for the conferencing activities. We subsequently evaluated this as a negative aspect of the tasks designed by ourselves and the tutor.

Activity 3 posed the following questions:

What purpose did the authors [Lightbown and Spada] have in writing about language learning (e.g., arguing a point of view? disagreeing with other research?)? What purpose did you have in talking electronically about language learning? What purpose will you have in writing about language learning in your first [assignment]?

This activity was designed to begin the process of metacognitive reflection, encouraging students to consider the distinctive purposes of writing in different situations and different text types, particularly with reference to how arguments are put forward and supported in an academic context. In Figure 12.6, we see a student making specific links between CMC and writing for assessment, which is evaluated positively by one of her peers. In terms of active, critical reflection, the response that follows would appear to indicate a successful outcome for the task, at least for this student.

However, peer feedback in general was uncommon at this stage in the conference. Activity 3 called forth detailed responses but little or no

RDP:	The following statement seems rather forceful to me. The use of 'obviously . . . they will' implies that we are all of the same opinion. Perhaps it would have been better expressed using words something like 'in my experience', or 'according to many colleagues'.	Peer feedback: Hedged negative evaluation + alternative suggestion
	"Obviously, if students are presented with teaching materials, whether text books, authentic texts, videos, literary extracts, or whatever, they will respond with more enthusiasm, and as a result learn something from them, if the content "speaks" to their own experience." (DS, E841 pjb353 Tutorial 1, 12th February 2002a).	
	A comment about this exercise. We were asked to find examples categorical / non categorical statements. While writing . . . I realised I was qualifying my language. Instead of saying, "This is a categorical statement.", I found myself writing, "It seems to me etc." Maybe this was the purpose of the exercise!!??	Metacognitive reflection (personal observation on own writing practice)

Figure 12.7. Student's feedback on categorical statement.

feedback on those responses. It was in Wertsch's (2002) terms "extended, reflective commentary" – students had the opportunity to craft their often-lengthy answers offline. As a result, the dialogic character of the conference declined for a time. Some of the reflection, however, dealt with the students' views of the activities and feedback generally and will be dealt with at the conclusion of the discussion of Group C.

The final activity focused on the linguistic realizations of argument, principally on the need to consider the position of the reader in response to arguments put forward. The following instruction was provided.

Find examples from the conference (a) of instances where people have put forward a statement in categorical, non-negotiable terms (b) of instances where people have put forward a statement in a way that anticipates and invites alternative perspectives.

Students were thus feeding back to each other their interpretations of specific linguistic choices. This activity rekindled some of the dialogic energy of the conference, with the postings developing an interactional momentum that led from listing negotiable and nonnegotiable statements to analysis of what made some statements negotiable and others not and to discussion of disciplinary, cultural, and genre influences on academic discourse. For example, student RDP lists and analyzes a number of

LMP:	Before listing examples, I'd like to mention a couple of things that struck me during this task....I found it much more difficult to find categorical affirmations from participants of British origin which made me wonder whether this depends on cultural academic traditions (I'm also a British ex-pat). After all, if we are to give any credit to Kachru's idea of concentric circles (Kachru B. B., 1985), some students on this course would belong in the 'inner circle' (native English-speaking countries such as Britain, U.S.A., Canada, etc.), others would be in the 'expanding circle' (countries where English is becoming a dominant language in education, science and technology) and still others would hover somewhere between (as far as I know nobody is from 'outer circle' countries, like India and Kenya, where English has achieved some official status). So we would have differing ideas about academic style and form. Further implications of this are that the tutor of this course, who will judge our assignments, is from the 'inner circle'.	Student response: Metacognitive reflection (personal observation related to academic theorizing)

Figure 12.8. Another student's feedback on categorical statement

statements from other students. The final extract and analysis is reproduced in Figure 12.7. Following the analysis, she goes on to reflect on
the exercise itself in relation to disciplinary expectations.

In Figure 12.8, a student begins her response to the task with observations and reflection. In particular, she reflects on the implications of her
observation that more nonnative students used categorical affirmations.
She follows this with an analysis of specific examples (not shown).

These examples focus attention on students' developing awareness of
how disciplinary knowledge in applied linguistics is expressed in English-
medium academic contexts and how this expression creates difficulties
for some NNS students or those from other different cultural backgrounds. Students whose ideas were discussed benefited from feedback
not just on their ideas but also on their expression of those ideas. In this
way, content-related and textual considerations were both subjects of
careful reflection. For all students it provided a forum to explore issues
about U.K. academic writing conventions in this discipline.

Feedback from both peers and the tutor had reached a sophisticated
level by this point in the conference. The overtly supportive type of
exchange was no longer as necessary, because all participants had had a

chance to develop good working relationships through the earlier activities. The cumulative nature of these activities had acted as a scaffold to both collaborative interaction and reflective thinking. In particular, students from diverse cultural backgrounds were reflecting on their own writing and whether it would be deemed appropriate in their discipline in the U.K. higher education context.

It is interesting to note that NNS students who expressed views through the questionnaires were positive about conferencing, with one noting that electronic tutorials were much easier. "I had the opportunity to better express myself in English and at my own pace." Students in Group B also gave positive feedback on the conferencing process overall, particularly the time and space given for reflection before contributing, but they did not make specific mention of academic writing skills or possible influences on their essay assignments. It seems then that whereas the role and feedback style adopted by the tutor in Group B was successful in stimulating interaction, the specific activities in Group C may have been responsible for students' increased metacognitive reflection on disciplinary writing.

Despite what seems to have been successful interaction in Group C, particularly with peer feedback helping to deepen the discussion, there were a number of politely phrased questions and comments that indicated difficulty, particularly during the responses to Activity 3. Here, students were encouraged to reflect on the purposes of "talking electronically," and some noted that such "talking" opened up the possibility for feedback. In line with concerns reported earlier by Lea (2001) and others, there were students who felt uncomfortable with the lack of an authoritative right or wrong decision from the tutor, as stated here:

Tutor feedback. This bothers me the most. Not having appraisal for the activities makes appraisal for the [assignment] an all or nothing.

When do we get your comments on our work so that we can make things right next time? . . .

Others were clearly satisfied with peer feedback:

Hello, I know I'm behind on this conference, but I would like to make a brief contribution to Activity 2 before getting stuck into the others. I would also appreciate a little feedback from anyone who has the time to do so. Thanks.

The comment in the following example is less clear-cut, recognizing the value of peer feedback but suggesting the lack of an authoritative voice. Interestingly, the student also compares the quality of the interaction to that of face-to-face situations.

Reading each others comments I think gave, in a way, peer feedback. If this had only been a spoken debate, then maybe there would have been less quality in the information (because we could go away and think about our responses), more aggression in the arguing, noise, turn giving disputes, etc. . . . We avoided all of these and aided motivation at the same time. Looking back at our initial contributions the quality has improved the more we have got into the topic. However the position of the tutor has not been supplanted by any one of us students.

It would appear that encouraging peer feedback and a symmetrical structure in CMC has to be balanced by recognizing the students' understandable wish to know whether they are on the right track. At one end of the spectrum we saw that Tutor A's desire to leave the floor open for peer interaction resulted in relatively little activity and that most of it remained at the level of personal experience. Tutor B was much more of a presence in his conference, although he took a generally nonjudgmental role in feedback. He used interpersonal strategies such as humor and open questions to the whole group to encourage participation and promote deeper and more critical reflection on key concepts. In the questionnaire survey, he specifically mentioned the tensions inherent in keeping the conference alive and getting it to be reflective. Like Tutor A, Tutor C provided little in the way of evaluative feedback but had structured the tasks to enable successful peer feedback and intervened more in the discussions, putting forward his own views and encouraging others. Although some students registered a degree of dissatisfaction with his level of input, there was an acknowledgment of the learning that had taken place and the way in which formative CMC could be built into summative assessment writing.

Summary and conclusions

Starting from a position of valuing the role of interaction in learning, we have looked at the potential for CMC to promote dialogic tutor and peer feedback on both subject matter and the disciplinary discourse. The written nature of asynchronous CMC provides opportunities not available in face-to-face discussions: to reflect at greater leisure on content; to create, in effect, an archive of other people's thoughts and responses; and to review content critically in the light of expanding awareness of disciplinary expectations. These affordances of CMC are not realized automatically and can be influenced by the tutor and by the tasks set.

As we have seen in looking at three different tutor groups, there is great variation in the types of responses and feedback. In Group A, the responses received only minimal feedback from tutor or students. In Group B, the feedback style modeled by the tutor and his frequent postings appeared to encourage much greater peer involvement in putting forward ideas and responding to others. The contributions were often relatively short and the overall feel of the conference was quite dynamic. Group C's tasks and tutor modeling encouraged more reflection at the expense of the dynamism of Group B. However, as a result of the greater reflection, students were able to consider how they were constructing disciplinary knowledge through sharing their own experiences, commenting on published work, and unpacking the implications of the tutor's expectations. This process seemed to be particularly helpful for NNS students unfamiliar with the traditions of writing at a U.K. university. It could apply equally well to any novice writer reflecting on disciplinary writing.

By focusing on peer and tutor feedback, we have seen how interactivity can vary substantially. The discussion of different tutorial styles across the same course illustrates the diversity of practices and how these might relate to the role of the tutor and to the structure of the activities. The analysis presented has sought to illustrate how factors broadly within the control of the tutor may facilitate open feedback dialogues in which students can deal with academic literacy issues. In particular, we would highlight the following factors:

- The need for a visible tutor presence in the conference
- The value of modeling interaction and feedback styles for students to adapt
- The role of open questions in encouraging dialogue without reinforcing an overly dominant teacher role
- The feasibility of making appropriate academic writing and argumentation strategies a focus for learning, alongside content considerations

We note that where there was an absence of feedback the interactions did not take on the reflective or dialogic character that research suggests promotes deeper and more critical thinking. We recognize, however, that in different contexts and at different points in the teaching and learning process, the pedagogic aims will vary and that feedback may not always be the priority. In addition, we acknowledge that applied linguistics and teacher education may lend themselves particularly well to reflection on content and writing. Further research is needed to investigate its applicability in other disciplines.

The successes and failures of the feedback techniques employed in the three groups, together with the types of activities undertaken, leaves us with the sense that there is great potential for CMC in encouraging both reflection on content and disciplinary writing at the tertiary level. The interactions captured by this study illustrate that both NS and NNS students can support each other through the exchange of views on writing and content, at a sophisticated level. Research is still required to trace the effect of formative feedback, particularly that relating to academic writing, on the students' summative assignments (see, however, Coffin

& Hewings 2005). Much also remains to be learned about how to refine the CMC tutorial process to promote deeper reflection without overburdening the students or the tutors with work, that is, how to promote focused dialogic interaction.

Notes

1. The research was supported by grants from the Open University Learning and Teaching Innovation Committee.
2. Note that for the purposes of the first tutorial, Group A was a combination of two groups.
3. "Well, that's it, honey. I'm going home."

References

Becher, T. (1994). The significance of disciplinary differences. *Studies in Higher Education, 19(2),* 151–161.

Belcher, D. (2001). Cyberdiscourse, evolving notions of authorship, and the teaching of writing. In M. Hewings (Ed.), *Academic writing in context: Implications and applications, papers in honor of Tony Dudley-Evans* (pp. 140–149). Birmingham, UK: University of Birmingham Press.

Bruner, J. S. (1986). *Actual minds, possible worlds.* London: Harvard University Press.

Coffin, C., Curry, M. J., Goodman, S., Hewings, A., Lillis, T., & Swann, J. (2003). *Teaching academic writing: A toolkit for higher education.* London: Routledge.

Coffin, C., & Hewings, A. (2005). Engaging electronically: Using CMC to develop students' argumentation skills in higher education. *Language and Education, 19(1),* 32–49.

Gee, J. P. (1990). *Social linguistics and literacies: Ideology in discourses.* London: Falmer Press.

Gee, J. P. (1994). Discourses: Reflections on M. A. K. Halliday's "Towards a language-based theory of learning." *Linguistics and Education, 6,* 33–44.

Gee, J. P. (2000). The new literacy studies and the social turn. In D. Barton, M. Hamilton, & R. Ivanic (Eds.), *Situated literacies: Reading and writing in context.* London: Routledge. Online at: www.schools.ash.org.au/litweb/page300.html. Retrieved November 2004.

Goodfellow, R. (2004). The literacies of online learning: a linguistic-ethnographic approach to research on virtual learning communities. *Proceedings of the Networked Learning Conference,* Lancaster University, April 2004. Online at: www.shef.ac.uk/nlc2004/Proceedings/Contents.htm. Retrieved September 2004.

Halliday, M. A. K. (1994). *An introduction to functional grammar,* 2nd ed. London: Edward Arnold.

Hara, N., & Kling, R. (1999). Students' frustration with a web-based distance education course. *First Monday, 4, 12.* Online at: http://firstmonday.org/issues/issue4_12/hara/index.html. Retrieved November 2004.

Harasim, L. (1989). On-line education: A new domain. In R. Mason and A. Kaye (Eds.), *Mindweave: Communication, computers and distance education*. Oxford: Pergamon.

Henri, F. (1995). Distance learning and computer mediated communication: interactive, quasi-interactive or monologue? In C. O'Malley (Ed.), *Computer supported collaborative learning*. Berlin: Springer-Verlag.

Hewings, A. (2004). Developing discipline-specific writing: An analysis of undergraduate geography essays. In L. Ravelli and R. Ellis (Eds.), *Academic writing*. London: Continuum.

Hyland, K. (2000). *Disciplinary discourses: Social interactions in academic writing*, Harlow, UK: Longman.

Jones, A., Scanlon, E., & Blake, C. (2000). Conferencing in communities of learners: Examples from social history and science communication. *Educational Technology and Society, 3(3)*, 215–226.

Lea, M. R. (2001). Computer conferencing and assessment: New ways of writing in higher education. *Studies in Higher Education, 26*, 2, 163–181.

Lea, M., O'Shea, T., Fung, P., & Spears, R. (1992). Flaming in computer-mediated communication: Observations, explanations, implications. In M. Lea (Ed.), *Contexts of computer-mediated communication*. London: Harvester Wheatsheaf.

Light, P., Colbourn, C., & Light, V. (1997). Computer mediated tutorial support for conventional university courses. *Journal of Computer Assisted Learning, 13*, 219–227.

Light, V., Nesbitt, E., Light, P., and Burns, J. R. (2000). "Let's you and me have a little discussion": Computer mediated communication in support of campus-based university courses. *Studies in Higher Education, 25(1)*, 85–96.

Lillis, T. M. (2001). *Student writing: Access, regulation, desire*. London: Routledge.

MacDonald, S. P. (1994). *Professional academic writing in the humanities and social sciences*. Carbondale and Edwardsville: Southern Illinois University Press.

Marttunen, M., & Laurinen, L. (2001). Learning of argumentation skills in networked and face-to-face environments. *Instructional Science, 29(2)*, 127–153.

Mercer, N. (2000). *Words and minds*. London: Routledge.

Myers, G. (1990). *Writing biology: Texts in the social construction of scientific knowledge*. Madison, WI: University of Wisconsin Press.

Painter, C., Coffin, C., and Hewings, A. (2003). Impacts of directed tutorial activities in computer conferencing: A case study. *Distance Education(4) 2*, 159–174.

Salmon, G. (2003). *E-moderating: The key to teaching and learning online*, 2nd ed. London: Taylor and Francis.

Sinclair, J., & Coulthard, M. (1975). *Towards an analysis of discourse: The English used by teachers and pupils*. London: Oxford University Press.

Thorpe, M. (2002). Rethinking learner support: The challenge of collaborative online learning. *Open Learning, 17(2)*, 105–119.

Tolmie, A., & Boyle, J. (2000). Factors influencing the success of computer mediated communication (CMC) environments in university teaching: A review and case study. *Computers and Education, 34(2)*, 119–140.

Vygotsky, L. S. (1962). *Thought and language.* Cambridge, MA: Massachusetts Institute of Technology Press.

Warschauer, M. (2002). Networking into academic discourse. *Journal of English for Academic Purposes, 1,* 45–58.

Wertsch, J. V. (2002). Commentary – computer mediation, PBL, and dialogicality. *Distance Education, 23(1),* 105–108.

Wilson, T., & Whitelock, D. (1998). What are the perceived benefits of participating in a computer mediated communication (CMC) environment for distance learning computer science students? *Computers and Education, 30,* 259–269.

13 Scaffolded feedback: Tutorial conversations with advanced L2 writers

Robert Weissberg

As research in developmental literacy and biliteracy moves forward, a recognition of the influence of oral language on learners' writing development has become widespread. Those who espouse a dialogic view of writing, and of teaching writing, assign a central role to social conversation in the planning, production, and revision of written texts (Bruffee, 1995; Wells, 1990). Indeed, some within this school of thought posit oral language as the point of origin for all literacy activities (Barnes, 1990; Dickinson et al., 1993; Kroll, 1981; Shuy, 1987).

According to this view, oral discourse provides us with the ideas we write about, the rhetorical modes we use to frame those ideas, and the voice that gives our writing its individual character. Even the words and expressions that find their way into our written texts ultimately derive from conversations we have had with others (see Gillam's 1991 and Herdman's 1997 discussions of Bakhtin's views of writing), and internally with ourselves (see Wertsch's 1991 treatment of Vygotsky's sociocultural theory of cognitive development, particularly his notion of inner speech).

To what extent this view of writing is valid for second language (L2) writers is open to question (Weissberg, 2000). Nevertheless, current theory and practice in L2 writing pedagogy depends to a large extent on social interaction in the form of conversational activities in the writing classroom. Oral brainstorming (Blanton, 1992), collaborative composing (Hirvela, 1999), and peer revision groups (see Williams's 2002 review) are just three examples of the deliberate use of oral language in L2 writing instruction.

The literature on L2 writing includes many research studies and pedagogical articles devoted to the role of oral language in the teaching and learning of writing. Areas treated include the role of teacher talk in the writing classroom (Boyd & Rubin, 2002; Cumming, 1992; Weissberg, 1994); conversational interaction among L2 writers working in peer groups (Donato, 1994; Guerrero & Villamil, 2000; Ohta, 1995, 2000, 2001; Storch, 2002; and this volume); and oral feedback provided by tutors or teachers in one-on-one writing tutorials and conferences with L2 writers (Goldstein & Conrad, 1990; Thonus, 1999; Williams, 2002). It is this latter setting that provides the context for the present discussion.

The conversation aspects of writing tutorials studied previously include the purposes and functions of tutor talk (Harris, 1995); the ways in which meaning is negotiated between tutor and student (Williams, 2002); how these negotiations affect the student's subsequent writing (Aljaafreh & Lantolf, 1994; Goldstein & Conrad, 1990); how dominance and control of the tutorial conversation is maintained (Powers, 1993; Thonus, 1999); and the role played by scaffolding in tutors' instructional talk (Williams, 2002).

The concept of scaffolding is central to the writing tutorial, since it is one of the principal features that distinguish tutorial talk from teachers' conventional, transmission-style classroom discourse (Wells, 1990). Williams (2002) defines scaffolding as the verbal support provided to the learner by the tutor that enables the learner to complete a new task (p. 85). Oral scaffolding in the writing tutorial is of particular interest here, because it constitutes a highly individualized, negotiated means of delivering oral feedback to L2 students on their writing. Through scaffolded dialogue, a tutor provides feedback that is uniquely tailored to an individual student working on a particular text (Aljaafreh & Lantolf, 1994). By providing such carefully calibrated assistance, tutorial conversations contrast dramatically with the ritualistic "language games" that typify much of the talk in teacher-fronted classrooms (Barnes, 1990, p. 42; Ohta, 1995).

Because oral scaffolding lies at the heart of tutorial dialogue, it takes on central importance for L2 writing tutors and their trainers. In particular, it is important to understand the specific linguistic and discourse features that characterize scaffolding as it occurs in writing tutorials, how they are implemented by expert tutors, and the roles that scaffolding plays in effective tutoring. In working toward these aims, this chapter reports on a fine-grained examination of conversational dialogues between writing tutors and their ESL college student clients. Before looking at the conversational evidence, however, we will try to pin down more precisely what the term *scaffolding* means in the context of writing conferences.

What scaffolding is and is not

Also known as "assisted performance" (Ohta, 2001; Wells, 1990), scaffolding is a familiar concept in the literature on sociocultural (Vygotskian) theory and its associated approaches to learning and teaching languages (Lantolf, 2000; Lantolf & Appel, 1994; Lee & Smagorinsky, 2000). The earliest reference to scaffolding in an educational context was its use by Jerome Bruner and his colleagues (Wood et al., 1976) in their attempt to specify the ways in which parents and tutors assist young children in learning new skills and concepts. They defined scaffolding as " . . . a process that enables a child or novice to solve a problem, carry out a task, or achieve a goal which would be beyond his unassisted efforts" (p. 90). They further limited the term by saying that it "consists essentially of the adult 'controlling' those elements of the task that are initially beyond the learner's capacity, thus permitting him to concentrate upon and complete only those elements that are within his range of competence" (p. 90). Bruner and his colleagues studied scaffolding by analyzing the kinds of help that parents gave their children in trying to arrange a set of toy blocks to form a pyramid shape. A physical example of scaffolding was when the mother in one experimental pair held the tower of blocks steady while her child attempted to fit in a new block.

Extrapolating from their experiment with wooden blocks, Wood et al. identified five crucial elements in the act of scaffolding (p. 98): *recruitment*, in which the tutor captures the child's attention; *reduction of degrees of freedom*, in which the tutor simplifies the task at hand; *direction maintenance*, in which the tutor keeps the learner on track; *marking critical features*, where the tutor draws the child's attention to key aspects of the task or its solution; *controlling frustration*, where the tutor provides the child with reassurance or a respite from the task; and *demonstration*, in which the tutor models a possible solution to the problem posed by the task. Later, Bruner (1978) amplified the notion of scaffolding to include *extension*, in which the parent or tutor presents the child with alternative situations for which an earlier solution will work, and serving as a "communicative ratchet" (p. 254), meaning that once the child has achieved a certain level of mastery over the task, the tutor does not let him or her slide back to a lower level.

Bruner's example is useful for illustrating scaffolding in situations in which child-adult pairs are engaged in close-ended tasks. However, some adaptation is required to make the concept meaningful in the context of acquiring L2 writing skills. Here we encounter some difficulty, as the term has been appropriated and expanded by many L2 practitioners – teachers and theorists – to the point that it seems in danger of losing its essential meaning. At a recent conference of ESL specialists, the term *scaffolding* was used at one time or another by participants to indicate such disparate items as a framework for learning, an outline, a temporary support, a mental schema, a curriculum progression – even a basal ESL text.

The definition problem is compounded by the fact that authors also disagree on how the term *scaffolding* should be applied to L2 teaching and learning situations. Wells (1998), for example, has argued that scaffolding should not be confused with "collaborative learning" as he claims some have done (e.g., Antón & DiCamilla, 1998). According to Wells, the scaffolding label is misapplied unless (1) it refers to a conversation involving *one participant who is more expert than the others*; (2) it is applied to situations where *the primary objective is to teach* someone something; and (3) it is carried out with the expert participant's intention of *making the novice participant self-sufficient* in managing the task at hand. It is this restricted sense of the term that is adopted for use here.

Agreement on essentials

Despite the lack of agreement on what constitutes scaffolding, second language researchers working within the sociocultural framework have helped to develop an understanding of the term that preserves its essential meaning, while specifying its application to L2 learning in general and L2 writing in particular. Donato (1994) provides a useful definition of scaffolding within the L2 tutorial context as: "social interaction [in which] a knowledgeable participant can create, by means of speech, supportive conditions in which the novice can participate in, and extend current skills and knowledge to higher levels of competence" (p. 40). In a later work, Donato (2000) captures more precisely the essential characteristics of scaffolding when he describes a kind of instructional dialogue in foreign language classrooms.

[The dialogue is] *conversational* in its attention to coherence, distributed turn talking, spontaneity and unpredictability ... [and] also ... *instructional* because teachers shape the discussion toward a curricular goal, build or activate background knowledge in students, engage at times in direct instruction or modeling, and promote more complex language expressions by using questions to help students expand, elaborate or restate (p. 34).

The dialogue must also have as its goal the "handing over control of the task to the learner" (p. 39). For socioculturalists, scaffolding is essentially the oral means by which a tutor or teacher helps the learner move through his or her zone of proximal development to "extend current knowledge and skills to a higher level of competence" (Donato, 1994, p. 40).

Once agreement has been reached on the meaning of scaffolding in the context of feedback on L2 writing, a subsequent task is to identify its constituent features. Williams (2002) provides a useful example of scaffolding in the context of an L2 writing tutorial, in which some of the most critical features of the concept are apparent.

1. L: This paragraph it's about ... he discover his father experience.
2. O: Mmhm. The discovery of his experience, right?
3. L: His father life, in the past.
4. O: He finds out the truth about his father's past?
5. L: The truth about Japanese.
6. O: About Japanese-Americans?
7. L: Uh huh ... being. It's about his father life.
8. O: Mmhm. His father's life.
9. L: Um ... (writes). The father's life.
10. O: Mmhm. So what's next? So all of this is about that one sentence?

11. L: Mmhm.
12. O: 'Kay. And this one is about...?
13. L: Relationship between, father. Of his father and himself.
14. O: About his father and his father's father?
15. L: Uh huh. So, it's...well... his father treated him like his grandfather treated his father...so it's like...relationship?
16. O: Mmhm. M' kay. So, his father had a similar relationship with his own father?

(from Williams, 2002, pp. 85–86)[1]

Williams points out that in the preceding exchange the tutor provides three different kinds of scaffolded support for the student writer: (1) recasting incorrect utterances (lines 7 and 8), extending and elaborating the student's utterances (lines 15 and 16), and identifying places in the student's text that may require revision (line 10).

Mechanisms of scaffolding

Other authors have attempted to identify the specific mechanisms of scaffolding in the context of L2 writing instruction. To do so, they have studied dialogues occurring between L2 writers in conference with tutors and teachers and among writers working together in pairs and in peer groups. Observing L2 writers and their tutors, Aljaafreh and Lantolf (1994) identified five levels of progression in the students' ability to complete grammar correction tasks, moving from the learner's total dependence on the tutor to self-regulated ability to perform the same type of task independently. Crucially, Aljaafreh and Lantolf note that effective scaffolded assistance is *contingent* (i.e., the help is offered only when needed and removed as soon as the learner is able to function independently), *graduated* (meaning that the tutor estimates early on the lower and upper limits of the learner's ability to manage the task and calibrates his or her own assistance to the learner's changing proficiency needs), and *dialogic* (i.e., the assistance is embedded in a conversation in which both tutor and learner are actively engaged) (p. 468).

Guerrero and Villamil (2000) made detailed studies of scaffolding dialogues between pairs of L2 writers engaged in reviewing a text written by one member of the pair. In an earlier study (Villamil & Guerrero, 1996), they identified 14 substrategies of scaffolding, from speech moves like "responding to advice" to negotiation-of-meaning strategies like "requesting clarification." In the latter study they identified six signs of scaffolding behavior on the part of the student in the role of reader / tutor: recruiting the writer's interest in the task; marking critical aspects of the text requiring correction by the writer; instructing, or giving mini-lessons; providing the writer with problem-solving heuristics; responding contingently, based on the tutor's judgments about the level of help needed by the writer at any given moment; and affective involvement, in which the tutor provided the writer with positive feedback and encouragement to persist in the task.

Like Aljaafreh and Lantolf (1994), Guerrero and Villamil limited their study to scaffolded dialogue directed toward problems in sentence-level grammar. And like Antón and DiCamilla (1998), Guerrero and Villamil may be guilty of Wells's (1998) charge of misdefining scaffolding, since the dialogues here are played out among peers, with little difference in expertise between the student readers and student writers. Nevertheless, Guerrero and Villamil's study is helpful because it focuses on instructional dialogue involving nonnative English-speaking writers and because it attempts to get at the specific mechanisms of scaffolding.

Although not specifically concerned with writing, Ohta (1995, 2000, 2001) isolated specific scaffolding behaviors employed by pairs of college students learning Japanese as a foreign language. She identified three important features of these students' collaborative dialogues: *explicit correction*; *requests for repetition* of a word or phrase; and *cueing possible responses*, in which one member of the pair gives the first syllable of the initial word in a possible response. Ohta also noted "subtle interactional cues" (2000, p. 53) that one partner used to provide scaffolded assistance to the other – behaviors such as pausing longer than normal to cue a response from the partner and using special intonation contours to signal the need (or the lack of need) for the partner's assistance.

A different approach to the study of scaffolding was taken by Antón and DiCamilla (1998), who observed students of Spanish as a foreign language engaged in a collaborative writing task. They studied students' use of their L1 (English) as a mediating device in their conversations as they cowrote an essay in Spanish. Antón and DiCamilla found that, far from being an impediment to their production of L2 text, the students' L1 served them as a scaffold to assist each other in completing the language task. Antón and DiCamilla identified three scaffolding functions of the L1: a means of generating content for the writing task; a way for students to evaluate and reflect on the text they had written; and its social use to create an atmosphere of mutual assistance.

Although studies of scaffolding in L2 writing contexts are few in number, it is evident from the foregoing review that various approaches to the analysis problem are possible. From the perspective of feedback on L2 writing, the approach taken by Williams (2002), which focuses on overt oral techniques employed by an expert tutor assisting a novice writer, seems the most promising. The study described in the following section takes a further step in the same direction. The objectives were two. The first was to expand on Williams's general categories by identifying specific discourse mechanisms used by tutors in their scaffolded conversations with L2 writers. The intention here was to provide as fine-grained a picture of scaffolding as possible by uncovering the particular linguistic elements and discourse functions embedded in a tutor's conversational turns that result in scaffolding.

Previous work on scaffolding in L2 writing contexts has focused mainly on sentence-level issues such as grammar and word choice. The second objective of the present study looks beyond the level of the sentence to examine how scaffolded feedback addresses global issues of academic writing, such as planning, organizing, revising, and the use of outside source materials. The study thus attempts to address the issue of scaffolding on two distinct but complementary levels. On the micro level, it pursues the question of how scaffolding is instantiated linguistically; on the macro level it responds to Aljaafreh and Lantolf's (1994) challenge to extend the notion of scaffolding to tutorial conversations about more "abstract properties" of L2 writing than have been dealt with previously.

Scaffolding analysis: Topics, mechanisms, and goals

To identify and isolate the linguistic features of oral scaffolding, conversational data was collected during four one-on-one, tutor-student writing conferences. The participants were a university writing instructor experienced in working with nonnative speakers of English and two international students, both enrolled in graduate programs at a midsize state university in the United States. The students were working on individual writing projects related to their programs of study. Najiba, an Egyptian woman (L1 Arabic), was working on a draft of the literature review chapter for her doctoral dissertation in special education. César, a Puerto Rican (L1 Spanish), was working on a series of experimental research reports for a graduate course he was taking in microbiology.

The tutorial conversations were audiotaped and analyzed for evidence of oral scaffolding, using a method of analysis designed for qualitative data known as *inductive analysis* (IA) (Bryman & Burgess, 1994; LeCompte & Preissle, 1993; Thomas, 2003). IA is an iterative process consisting of repeated cycles of data analysis and hypothesis revision. In this case, a portion of the tutorial transcripts was first examined for an initial set of discourse categories, then the resulting categories were modified and refined through further examination of the transcript data. Preliminary results of the IA yielded three layers of information in the audio transcripts (see Hatch, 1992, and Van Dijk, 1985, for more elaborate analyses of layers of discourse): a surface discourse level consisting of *scaffolding mechanisms* (i.e., overt conversational moves); a semantic-content level, also overt, consisting of *topical episodes* (i.e., a related sequence of utterances in the tutorial dialogue dealing with a single topic); and an underlying, implicit pragmatic level of *goals* (i.e., the pedagogic and social purposes implicit in a sequence of topically related episodes). These three layers of discourse are illustrated in Figure 13.1.

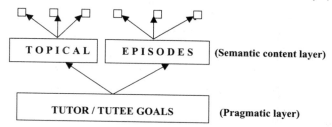

SCAFFOLDING MECHANISMS (Surface discourse layer)

Figure 13.1. Layers of analysis in writing tutorial conversations

As shown, a single topical episode may include multiple instances of scaffolding; similarly, multiple topical episodes may be devoted to a single instructional goal. Repeated examinations of the transcripts confirmed the validity of these three levels and identified some of the possible constituents of each, as shown in Table 13.1. For this analysis the conversational segments dealing with sentence-level errors ("mechanics") were ignored in favor of segments in which tutor and students dealt with more global issues of writing.

Of particular interest for this study was the surface "mechanism" level, since it was here that the actual dialogic moves resulting in scaffolding were found. Of these, the most interesting were those identified as "linking" moves (Table 13.1), since they seemed to instantiate the most salient feature of scaffolding in these conversations. The tutor created dialogic links with the tutees in various ways, as shown in the following excerpts from the recorded conversations.

Excerpt 1: Linkage through questions and summary / paraphrase statements[2]

Excerpt 1 shows the tutor working with César (C) on a draft report the latter had written about a microbiology laboratory experiment. Here, the tutor created links to the student's side of the conversation using both information questions and statements that summarized or paraphrased César's utterances. Excerpt 1 follows Table 13.1.

1. T: The most interesting, um, problem about this paper for me was not the grammar, because the grammar's probably just something you can, you can go back and pick up pretty, pretty quickly if you just read through it again, is the, um, . . . I think it's deliberate. . . . I think you're doing it on purpose and I wanted, I wanted to ask you about it. The deliberate use of personal involvement. You're using a lot of personal pronouns. You're using "I" and "we" a lot.
2. C: Uh huh.

Table 13.1. *General categories of writing conference tutorial discourse*

Topics	Mechanisms	Goals
• Style, "voice" • Mechanics (grammar, punctuation, paragraphing) • Arrangement and organization • Writing processes and procedures • Coherence • Use of source materials • Citations • Idea content • Text format	• Linking moves (lexical / phrasal repetition and paraphrase, expressions of affiliation, and acknowledgment of others' points) • Negotiating moves (requests for clarification, confirmation checks, comprehension checks) • Initiating moves (information questions, proposing a new topic)	• Framing (setting agenda, summarizing, identifying problem areas) • Instructing • Problem solving • Creating affiliation • Generating written text • Evaluating / reflecting on text • Establishing / maintaining speaker status

3. T: ...and I wonder if you're doing that for a reason, because you probably know, in technical writing, it's not usually done.

4. C: No. It's not usually done.

5. T: So [laughs] why are you...? Is your professor telling you to do it? Or do you just prefer to do it that way?

6. C: Okay. The, the.... One of the things that, that I decided for to write for in English, it was easier for me to use "I" and "we."

7. T: Ah. Obviously. Yeah. Right.

8. C: ...but the other reason is that, the, according to the professor, we should write those, this paper, similar to the papers that we already read [in class]. And some of the papers use "I" and "we." So....

9. T: These are published, published papers?

10. C: Published papers.

11. T: Really?

12. C: Yes. Not, not necessarily from USA, but, publishing in peer review, ah, journals from USA...so *Applied Environmental*...

13. T: Hmm. Interesting.

14. C: I, I think that...Probably some of the people are not, ah, I mean, ah, their first language is not English.

15. T: ...is not English. Right. But they write English very well.

16. C: Yeah. But according to him, we should use the same, more or less the same structures.

17. T: That's really interesting. Do you think the native speakers are using this differently from the non-native speakers? Do you think the non-native speakers tend to make it more pers, personalized than

the native speakers of English in the published, in the published papers?

18. C: Yeah. Yeah. I think so. And also, and also the native speakers of English are easier to read the papers and to understand, I mean the technical papers, than the non-native.... Some papers which come from the East and also from, from other places, such as Spanish places also are, are difficult to understand the English

19. T: So. Okay. So you're saying... Let, let me see if I've got this right. First thing you're saying... distinguishing between the native-speaker writers and the non-native-speaker writers.... You're saying that the,... that the non-native-speaking writers are using more personalized sentences than the native speakers?

20. C: That was my experience for this class.

21. T: Yes. Okay. Right. And then, number two, that the papers written by the non-native writers are less easy... are not as easy to read as the papers written by the native speakers?

22. C: Right. Um hmm. But, was a, was a... was a shock for me that those, those papers should be reviewed by the, but the editor so I don't know why,... why they.

23. T: Yes. It's very interesting and I wonder if some journals are more strict about the, the English language conventions than, than, than other journals... Like, like this level of personalization for me. If you... I you, If you submitted this, I mean I'm not a microbiologist..., but if you submitted this to me as an, as an editor and I was to look at it... and I said, "Yeah. It's a great paper but I would like you to depersonalize it."

24. C: Yeah. I didn't like it either...

Following the rubric in Figure 13.1, the discourse aspect of this excerpt may be identified as "choosing the appropriate style or voice." César's written text contrasted with the general trend of scientific reports in English to be written in the passive voice. The tutor's overall goal here was apparently to highlight and if possible resolve this contradiction. However, rather than pursue a directive approach, the tutor engaged César in an exploratory dialogue about the issue. The tutor used scaffolding mechanisms to link his side of the dialogue to César's in two ways: by using paraphrasing to ask questions directly related to César's contributions (lines 5 and 9) and by summarizing César's contributions (lines 19 and 21). The episode ends with the tutor making a direct instructional point ("... I would like you to depersonalize it").

Excerpt 2: Linkage through repetition

A second excerpt illustrates a scaffolding mechanism of a different kind. Here, the tutor is talking with Najiba (N) about the organization of the literature review chapter for her dissertation, which dealt with special education and Arab children attending U.S. schools.

1. T: Okay, here's an inconsistency. See, "Assessment" as a main topic is only one page and a little bit more. About one page.
2. N: Uh huh.
3. T: That's not enough. I don't think that's enough for one major topic. So it doesn't look like it's a major topic. It looks like it should be part of something [else] ... you know what I mean?
4. N: Okay.
5. T: Your other major topics are 3, 4 pages long, you know? ... until you get to this one. I mean this is big. This is the rest of the chapter ... just about ... but this one is only one page.
6. N: Yeah. So it's either, you mean like it shouldn't be either a main topic or ...
7. T: It should not be a main topic
8. N: It should be included or if I use it as a main topic so I should, you know, add more.
9. T: Right. The easy thing to do, I think, would be to include this in one of the other topics and take it out as a main topic.
10. N: Um.
11. T: Sub ... you know, ... subsume it under another, um, section. If you, if you did that, where would it most likely go? Would it, would it be better to put it here, under this topic or would it be better to put it under this topic?
12. N: No it would be ... Yeah ... before talking about the IQ and creativity. Because IQ and creativity are assessments also, like assessment, ... a way of assessing the kids.
13. T: Okay.

Here the discourse topic is the relative length of sections within Najiba's literature review chapter. Her draft presented a problem of balance – one of her sections was noticeably shorter than the others. The tutor's goal was apparently to find a solution to the balance problem.

Again, the tutor opted for a negotiated solution with the student, rather than imposing his own. In order to do so, he created conversational linkages by echoing phrases from Najiba's side of the conversation (lines 6 and 7; lines 8 and 9). In the latter instance, the tutor's repetition serves to acknowledge and build on Najiba's contribution. The teacher's instructional point (i.e., to include the short section of text as part of another, longer section rather than allowing it to stand on its own) rises directly from Najiba's previous remark (line 8); the tutor chooses one of the two options presented by Najiba as the best way to solve the balance problem.

Excerpt 3: Linkage through completion and extension

Another scaffolding mechanism revealed in the tutorial data is the creation of links by speakers completing or amplifying each other's utterances. In excerpt 3, both Najiba and the tutor employ this mechanism while discussing Najiba's use of citations in her literature review chapter.

1. T: Okay. Oh... This was a...
2. N: ... a citation?
3. T: Well, this was a question I had about the whole paper and it's something I want you to look at when you write the second draft. The reason why they use citations in this kind thing is so that it's really clear for the reader whose stuff is whose. Which stuff comes from you and which stuff comes from the sources.
4. N: Um.
5. T: So if you don't put a citation there, I assume that it's from you. If it's not from you, you better put a citation. Because the reader can't guess... you know.... I just don't know.
6. N: It can be... plagiarism.
7. T: Right. "This" was not clear here.
8. N: "in this research..."
9. T: Are you referring to Hubert's research, or are you referring to your [own] research?
10. N: It was mine.... to my research
11. T: Oh, okay. Then you need to say something else. You can't say "this" because "this" refers to this... because everything here talks about Hubert's...
12. N: You can say that, like, "the researcher will focus on,"...
13. T: "In the present study... In the present study,"... In other words, the one you're doing, "the researcher will focus on..."
14. N: "... in the present"
15. T: Yeah. Because "this" is... "this" is ambiguous.
16. N: Yeah.

The discourse topic in this excerpt is the strategic placement of citations within the text of Najiba's literature review and the use of foregrounding phrases to highlight her original research and to contrast it with the published work of others. The underlying goal for both participants appears to be the drafting of new text. The mechanism the speakers use to create linkage consists of completing and expanding each other's sentences. Najiba expands the tutor's sentence (lines 1 and 2; lines 7 and 8), and later the tutor employs the same tactic when Najiba suggests new text (lines 12 and 13).

Excerpt 4: Linkage through personal affiliation

In addition to linguistic links created by information questions, paraphrase, repetition, completion and expansion, scaffolding in these tutorial sessions also included the tutor's attempts to create personal links with the student. In the following excerpt, the tutor and Najiba are conferencing over a particularly difficult problem in academic writing: the integration of outside source material into one's own text.

1. T: When you started this, when you made the outline, did you try to, um... see, 'cause this is the problem that I work with too. You have all these sources here and then you have your outline, but did you try to put the sources together with the outline? In other words, did you try to look at the outline that you made and look at the sources and decide which source would go in which part of the outline? Did you ever do that?

2. N: You mean like have I started with the outline first or the sources?

3. T: Well, kind of. I don't know if that's the question 'cause you can certainly do either one. You can start with the outline first or you can start with the sources first.

4. N: Well, actually...

5. T: ...but at some point, it seems to me, you have to put them together. Did you ever try to do that?

6. N: Yeah, yeah. That was hard for me first because, like, I remembered a sentence and I don't know where is it, so I keep looking and read several articles and I couldn't do the cards, the index cards.... It didn't, you know...I couldn't put all the information I needed on that card.

7. T: Right, right...

8. N: So I had a blank paper at the beginning of every article...

9. T: Right, right...

10. N: ...and then I would write, like, the main points, like, in this article...like, um, covers mostly, you know, the lit review, something about, like, recommendations....

11. T: Well, I think you do the same thing I do. I was doing this, this morning. Let me show you what I was doing. I don't use a card...because there's not enough space. So I use sheets like this.

12. N: Exactly.

13. T: Well, when you make the outline, do you, do you physically write the outline on a piece of paper or do you just have it in...?

14. N: Um. First I said, yeah, I wrote, like, these points, 1, 2, 3, 4, 5, 6, 7, 8, and then they became in my mind.

15. T: So you had it memorized...basically.

16. N: Yeah. But, you know, I didn't mean...

17. T: This is what I was doing today. This is exactly what I was doing today.

18. N: ...but I didn't mean to memorize it. It just came to me.

19. T: No, it just...right, right...

20. N: Because, maybe because this is my topic of interest, you know...something that I'm interested in so I know what I'm going to cover.

21. T: Well I'm going to show you, I'm going to show you what I do, because I'm doing something very similar right now...to what you're doing. I'll take these notes and then I have a physical outline. I've got an outline that I type up like that, and then I, um, I try to key the sources to the outline, so I'll take, like here's the part about this one topic. I'm going to write some section about that. And I've got the names of all the guys I want to use here...

22. N: Yeah. It's overwhelming for me to through all these articles all ...
23. T: It *is* overwhelming. It's terrible. Yeah ...

Although the tutor uses lexical repetition to create a link (lines 22 and 23), the connection in this instance is more than a linguistic cohesion device. The tutor creates an affiliational tie with the tutee by comparing her writing processes to his own (lines 1, 11, 17) and empathizing with her frustration (line 23). This approach is akin to the "affective involvement" noted by Guerrero and Villamil (2000, p. 64) in their study of scaffolding among pairs of L2 writers. As he did with other types of links, the tutor here used affective links as a springboard for instruction, in this case providing Najiba with a model (his own outline) as an alternative to the planning procedure she was then using.

Scaffolded dialogue as feedback

The dialogues examined in this study illustrate a number of mechanisms by which tutors help L2 student writers find solutions to problems in their texts. Tutors create conversational links through questioning, repeating, rephrasing, completing, extending, and summarizing their students' contributions. We have also seen that tutors form linkages by expressing personal affiliation with their student clients. Taken together with the findings of earlier studies, these mechanisms help to fill out the picture of scaffolded L2 instruction that has emerged over the last decade.

To view these mechanisms in perspective, it is useful to return to a prototypical example of scaffolding at work (Wood et al., 1976): a mother's hand supporting a tower of blocks as her child attempts to complete the structure. From this view, scaffolding clearly emerges as a metaphor for *construction*, an altogether appropriate application of a term that in common use refers to a temporary structure attached to the exterior of a building in order to assist in completing it or repairing it. From the perspective of the construction metaphor, the scaffolding mechanisms observed here can be seen as having two essential functions: first, *attachment*, to forge connective links to the student's discourse at the lexical, ideational, and affective levels; and second, *extension*, to use those links as springboards to instructional points (a slightly different interpretation of extension from that used by Bruner, 1978). These two functions, attachment and extension, may be the core elements of oral scaffolding in instructional practice. (See a similar analysis of teachers' classroom talk by Boyd and Maloof, 2000.)

In considering these results, two caveats are in order. First, it is not clear whether the scaffolding behavior uncovered here is merely an artifact of a particular tutor's conversational style, or whether it is an inherent feature of expert-novice instructional dialogues. It must be said that scaffolding was not a ubiquitous feature of these dialogues; in the tutorial sessions with César, scaffolding occurred in a little over 20 percent of the topical episodes (eight out of 39), and in 30 percent of the episodes with Najiba (nine out of 30). (The non-scaffolded episodes dealt with the logistical issues of the tutoring sessions, direct instruction by the tutor, or informative talk by the students.) Scaffolding seemed most likely to occur either when the tutor did not have a ready solution to a particular problem in the students' texts, or when he took the time to lead his tutees to discover solutions on their own or to reach solutions mutually, rather than taking the easier route of providing his own quick fixes. It must be added that although the scaffolded episodes were relatively infrequent, they featured more and longer talk turns for both tutor and student than did the non-scaffolded episodes. Whether scaffolded episodes are more effective than more directive, overtly instructional episodes in prompting students to revise their texts is a question for future research to address.

The second caveat is that it is yet to be determined how effective oral scaffolding is in practical terms as a source of feedback for L2 writers. This study does not provide direct evidence of its efficacy in helping nonnative students become better writers of academic English. The only measure of success discernible here is the indirect evidence afforded by Najiba's and César's active participation in their tutorial sessions. One could assume with Aljaafreh and Lantolf (1994) that the mere fact of the students' intense involvement in dialogue with their tutor indicates that they benefited from the sessions. And evidence provided by Goldstein and Conrad (1990) supports the assumption that episodes of conferencing discourse in which tutees are actively engaged in negotiation can lead them to make positive changes in their subsequent drafts. However, the present study did not employ an input-output design; no pre- and post-tutorial writing samples were examined, and thus there are no definitive conclusions as to whether tutor scaffolding helped these students improve either the texts they brought to the tutorials or their general proficiency in written English. Neither is it possible, based on the evidence here, to determine whether scaffolded episodes were more effective than directive, overtly instructional episodes in prompting students to revise their texts.

The immediate objective of this study was to determine whether, and how, scaffolded dialogue functions as feedback in L2 writing conferences when the topics of conversation are other than surface problems of grammar and word choice. The tutorial conversations analyzed in this chapter focus on academic writing issues beyond the sentence level – organization and arrangement, coherence, documentation of outside sources, and pre-drafting strategies. The analyses indicate that scaffolded dialogue did indeed occur in discussions about these topics and that it played a role in finding solutions to the writing problems associated with them.

A larger goal for this study was to clarify what the term *scaffolding* signifies in the context of feedback on L2 writing. Clearly, the term is most meaningful when it is limited to its sociocultural sense, i.e., to the verbal mechanisms employed by an expert to assist a novice in moving upward through his or her zone of proximal development to a higher level of performance. It must be acknowledged, however, that the lexical and semantic linkages observed in the tutor's scaffolded conversations with Najiba and César are not substantially different from discourse elements found in native-speaker–nonnative speaker conversations in noninstructional settings. The use of questions, requests for clarification, confirmation checks, and sentence or phrase completions are similar to the "negotiation of meaning" described by Williams (2002) and the "care-giver" speech described by Ochs and Schieffelin (1984) and Hudson (2000). What distinguishes these discourse features in the context of L2 writing tutorials is their use by the tutor to accomplish an instructional agenda and by the students to achieve the practical and immediate objective of getting a written assignment into acceptable shape.

Scaffolding in L2 writing tutorials is thus a purposeful kind of instructional conversation resulting in a unique form of feedback otherwise unavailable to student writers. Feedback delivered in the writing classroom, in peer revision groups, or through an instructor's written comments all have their place in L2 writing instruction, but tutor feedback delivered in a one-to-one setting through scaffolded dialogue tailored to a particular student writer constitutes an unparalleled opportunity to provide targeted, individualized instruction.

The ability to provide scaffolded instruction is not a special gift that only certain tutors possess. Like any instructional skill, it can be described, identified in context, practiced, and refined. However, to provide their student clients with well-calibrated, scaffolded feedback, writing tutors may need assistance in developing mastery of its mechanisms. Neophyte tutors would be well-served by pre- and in-service workshops designed to acquaint them with the concept of scaffolding, its value as a tutorial tool, and the techniques necessary to carry it off. And since even highly experienced educators are often unconscious of their own patterns of instructional talk (Cazden, 1988), it would be worthwhile for all tutors to reflect on the extent to which scaffolding plays a part in their practice. With their clients' consent, tutors might record selected sessions and analyze them later to determine the degree to which they make use of scaffolding in their interactions with learners. Students' subsequent drafts can also be examined to evaluate the effectiveness of scaffolded feedback in the revision process. Through such applications, it is hoped that this study and others like it will serve as catalysts for the further study of oral scaffolding as a source of feedback for L2 writers.

Summary

This chapter has examined feedback on L2 writing in the context of the writing tutorial. Special attention has been given to the concept of oral scaffolding. It has been claimed that scaffolding is a central feature of the writing tutorial, since it is through scaffolded dialogue that expert tutors make their unique contributions to the writing development of their student clients.

The following points were also covered in the chapter:

- The term *scaffolding* implies a sociocultural view of learning and teaching and assumes a more knowledgeable tutor working with a less expert student to provide oral feedback on a text written by the learner. Scaffolding also assumes the existence of a pedagogical goal, or goals, on the part of both tutor and learner. Although scaffolding may occur during peer interaction, it is not to be confused with collaborative learning.
- The study of tutor–L2 learner discourse in writing conferences described here shows that scaffolding can be implemented as a set of *observable discourse mechanisms* practiced by a tutor during conversation with a learner. Among the most salient of these mechanisms are the verbal linkages created by the tutor through lexical and phrasal repetition, questioning, phrase completion and extension, summary and paraphrase statements, and statements of personal affiliation.
- Viewing scaffolding as essentially a construction metaphor, its essential components in an L2 writing conference appear to be *attachment*, by which the tutor makes explicit linkages to the learner's side of the conversation, and *extension*, by which the tutor uses the links as springboard to making instructional points.
- The writing tutorial is a unique opportunity to address the needs of individual L2 writers through dialogic scaffolding. However, the impact of scaffolding on students' later written drafts remains to be determined.

Notes

1. In this excerpt O is the tutor and L is the student. The transcription conventions are taken directly from Williams, 2002, pp. 85–86.
2. These excerpts employ a loose transcription of the audiotapes. Editorial insertions are indicated by brackets [ ], pauses, interruptions (cross-talk), and omitted sequences are indicated by.... A period indicates falling, sentence-final intonation. The speakers' self-repetitions and hesitations are retained whenever possible.

References

Aljaafreh, A., & Lantolf, J. (1994). Negative feedback as regulation and second language learning in the zone of proximal development. *The Modern Language Journal, 78,* 465–483.

Antón, M., & DiCamilla, F. (1998). Socio-cognitive functions of L1 collaborative interaction in the L2 classroom. *Canadian Modern Language Journal, 54(3),* 314–342 Available at www.utpjournals.com/jour.ihtml?lp=product/cmlr/543/543-Anton.html

Barnes, D. (1990). Oral language and learning. In S. Hynds and D. Rubin (Eds.), *Perspectives on talk and learning* (pp. 41–54). Urbana, IL: National Council of Teachers of English.

Blanton, L. (1992). Talking students into writing: Using oral fluency to develop literacy. *TESOL Journal, 1,* 23–26.

Boyd, M., & Maloof, V. (2000). How teachers build on student-proposed intertextual links to facilitate student talk in the ESL classroom. In J. Hall & L. Verplaetse (Eds.), *Second and foreign language learning through classroom interaction* (pp. 163–182). Mahwah, NJ: Lawrence Erlbaum.

Boyd, M., & Rubin, D. (2002). Elaborated student talk in an elementary ESoL classroom. *Research in the Teaching of English, 36,* 495–530.

Bruffee, K. (1995). Peer tutoring and the "conversation of mankind." In C. Murphy & J. Law (Eds.), *Landmark essays on writing centers.* Davis, CA: Hermagoras Press.

Bruner, J. (1978). The role of dialog in language acquisition. In A. Sinclair, R. Jarvella, & W. Levelt (Eds.), *The child's conception of language* (pp. 241–255). Berlin: Springer-Verlag.

Bryman, A., & Burgess, R. (1994). Developments in qualitative data analysis: An introduction. In A. Bryman & R. Burgess (Eds.), *Analyzing qualitative data* (pp. 1–17). London: Routledge.

Cazden, C. (1988). *Classroom discourse: The language of teaching and learning.* Portsmouth, NH: Heinemann.

Cumming, A. (1992). Instructional routines in ESL composition teaching: A case study of three teachers. *Journal of Second Language Writing, 1,* 17–35.

Dickinson, D., Wolf, M., & Stotsky, S. (1993). Words move: The interwoven development of oral and written language. In J. Gleason (Ed.), *The development of language,* 3rd ed. (pp. 369–420). New York: Macmillan.

Donato, R. (1994). Collective scaffolding in second language learning. In J. Lantolf & G. Appel (Eds.), *Vygotskian approaches to second language research* (pp. 33–56). Norwood, NJ: Ablex.

Donato, R. (2000). Sociocultural contributions to understanding the second and foreign language classroom. In J. Lantolf (Ed.), *Sociocultural theory and second language learning* (pp. 26–50). Oxford: Oxford University Press.

Gillam, A. (1991). Writing center ecology: A Bakhtinian perspective. *The Writing Center Journal, 11,* 3–12.

Goldstein, L., & Conrad, S. (1990). Student input and negotiation of meaning in ESL writing conferences. *TESOL Quarterly, 24,* 443–460.

Guerrero, M. C. M. de, & Villamil, O. (2000). Activating the ZPD: Mutual scaffolding in L2 peer revision. *The Modern Language Journal, 84,* 51–68.

264   *Robert Weissberg*

Harris, M. (1995). Talking in the middle: Why writers need writing tutors. *College English, 57,* 27–42.

Hatch, E. (1992). *Discourse and language education.* Cambridge: Cambridge University Press.

Herdman, N. (1997). Community texts: Bakhtin in the writing center. Paper presented at the Conference on College Composition and Communication, Phoenix, March 12–15. ERIC: ED 408 595.

Hirvela, A. (1999). Collaborative writing instruction and communities of readers and writers. *TESOL Journal, 8,* 7–12.

Hudson, G. (2000). *Essential introductory linguistics.* Malden, MA: Blackwell.

Lantolf, J. (Ed.). (2000). *Sociocultural theory and second language learning.* Oxford: Oxford University Press.

Lantolf, J., & Appel, G. (Eds.). (1994). *Vygotskian approaches to second language research.* Norwood: Ablex.

Kroll, B. (1981). Developmental relationships between speaking and writing. In B. Kroll & R. Vann (Eds.), *Exploring speaking-writing relationships: Connections and contrasts* (pp. 32–54). Urbana, IL: National Council of Teachers of English.

LeCompte, M., & Preissle, J. (1993). *Ethnographic and qualitative design in educational research.* San Diego: Academic Press.

Lee, C., & Smagorinsky, P. (Eds.). (2000). *Vygotskian perspectives on literacy research.* Cambridge: Cambridge University Press.

Ochs, E., & Schieffelin, B. (1984). Language acquisition and socialization: Three developmental stories and their implications. In R. Shweder & R. LeVine, (Eds.), *Culture theory: Essays on mind, self, and emotion* (pp. 276–320). Cambridge: Cambridge University Press.

Ohta, A. (1995). Applying sociocultural theory to an analysis of learner discourse: Learner-learner collaborative interaction in the zone of proximal development. *Issues in Applied Linguistics, 6,* 93–121.

Ohta, A. (2000). Rethinking interaction in SLA: Developmentally appropriate assistance in the zone of proximal development and the acquisition of L2 grammar. In J. Lantolf (Ed.), *Sociocultural theory and second language learning* (pp. 51–78). Oxford: Oxford University Press.

Ohta, A. (2001). *Second language acquisition processes in the classroom: Learning Japanese.* Mahwah, NJ: Lawrence Erlbaum Associates.

Powers, J. (1993). Rethinking writing center conferencing strategies for the ESL writer. *Writing Center Journal, 13,* 39–47.

Shuy, R. (1987). Dialogue as the heart of learning. *Language Arts, 64,* 890–897.

Storch, N. (2002). Patterns of interaction in ESL pair work. *Language Learning, 52,* 119–158.

Thomas, D. (2003). A general inductive approach for qualitative data analysis. Available at www.health.auckland.ac.nz/hrmas/resources/Inductive2003.pdf.

Thonus, T. (1999). NS-NNS interaction in academic writing tutorials: Discourse analysis and its interpretations. Conference paper, American Association of Applied Linguistics.

Van Dijk, T. (1985). (Ed.). *Handbook of discourse analysis: Dimensions of discourse,* Vol. 4. London: Academic Press.

Villamil, O., & de Guerrero, M. C. M. (1996). Peer revision in the L2 classroom: Social-cognitive activities, mediating strategies and aspects of social behavior. *Journal of Second Language Writing, 5*, 51–75.

Weissberg, R. (1994). Speaking of writing: Some functions of talk in the ESL composition class. *Journal of Second Language Writing, 3*, 121–139.

Weissberg, R. (2000). Developmental relationships in the acquisition of English syntax: Writing vs. speech. *Learning and Instruction, 10*, 37–53.

Wells, G. (1990). Talk about text: Where literacy is learned and taught. *Curriculum Inquiry, 20*, 369–405.

Wells, G. (1998). Using L1 to master L2: A response to Antón and DiCamilla's 'Socio-cognitive functions of L1 collaborative interaction in the L2 classroom.' *Canadian Modern Language Review, 54(3)*. Available at www.utpjournals.com/jour.ihtml?lp=cmlr/cmlr543.html.

Wertsch, J. (1991). *Voices of the mind: A sociocultural approach to mediated action.* Cambridge, MA: Harvard University Press.

Williams, J. (2002). Undergraduate second language writers in the writing center. *Journal of Basic Writing, 21(2)*, 73–91.

Wood, D., Bruner, J., & Ross, G. (1976). The role of tutoring in problem solving. *Child Psychology and Psychiatry, 17*, 89–100.

14 "You cannot ignore": L2 graduate students' response to discipline-based written feedback

Ilona Leki

Graduate students studying in a second language may find themselves knowing a great deal about the subject matter they study, yet feeling much less in command of the writing skills required to display and to further develop that knowledge within their disciplines. Their awareness of this discrepancy may be painful or embarrassing as well as frustrating (Braine, 2002; Cho, 2004; Hirvela & Belcher, 2001; Ivanic & Camps, 2001; Schneider & Fujishima, 1995; Silva, 1992). Some L2 graduate students, particularly science and technology students, may not only be writing in English for the first time but also writing for the first time at all at any length (Dong, 1998). Furthermore, these L2 graduate students may find themselves called upon to write sophisticated discipline-specific texts, including theses and dissertations, with the curricular aid of only elementary and general-focus L2 writing courses (Hansen, 2000). The difficulty these students face is exacerbated by the fact that literacy requirements at the graduate level in disciplinary courses are often implicit (Carson, 2001; Raymond & Parks, 2002). How do they learn the genres, disciplinary language, and discourse conventions for papers in graduate courses, articles for publication (sometimes in collaboration with advisors), and theses and dissertations?

One formative aspect of graduate literacy education is feedback on writing, as clearly exemplified in L1 by Berkenkotter, Huckin, and Ackermann's study (1988) of a graduate student's development of expertise in a discipline's written genres. A fairly extensive literature exists on feedback to L2 student writing as well, for both ESL and FL. (See Ferris, 2003, for an overview.) This research has examined efficacy and students' preferences for a variety of approaches to providing feedback, hoping to determine which kinds of feedback benefit L2 writers most with revising the same document or improving their writing and language proficiency generally (Ferris, 1997; Ferris et al., 1997; Hedgcock & Lefkowitz, 1994; Hyland, 1998; Leki, 1991; Radecki & Swales, 1988). Given its orientation toward general language and writing pedagogy, most of the research has focused on feedback responses of English, ESL, or writing teachers rather than on the responses of disciplinary

266

faculty to L2 student writing and has not distinguished between under-graduate and graduate needs.

One exception is Prior's (1995, 1998) microanalyses of text-based interactions in graduate geography and sociology courses, which uncovered some of the ways commentary by peers and professors was eventually laminated into texts produced by both English L1 and L2 graduate students. Riazi's (1997) study of the disciplinary enculturation of four Iranian graduate students in education also included a brief discussion of some of the feedback they received on their written course work. Other studies of graduate students have tended to be closely focused case studies such as those of Belcher (1994) and Casanave (1992, 1995), which reveal specific, and complex socio-academic interactions between students and their advisors or their course professors but do not highlight the faculty's written responses to graduate student writing.

If L2 graduate students come to their graduate course work with little experience writing for a discipline or with only general language or L2 writing course work, and if graduate literacy requirements remain implicit, information on how to perform disciplinary literacy tasks is likely to come from one or a combination of the following sources: detailed descriptions of what the task requires, models of completed tasks (including readings in the discipline), and feedback on attempts to complete a task. Arguably, however, regardless of the care with which task directions are created and followed, and regardless of the quality of models to which the L2 graduate student might be referred, it is the response to the attempted completion of the task – the grade, the commentary, the praise or criticism – that will send the strongest message about whether the attempt has matched disciplinary expectations. Thus, the response is likely to have the greatest impact on the writer's developing sense of where to go with the next writing attempt. While a variety of factors may influence a writer to reject intervention or appropriation, Dong (1998) noted that in general the L2 English science and technology graduate students she studied sought and got less help with their writing than did other students, although their advisors did not perceive this difference and although the students themselves generally craved more, not less, intervention in their work.

In the interview and text-based study reported here, I have worked from the assumption that written feedback from professors in a student's discipline has a significant role to play in the development of advanced L2 literacy skills in English. The research goal was twofold: to gain a better sense of the extent and variety of written commentary made by disciplinary faculty on course work submitted to them by a group of L2 graduate students studying in a U.S. institution and to sound the students' sense of the role of written feedback in the development of

Table 14.1. *Interviewee demographic data*

Total student interviews	21
Women	8
Men	13
Master's students	8
Ph.D. students	13
1 year at university	14
2–7 years at university	7

their disciplinary literacy. The following research questions guided the study:

- How much feedback did these students receive on their writing in courses in their majors during one semester? What kinds of feedback did they receive?
- How did these students use the feedback they received?
- How valuable did these students perceive this feedback to be for the development of their disciplinary literacy?

Description of the study

This section describes the methods and approach to data analysis.

Methods

This study took place at a large, research-oriented state university that has about 800 international students enrolled at any one time, including about 500 graduate students. All 61 of the L2 graduate students enrolled in writing classes in fall of 2003 were contacted and invited to be interviewed or to contribute documents for the project. Six said they had not done any written work in graduate school outside of their English classes. Of 55 who had, 21 agreed to the interview and one contributed documents but declined to be interviewed. Of the 21, 14 were in their second semester of graduate work and 7 had been attending classes at this university for between two and seven years.

The interviews lasted about 30 minutes (see Appendix for interview guide questions) and were either tape-recorded with permission and transcribed (18) or reconstituted immediately after the interview from notes (3). Interviewee demographics are displayed in Table 14.1.

The students were also asked to select and submit course papers over two pages long that had been returned to them with written commentary. The purpose of this request was to permit analysis of the commentary

Table 14.2. *Summary of document data*

Number of students submitting papers	13
Number of pages submitted	311
Number of courses represented	18
Number of non-prose pages	60
Types of documents	Reports
	Research papers
	E-mail exchanges
	Lab reports
	Executive summaries
	Exams

the students had received. Although 14 sets of documents (including a set from the student not interviewed) were submitted, eight students had no papers to contribute because what they turned in was never returned to them, what they submitted was returned but with no markings other than a grade, or they had not kept any written work.

While numbers and types of contributions from individual students varied widely, the total number of text pages submitted was 311 and it came from 18 different graduate courses. See Table 14.2. Of the 311 pages, 60 were non-prose but also subject to professor commentary.

Data analysis

The 311 pages of text the students submitted were the basis of the analysis intended to answer the first research question: How much and what kinds of written feedback did these graduate students get on papers in their major? Each student paper was read through first in an attempt to grasp what the content of the document was intended to convey.

Next, each paper was analyzed for the professor's written commentary, the focus of the documentary analysis. The commentaries were clustered into idea units, the unit of analysis we use here. Each mark, word, phrase, sentence, or group of sentences on the pages was considered a unit if it appeared to stand alone in communicating a response to what the student had written. For example, a single check mark next to a calculation or written on top of a word was analyzed as one unit. A series of comments on just one section of a paper that maintained a single focus while giving advice, challenging, or critiquing the idea or formulation communicated in that section was also considered a single unit. For example, the following is an excerpt from a paper in educational psychology. The student's unaltered text is on the left and the professor's commentary on the right. The items in the teacher's commentary are numbered to show division by units.

Student	Teacher
Communication is another concept related to environment. Children assimilate and internalize the language through communication. The process is gradual. They construct generalizations from the more simple to the more complex. Gradually the children are able to master the necessary skill "so, as a result children at different stages of their development do not yet posses a system of communication with adults which is sufficiently compatible." (Vygotsky, 1994, p. 345). **Skinner's theory** [new subhead] In Skinner's theory the idea of environment is strictly . . .	[1] in Vts theory? [2] V emphasizes the role of a mediator who shares the ideal form of the language. This is not clear in your paragraph. [3] This quote does not fit clearly the point you made in this paragraph – I think you can find a better quote. [4] You need a sentence or paragraph to help the reader follow you to Skinner. [5] [deletes 's, adds] ian

Figure 14.1.   Idea units in a sample of student text and teacher written response

Similar idea units were grouped in initial categories such as "gives information," "requests elaboration," "expresses opinion," "evaluates positive or negative." These categories were then collapsed into broader ones. Although other categorization schemes exist for analyzing feedback on L2 writing (notably Ferris, 1997), they focus on feedback from writing or language teachers and were judged inadequate to capture the concerns of disciplinary readers. The categorizations developed here arose from multiple reviews of the data and reflect disciplinary orientations beyond those of writing or language teachers.

To answer the remaining research questions, the interview data were analyzed in two ways. First, the audiotapes of the recorded interviews were reviewed twice, noting particularly salient or interesting comments as potential themes or categories to be cued against transcripts. Repeated review of oral data adds a dimension to interview data interpretation that seems to disappear when the transcripts alone are analyzed. The interviewee's emphases and emotional responses are not caught in the transcripts but are apparent in the recordings themselves. They create a kind of emotive frame for the transcribed words and thus permit a depth of understanding otherwise difficult to achieve. Second, the interview transcripts themselves were read repeatedly against the interview questions, with straightforward responses tabulated and elaborations examined for themes and potential analytic categories to be correlated with themes and categories noted in the oral recordings.

Table 14.3. *Number of written comments*

Student number	Number of pages	Pages with comments	Number of comments per page	Average number of comments per page	Student major	Home country
1	30	30	280	9.3	TESL-ED	Korea
2	50	44	263	5.3	TESL-ED	Taiwan
3	25	25	112	4.5	Biomedical science	China
4	15	15	39	2.6	Speech pathology	Korea
5	4	4	57	14.3	Genome science	China
6	15	7	10	0.7	Engineering	China
7	4	3	9	2.3	Statistics	India
8	11	11	30	2.7	Counseling	Korea
9	11	10	111	10.1	Educational psychology	Argentina
10	2	2	5	2.3	Biochemistry	India
11	16	7	23	1.4	Management	India
12	54	40	95	1.8	Computer science	China
13	18	12	45	2.5	Engineering	China
14	56	34	72	1.3	Management	India
15	0	0	0	0	Graphic design	Germany
16	0	0	0	0	Engineering	Taiwan
17	0	0	0	0	Engineering	Uruguay
18	0	0	0	0	Marketing	Turkey
19	0	0	0	0	Logistics	Thailand
20	0	0	0	0	Engineering	Yemen
21	0	0	0	0	Engineering	China

Study: Content analysis

Fourteen students submitted papers for analysis. The number of pages submitted was 311, ranging from a low of two pages per student to a high of 56, with an average of 22 pages (median = 15.5). The total number of idea units in the form of comments on the students' papers came to 1,151, ranging from a low of five comments to a high of 280 comments. The average number of comments per page for each student submission ranged from a low of less than one to a high of more than 14 per page. Table 14.3 shows the number of pages submitted for review, the number of comments written on those pages, and the majors and home countries of all 21 students. In the sections following Table 14.3, the numbers in parentheses correspond to the student numbers listed in the table.

Written responses were divided into three categories: absolute minimal response (less than one notation per page; student 6 in engineering), an intermediate level of response (1 to 5 notations per page; students 2, 3, 4, 7, 8, 10, 11, 12, 13, 14), and intensive feedback where nearly every page was extensively annotated (9 to 14 notations/page, student 5 in genome science and student 9 in educational psychology).

The comments were grouped into the nine nonexclusive categories: Again, numbers in parentheses identify the student respondents (see Table 14.3).

1. Substantive response
     Like how? You must let me know. (2)
     Note [x]. Your comments ignored this. (12)
     These are way off. How did you calculate them? (13)
2. Professional enculturation
     Bad notation. Use this form [+ formula]. (12)
     Too long a quote to write this way. See APA for format of long quote. (9)
3. Language/writing
     [student text] . . . *sighted by EPA.* [in margin] *cited?* (14)
     Don't split the word. (2)
4. Checks, underlines, circles, question marks, OKs, squiggly lines, arrows, or a line along the side of a stretch of text without further comment
5. Task management
     Just give the finite state diagram. It's easier when one has 60 papers to look at. (12)
     Do not staple three times, only once. I told you this many times. (1)
     Follow instructions! Exceeded 2 page limit. (14)
     In one case the student herself wrote a note to the professor stating her inability to stay within designated page limits.
6. Illegible comment
     Candidates for this category initially included idiosyncratic abbreviations such as *R'ch*, *impo't*, and *howr*, as well as statements that were self-contradictory or appeared to make no sense possibly because of missing the word *not*. Since it was possible, however, that these were transparent to the students, I included only illegible writing here.
7. Evaluative comment
     Positive: *Bravo!* (12)
     Negative: *Wrong.* (14)
     Not very convincing. (14)
8. Grades
     Grade marks included notations such as *4 / 5*.
9. Name use
     Professor signs name (always prefaced with *Dr.*) or addresses student by name. In two of these instances the professor used the wrong name and in two others addressed the student as "Dear Writer."

     As already, noted these categories were not mutually exclusive, since comments occasionally fell into more than one category. For example, a comment might criticize incorrect use of APA citation style or of some disciplinary formula (classified as both negative evaluation and enculturation), as in "Bad notation. Use this form [+; formula] (12)."

Table 14.4 displays the numbers of comments placed in each of the nine categories.

As Table 14.4 shows, comments on language and writing headed the frequency list, followed by the more ambiguous checks and other such

Table 14.4. *Numbers of written comments by category*

Language and writing	299
Checks, underlines, etc.	287
Substantive response	275
Evaluative comment	113
Grades	102
Professional enculturation	63
Task management	47
Name use	14
Illegible comment	3
Total	1,203

Table 14.5. *Substantive comment types (instances = 275)*

Type of comment	Number of instances	Percentage represented by column 1	Number of professors
Correcting student's interpretation	48	17	8
Elaborating content	47	17	8
Requesting clarification	39	14	7
Requesting elaboration	33	12	10
Correcting / rejecting calculation	16	6	3
Requesting information	5	2	3

graphics, apparently signaling that something was found, reviewed, and correctly executed or included or indicating agreement (as in Raymond & Parks, 2002). Question marks no doubt indicated puzzlement or a challenge to what was written, but it was not always possible to tell what the question was or what word, calculation, or precise section of text it referred to, although the message may have been clear to the student. Underlinings pinpointed the area of reference but not the message. So, although these markings were second in frequency, after feedback on language and writing, what to make of them was not so clear.

The third-largest category of comments, close behind the first two in number of appearances, was substantive comments referring to the content (including calculations and tables) of the student's text. This category also subsumed the largest variety of subcategories; those found most frequently are displayed in Table 14.5.

Presumably, correcting an interpretation and elaborating content gave the student a clear indication of where and how the professor expected him or her to alter or expand understanding of the course material. That feedback was likely to be appreciated by the students looking for guidance from their professors, an appreciation reflected in the students' comments.

The two next-highest-frequency interventions, requesting clarification and requesting elaboration, present a potentially different situation. In their analysis of student revision after teacher response, Conrad and Goldstein (1999) found that the feedback response least likely to result in successful student revision was a request for elaboration / explanation, presumably because the student did not quite know how to address these requests. Conrad and Goldstein's students were undergraduates writing for an English class that required revision. They probably would have had to do more guessing to fathom what their teachers were requesting and do so with fewer informational and strategic resources than those available to the graduate students in the present study.

Such superficially similar feedback from writing and disciplinary responders may in fact represent fundamental ontological differences. Furthermore, the graduate students were not typically expected to revise the work they turned in to their professors. It is interesting to note that faculty relied relatively heavily on a response technique that had, at least in some other contexts, proved to be less helpful than anticipated. And in fact, one student respondent specifically expressed her problem with questions requesting clarification.

I want [my professor to show me where clarification is needed] but I cannot handle those things. (Category 2)

Study results interview analysis

Was it feedback?

An examination of the students' documents indicates that feedback on their work came in a range of forms, from simple check marks to extensive prose commentary. Their interview comments, however, suggest that the students' perceptions of what constitutes written work and feedback were less broad. When asked whether they ever did writing in their majors, eight students said they wrote only lab reports or answers to questions. Five of the eight students nevertheless submitted written work for this study. A text (an answer to a question, for example) that they felt did not constitute writing might extend to half a page and have responses written in the margin; to these students "writing" appeared to mean the type of extended prose they experienced in English and writing classes.

Similarly, although 13 of the students who agreed to be interviewed also submitted course papers and every document carried markings of some kind by the professor, only nine of them regarded those markings as feedback, whereas six said they never received any feedback at all. Perhaps the nature of some of these submissions – short answers to questions or non-prose elements (e.g., calculations, equations, or tables) introduced or explained by short texts – precluded the students' recognition of response to that work as real feedback.

To look more closely at two cases, I compared the interview transcripts and the papers submitted by the students who had the highest and the lowest average number of comments per page on their submitted texts. Student 5, in genome science, received an average of 14.3 comments per page, covering a wide range of categories: corrections of language, corrections of content, elaborations of content, positive and negative evaluations, disagreements with content, questions, expression of opinions. Strangely, the student felt that in his major his professors tended not to give much feedback ("They just probably read our homework and give us scores . . .") and none on language issues. The student's experience was not in keeping with the evidence of the text he submitted, which included 16 language-related markings of the 57 total. He also mentioned that he not only wished for more commentary but also wished for the commentary to be written in handwriting he could read.

The student with the lowest average number of comments per pages (0.7) also wished for more feedback, particularly on language issues. However, of the 10 feedback units on the paper she submitted, four were language corrections, four were items of professional enculturation, and two were evaluations.

Post-feedback action: The role of revision

Only three students had experienced rounds of writing / feedback / re-writing more than once; all of them considered this effort useful.

I: When you get these papers back for your major course, do you ever rewrite them?
R: [with enthusiasm] Oh yeah, I did. Almost every single time. (19)

Three other students had this experience once, but not as part of course work; one student revised only as a part of a corporate internship, and two other students revised only as part of their dissertation work.

Post-feedback action: The role of attention

Even students who did not revise reported reading the feedback comments with close attention. Typical answers emphasized the importance of feedback in guiding content, writing, and language.

Yes, I want to know what the professor expects. There are several ways to do, several equations. Which is preferred, which is recommended? . . . Without comments, I don't know what I did wrong or what I did right . . . what is expected from the project, what is suitable. (14)

R: OK, first I try to look at it and think what can make improvement
    here. . . . They have two kind of professor, some of them very concept
    oriented and they just read through it and they know what you talk about
    and they like the idea and they ignore like the grammar because they say
    that is not your language. But some of them look further than that and say,
    Duke, you need this one to look like ready for publish so those kind [of]
    professor, like you know the one that publish a lot, they correct grammar,
    they correct concept, they do everything. So I think you follow them . . . and
    you can see improvement.
I: Are there any comments that you ignore?
R: You cannot ignore. (19)

I read it very carefully, like every word . . . I'm thankful for every
help . . . teachers in Germany don't do that carefully and teachers do it here,
and I really appreciate that. I mean it's very special. And I'm not sure if
students here are really aware of the, all the work and effort professors are
really putting into. (15)

Not all the students were so lucky as to get careful feedback, but nearly all were extremely attentive to the feedback they did get. Two students remarked that in their experience feedback was so rare that when course work came back to them with any kind of commentary whatsoever, they each read it carefully, assuming that if the professor bothered to make comments they must be especially important ones.

However, not all the students accepted the feedback uncritically. Three students noted that, although they tried to read feedback they received, the professors' handwriting was nearly unintelligible to them. Another student, perhaps reacting to the aggressive tone and sheer abundance of her professor's comments, said she did not read them. And one submitted the comments to critical scrutiny, noting:

R: . . . at the beginning I think my professor's feedback absolutely accurate.
    Then I will [change] according [to] them and re-correct them. But after a
    while I have been to here, sometimes I will thinking about if, is his feedback
    right? (13)

Longing for more

One of the interview questions asked whether the students wished for any kind of feedback they were not getting. Of the 21 students interviewed, six students said they were happy with the amount and type of feedback they were receiving. Another 11 stated directly that they simply wished for *more* feedback: more help in identifying problems and errors, more information about expectations, more indication of how native speakers would express the same ideas. They clearly saw feedback as a form of instruction and wanted more direction and guidance, as well as a sense of what the target they were aiming for looked like.

I: ...Do you wish that you got more written comments or are you happy with what you get?
R: I hope to get more.... [a] standard... to compare against, and you can get that one from your major professor.... So if they give you less comments, it's like it's not complete picture. (19)

R: [Yes, about] the way I express. Did I express clearly? But I don't get, not much comment on verbal.
I: Why do you want that kind of feedback?
R: To be sure I am properly understood. (12)

In terms of content, two students noted that they wished they could get different perspectives on material in their disciplines. However, when one of them asked a professor on his Ph.D. exam committee whether he would be willing to give the student feedback on something he had written, the professor replied that he would do so – at the dissertation defense! Other students expressed frustration generally at not getting as full a response to their written work from faculty as they had hoped.

I: Did they return the work to you with written comments?
R: Some, but that is not a common practice; I expected more and would like more. I would like to know what I did wrong and what I could do better.... [Noting that he did not have any commented-on written work to give me for this project because his professors had not returned any, he said] I *really* don't like that way. (21)

R: ...professor didn't provide many comments...She just write overall evaluation. She said, "Wonderful paper." The result of the paper is good, but I don't know what is good or what is bad. (8)

The last comment here makes it clear that praise is not enough; this student craved more guidance. On the other hand, one student remarked jokingly that she would like "exuberant praise," a wish probably shared by many writers.

Expectations for language feedback

In terms of where they wanted feedback focused, a very large number felt more confident in the content of their writing than in the expression of their ideas. Only four wished for more feedback on content; nine wished for more on language, and nine for more on writing, including genre features.

On the other hand, 11 students said that they either were happy enough with the amount they were getting or that they never expected any, particularly help with language. As some students said, they did not see language improvement as part of their major professors' job descriptions.

R: They are not in charge of my writing improve. (13)

R: I'm sure probably they don't have time to correct our English. . . . if they have time [it would help], but that's not their work. (5)

R: My professor is not my grammar teacher so I cannot expect him to correct my English. (18)

Discussion

What is writing?

The object of this study was the feedback these L2 graduate students received on papers written in their specialty areas. One of the most striking results of the study was how often students claimed to have submitted no writing at all in their discipline during a semester. Several students were unable to participate because they had written no papers in their majors; others did not receive feedback or never had papers returned to them. This is striking, in part because of the general insistence among L2 writing professionals that L2 writing instruction is crucial, since L2 students will face a great deal of demand for writing in both graduate and undergraduate programs in English-medium universities. Apparently, for at least some students in this study, particularly those in their first semester, the need to write was being deferred.

But the students' assertion that they had done no writing in their graduate course work may also reflect these students' rather narrow definition of disciplinary writing, excluding short answers or the summary comments that introduce non-text material. The question that arises for L2 writing practitioners is how broad our own view of writing is, and whether when we teach writing, we also exclude such types of disciplinary writing in our definition in favor of the more discursive prose typical in the humanities and more familiar to writing teachers. In their discussion of the differences between "Continental" and "Anglo-American" university writing traditions, Rienecker and Jorgensen (2003) characterize Anglo-American university writing as more problem-oriented and less hermeneutical or interpretive than its European counterpart. The European perspective on what real academic writing entails may be more pervasive than the authors suggest, at least among these L2 graduate students, and perhaps among L2 English writing practitioners.

Response to the feedback

Nearly all the students claimed to read any feedback they received carefully. For the most part, then, we got a picture of these students as highly motivated to produce better written work, very responsive to any feedback they got, and craving more. What they hoped for from the feedback was a clear sense of expectations and of standards, information about where they were falling short, and where they were performing adequately. Interestingly, sociocultural models of situated learning, apprenticing (Lave & Wenger, 1991), and collaborating in the "zone of proximal development"(ZPD) (Vygotsky, 1962) emphasize novice development as a function of interaction with expert performance, if only through observation. Yet the novice's questions "How did I do?" or "How am I doing?" both requesting evaluation of solo performance apart from or in addition to interaction with expert performance, appear to be widespread and even urgent.

The analysis of the students' papers presents an interesting contrast with the students' comments in their interviews. From the documentary evidence, it would seem that some of these students were drowning in feedback from professors in their disciplines; yet every one of those drowning students, like nearly all of those interviewed, wished for more. This finding certainly concurs with Dong's (1998) conclusion that L2 graduate students seek support in the form of intervention in their texts, thus raising the issue of appropriation of student text. Does this issue pose itself differently in writing for writing classes and in writing for disciplinary courses? Possibly. In writing courses students are seldom held responsible for learning the content of what they write (Leki & Carson, 1997); presumably, they are much more likely to be held responsible for doing so in a disciplinary course. The need to feel sure that they are learning or in some way taking on the correct information or concepts or values, and phrasing them in the correct discipline-appropriate language, may help to account for the insecurity suggested by these students' intense desire for even more feedback.

Prior's (1995) description of the situation of one of his research participants is suggestive. Liz received high evaluations in her graduate geography class but seemed unconvinced of her mastery of the material, noting that in her seminar paper she had used disciplinary terms whose meaning she did not fully grasp. She suggested that her professor, who of course did know the complete meaning of the term, might have been reading into her use of the term his own grasp of it. Prior suggests that disciplinary faculty must respond to their students' writing by filling in the knowledge gaps in just the way Liz suggested, both to enculturate and to keep the conversation going between two people with highly asymmetrical knowledge bases. It is perhaps in part this vague awareness that the professor might be reading more into their work than they themselves could at this stage of their development that gave the students in this study a sense of insecurity about what they wrote and prompted such insistence on more feedback. Despite the time some faculty spent on providing feedback (and excluding students who were working with thesis or dissertation advisors and thus revising repeatedly), only three students were required to revise based on the feedback or took the opportunity to do so.

Course work and its attendant literacy development, which is part of graduate students' socialization process (Casanave, 1992), culminates in the thesis or dissertation. It seems unfortunate, even illogical, that so much effort on the part of the students and their advisors goes into revising the thesis or dissertation (Belcher, 1994; Dong, 1996) after years spent *not* reworking course papers. It would seem that the great final effort might better be spread across time. In the meantime, most of the academic literacy these students are developing through their reading and through the responses they get to their writing appears to be what Dong (1996) has referred to as "probing in the dark and learning from mistakes" (p. 453).

Somewhat astonishing was the number of claims that written work was submitted and never returned or returned with only the barest response, such as a grade. Were the students too intimidated or incurious to try to find out more about the professor's reaction to their work? During the interviews, none of the students volunteered that they had done so.

Conclusion

Many years ago, Raimes (1985) commented that the L2 students she was studying appeared to need more of everything in order to succeed. The research reported here indicates these L2 graduate students also wanted more, if not of everything, at least of feedback to give them assurance that they were on the right track and to offer indications of which track to get on if they were not.

For L2 writing practitioners and curriculum developers, one of the most vexing unresolved questions in the field is the issue of what skills, abilities, knowledge, and experience can transfer from an EAP writing course to writing for disciplinary contexts. I have argued elsewhere (Leki, 1995) that writing teachers are necessarily functioning as representatives of some discourse community and bringing that community's values to bear on their responses to student texts. Yet, the community that writing teachers belong to, and so can legitimately represent, is not typically the one students care to enter. Even when EAP classes attempt to accommodate L2 graduate students by having them write on topics in their disciplines, it may be difficult at best to provide an authentic context for that writing as we see, for example, in Hansen's (2000) study of Mei-Huei's frustrations and confusion in attempting to write about math in her EAP course. Her EAP teacher asked her to write in a way that was inconsistent with what Mei-Huei knew to be appropriate in math; thus, EAP demands clashed with disciplinary demands. For the EAP course, Mei-Huei ultimately decided simply to accommodate her writing instructor in order to get a good grade. But surely no one would argue that the point of a writing class is to help L2 students write well only for the writing class.

The study shows us that the L2 graduate students would like more feedback on their written work, do not expect their major professors to give it (although they clearly do give feedback), and, because EAP teachers are not in the students' disciplines, cannot expect EAP teachers to be positioned to give it. What solutions are there to such a dilemma? The solution that seems to come most readily to the institutional mind, yet seems doomed to be least effective, is a freestanding EAP course (at worst, not even separating graduate from undergraduate students) that attempts to teach either disciplinary writing from a position outside the discipline or, failing that, general writing skills. By free-standing, I mean a course that is not associated or team-taught in any way with the disciplinary department. In such courses, the commonality between EAP writing and authentic disciplinary writing may be merely superficial, possibly limited to some genre features and language. While the students in this study did appreciate feedback on language, the profession frowns at this time on excessive interest in language in a writing course, and for good reason.

One potentially useful approach, though less easily implemented, would be for disciplinary areas to set up their own writing classes, assisted by writing experts (including L2 writing experts) in consulting roles. The classes would be staffed by teachers who are familiar with disciplinary discourse and can give informed feedback. The college of business at my institution has such a program, required of all MBA students, with additional tutorial hours set aside for L2 students who need extra help. Attention is given not only to writing, including language issues, but also to other forms of disciplinary communication, such as working in teams, making oral presentations, and participating in required peer response.

With or without such well-focused remedies, L2 professionals can play a role in making disciplinary faculty aware of L2 students' desire for more feedback. They can also address L2 students' silence about that need, thus making it the faculty's responsibility to initiate negotiations with students to determine the quantity and character of intervention that will be most efficacious for the professor and most useful for the student.

In addition, it appears that disciplinary faculty could support the development of disciplinary writing skills in the following ways:

- Legible exchanges, promoting electronic submissions and response over handwritten work
- Return of work submitted
- Commitment to respond more to L2 students' language needs, especially by modeling appropriate disciplinary discourse
- A stated policy and practice of inviting students to consult about returned work
- Encouragement to students to share post-feedback papers and discuss the responses with peers, perhaps thereby clarifying the feedback
- Offering of opportunity for revision, even if only a paragraph or two, thus encouraging a focus on disciplinary writing and decreasing the language burden for both student and professor

Some students in this study devised their own means for dealing with lack of feedback, such as paying close attention to what feedback there was or comparing the feedback to class notes. L2 professionals might question concerned students like these about their tactics and share the suggestions with newly enrolled graduate students. Teachers also need to be sure that L2 students are aware of resources on campus that offer writing help; most of the students in this study were only dimly aware of the university's writing center, for example.

Such an approach is not institutional, but individual, making it potentially quicker and easier to make and implement suggestions and to bring students and faculty together in the same space. The research on L2 graduate students repeatedly emphasizes the importance of students' individual encounters and relationships with faculty, advisors, and peers. Written feedback is one form of socioacademic interaction that these L2 graduate students want, need, and deserve.

References

Belcher, D. (1994). The apprenticeship approach to advanced academic literacy: Graduate students and their mentors. *English for Specific Purposes, 13,* 23–34.

Berkenkotter, C., Huckin, T., & Ackerman, J. (1988). Conventions, conversations, and the writer: Case study of a student in a rhetoric Ph.D. program. *Research in the Teaching of English, 22,* 9–44.

Braine, G. (2002). Academic literacy and the nonnative speaker graduate student. *Journal of English for Academic Purposes, 1,* 59–68.

Carson, J. (2001). A task analysis of reading and writing in academic contexts. In D. Belcher & A. Hirvela (Eds.), *Linking literacies: Perspectives on L2 reading and writing connections* (pp. 48–83). Ann Arbor: University of Michigan Press.

Casanave, C. (1992). Cultural diversity and socialization: A case study of a Hispanic woman in a doctoral program in sociology. In D. Murray (Ed.), *Diversity as resource: Redefining cultural literacy* (pp. 148–182). Washington, DC: TESOL.

Casanave, C. (1995). Local interactions: Constructing contexts for composing in a graduate sociology program. In D. Belcher, and G. Braine (Eds.), *Academic writing in a second language* (pp. 83–110). Norwood, NJ: Ablex.

Cho, S. (2004). Challenges of entering discourse communities through publishing in English: Perspectives of nonnative-speaking doctoral students in the United States of America. *Journal of Language, Identity, and Education, 3,* 47–72.

Conrad, S., & Goldstein, L. (1999). ESL student revision after teacher-written comments: Text, contexts, and individuals. *Journal of Second Language Writing, 8,* 147–179.

Dong, Y. (1996). Learning how to use citations for knowledge transformation: Non-native doctoral students' dissertation writing in science. *Research in the Teaching of English, 30,* 428–457.

Dong, Y. (1998). From writing in their native language to writing in English: What ESL students bring to our writing classrooms. *College ESL, 8,* 87–105.

Ferris, D. (1997). The influence of teacher commentary on student revision. *TESOL Quarterly, 31,* 315–339.

Ferris, D. (2003). *Response to student writing: Implications for second language students.* Mahwah, NJ: Lawrence Erlbaum.

Ferris, D., Pezone, D., Tade, C., & Tinti, S. (1997). Teacher commentary on student writing: Descriptions and implications. *Journal of Second Language Writing, 6,* 155–182.

Hansen, J. (2000). Interactional conflicts among audience, purpose, and content knowledge in the acquisition of academic literacy in an EAP course. *Written Communication, 17,* 27–52.

Hedgcock, J., & Lefkowitz, N. (1994). Feedback on feedback: Assessing learner receptivity to teacher response in L2 composing. *Journal of Second Language Writing, 3,* 141–163.

Hirvela, A., & Belcher, D. (2001). Coming back to voice: The multiple voices and identities of mature multilingual writers. *Journal of Second Language Writing, 10*(1/2), 83–106.

Hyland, F. (1998). The impact of teacher-written feedback on individual writers. *Journal of Second Language Writing, 7,* 255–286.

Ivanic, R., & Camps, D. (2001). I am how I sound: Voice as self-representation in L2 writing. *Journal of Second Language Writing, 10*(1/2), 3–33.

Lave, J., & Wenger, E. (1991). *Situated learning: Legitimate peripheral participation.* Cambridge: Cambridge University Press.

Leki, I. (1991). The preferences of ESL students for error correction in college-level writing classes. *Foreign Language Annals, 24,* 203–218.

Leki, I. (1995). Good writing: I know it when I see it. In D. Belcher & G. Braine (Eds.), *Academic writing in a second language: Essays on research and pedagogy* (pp. 23–46). Norwood, NJ: Ablex.

Leki, I., & Carson, J. (1997). "Completely different worlds": EAP and the writing experiences of ESL students in university courses. *TESOL Quarterly, 31*(1), 39–69.

Prior, P. (1995). Redefining the task: An ethnographic examination of writing and response in graduate seminars. In D. Belcher & G. Braine (Eds.), *Academic writing in a second language: Essays on research and pedagogy* (pp. 47–82). Norwood, NJ: Ablex.

Prior, P. (1998). *Writing/disciplinarity: A sociohistoric account of literate activity in the academy.* Mahwah, NJ: Lawrence Erlbaum.

Radecki, P., & Swales, J. (1988). ESL student reaction to written comments on their written work. *System, 16,* 355–365.

Raimes, A. (1985). What unskilled ESL students do as they write: A classroom study of composing. *TESOL Quarterly, 19,* 229–258

Raymond, P., & Parks, S. (2002). Transitions: Orienting to reading and writing assignments in EAP and MBA contexts. *Canadian Modern Language Review/La Revue canadienne des langues vivantes, 59,* 152–180.

Riazi, A. (1997). Acquiring disciplinary literacy: A social-cognitive analysis of text production and learning among Iranian graduate students of education. *Journal of Second Language Writing, 6,* 105–137.

Rienecker, L., & Jorgensen, P. (2003). The (im)possibilities in teaching university writing in the Anglo-American tradition when dealing with Continental student writers. In B. Lennart, G. Brauer, L. Rienecker, & P. Jorgensen (Eds.), *Teaching academic writing in European higher education* (pp. 101–112). Boston: Kluwer Academic Publishers.

Schneider, M., & Fujishima, N. (1995). When practice doesn't make perfect. The case of an ESL graduate student. In D. Belcher, and Braine, G. (Eds.), *Academic writing in a second language: Essays on research and pedagogy* (pp. 3–22). Norwood, NJ: Ablex.

Silva, T. (1992). L1 vs. L2 writing: ESL graduate students' perceptions. *TESL Canada Journal, 10,* 27–47.

Vygotsky, L. (1962). *Thought and language.* Cambridge, MA: Harvard University Press.

Appendix

The following shortened interview guide does not include probes. Interviewees received a copy of the guide by e-mail before the interview.

Disciplinary writing in a specific course

1. Think of a course you took in your major that required writing at least two pages. Did you get written comments?
2. Describe the kinds of comments.
3. Describe what you did with those comments.

4. Did you rewrite that paper again for your professor? If so, did you use the written comments? Which kinds? Were there some you ignored? Why?
5. What do those written comments help you improve? Writing? Understanding of concepts? New ideas? Calculations?
6. Are there any kinds of written comments on your papers in your major that you wish you could get that you don't get?
7. What kinds?
8. Is there any other kind of feedback you wish you could get on your papers in your majors? From peers? Do you ever go to the Writing Center? To work on what? Do you ever have conferences with your professor? About what?
9. What do you think has helped you the most to improve your English writing in your major?

Author index

Subject index